I0812829

POSTCARD HISTORY SERIES

Along the Brandywine River

POSTCARD HISTORY SERIES

Along the Brandywine River

Bruce Edward Mowday

ARCADIA PUBLISHING

ISBN 978-0-7385-0940-2

Published by Arcadia Publishing
Charleston, South Carolina

Printed in the United States of America

Library of Congress Catalog Card Number: 2001091702

For all general information contact Arcadia Publishing at:
Telephone 843-853-2070
Fax 843-853-0044
E-mail sales@arcadiapublishing.com
For customer service and orders:
Toll-Free 1-888-313-2665

Visit us on the Internet at www.arcadiapublishing.com

Contents

ACKNOWLEDGMENTS

As with the publication of any book, many people are responsible for bringing the pages to life, and *Along the Brandywine River* is no different. I have long collected postcards—especially of Chester County, where the Brandywine originates—as a way to relax and also to have and hold a part of my home county's heritage.

The idea of collecting postcards seemed a little odd to my wife, Katherine Harlan, when we married in the mid-1990s. She agreed to attend a few postcard shows and soon began her own special collections relating to her college years at Agnes Scott College in the Atlanta area.

As I anxiously scrambled around the region looking for those final few postcards that would enhance and complete *Along the Brandywine River,* Katherine offered valuable assistance. At several postcard shows, she started at one side of the room while I went to the vendors on the other side of the room. She segregated all of the cards on the Brandywine for my review. Her help and cooperation made the hectic final days a lot easier.

The postcard community is a friendly bunch in the Brandywine region. Joe Lordi, a librarian at the Bayard Taylor Memorial Library in Kennett Square, is a first-rate collector who was always ready to answer a question and point me to possible sources of cards to add to my collection. Dolores and Leon Rowe of Kennett Square, friends of Joe, kept an appointment they made for me to review their collection even though, only a few hours earlier, a fire had destroyed a relative's home and they were both sleep deprived. Bill Martin, owner of Mary Martin Vintage Postcards in Perryville, Maryland, allowed me to explore his vast collection of postcards. Marion of Marion's Postcards of Morgantown, Pennsylvania, was helpful and cheerful.

Chester County and the Brandywine Valley are rich in recorded history and date back to William Penn. Special thanks go to my valued friend Elizabeth Humphrey, who more than a decade ago wrote her own history of the Brandywine, for sharing her insights of the region. Besides working as journalists for the same paper, we share a Welsh heritage and together have celebrated many St. David's Days.

A search was conducted for a map to accompany this book. After a period of time, it was clear that one would have to be created especially for this book, and Diana Cirafesi of Cirafesi Designs of West Chester did a great job, under a tight deadline, of researching and designing an original map to be used here.

My two daughters, Melissa and Megan, were both "treated" to collecting excursions in their youth, with Melissa becoming somewhat of a devotee. Megan never considered those trips to antique shows as a treat but was always a good sport. My collection and many cards in this book began during those days.

Special thanks go to Arcadia Publishing and Peter Turco, acquisitions editor at Arcadia. They encouraged me in the production of this book. More importantly, Arcadia brings history to life, and our country's heritage should be extremely important to all who live here.

INTRODUCTION

The Brandywine River may not rate as one of the most powerful rivers of this nation, as does the mighty Mississippi, but it certainly ranks as one of the most historic rivers in the United States. The origin of the river is in the higher elevations of Chester County, which is one of the original three counties founded by William Penn in November 1682. Native Americans, especially the Lenape tribe, roamed the Brandywine River Valley when the colonization of the commonwealth began. Many of the first settlers were Quakers, and their descendants still have considerable influence in Chester County today. The Mason-Dixon line, separating the North from the South and acting as the southern boundary of Pennsylvania, was formed through the use of the Stargazers' Stone, which is located not far from the banks of the Brandywine.

Early American farmers needed mills to turn their grain crops into flour, and those mills needed power. The Brandywine helped to supply that power. Later, an early steel mill was founded in Coatesville by Rebecca Lukens, one of the pioneers of women in business in this country. Again, the Brandywine played a part in the early success of the steel mill that still operates today. The Brandywine actually begins with two separate branches. The eastern branch winds it way through Downingtown, which was a way station for earlier travelers commuting between Philadelphia and Lancaster, but was later known for its paper mills along the Brandywine.

Chester County has often been described as bucolic, being one of the most scenic areas in the United States. Today, the county is fighting sprawl and an ever-expanding population, but the scenic vistas still survive along the Brandywine. Canoeing on the Brandywine is still a favorite pastime of many area residents. The Brandywine at Lenape has been a recreational spot for more than a century. Families have long relaxed along the Brandywine's shore, and the Lenape amusement park has offered many young West Chester residents their first paying summer jobs.

Where the two branches of Brandywine join to make its final way through Chester County and Delaware to Wilmington, one of the most important battles of the American Revolution took place. The Battle of Brandywine pitted American general George Washington against British generals William Howe and Lord Charles Cornwallis and Hessian general Baron Wilhelm von Knyphausen. The first major battle of the Philadelphia campaign began during a hot summer day with a dense early-morning fog. While Howe and Cornwallis departed early in the morning of September 11, 1777, with half of the British army from Kennett Square in a flanking movement, the other half, under Knyphausen, marched straight toward Washington, who was using the Brandywine for his main defense.

The day belonged to the British, even though a young French officer, Lafayette, made his debut with the American army. He was wounded in the fields just south of the Birmingham meetinghouse, which was turned into a hospital. The flanking movement by Howe and Cornwallis and Washington's lack of credible intelligence as to the movements of the British army led to a defeat. However, the day's action did give enough time to Congress, sitting in Philadelphia, to escape. Howe's plan to destroy Washington's army and take Philadelphia and the American government failed, and Washington's troops made it to Valley Forge for the winter.

The du Pont family made its fortune along the banks of the Brandywine with its powder mills. Du Pont is now a major international company, and many of the descendants of the du Ponts still inhabit the lands surrounding the Brandywine. They have also helped to fund some of the great cultural institutions, museums, and gardens in the area, including the world-famous Longwood Gardens.

The Brandywine at Chadds Ford has (besides its claim to fame in the American Revolution) its own family of world-class artists. N.C. Wyeth studied under Harold Pyle and his Brandywine School of artists. Wyeth's illustrations adorned Scribner children's books in the early 1900s, and his other works are known as masterpieces. N.C. Wyeth's children added to the fame of the family, especially Andrew. Andrew Wyeth and his wife, Betsy, helped to establish the Brandywine River Museum, near where Washington's troops desperately engaged Knyphausen. Jamie Wyeth, Andrew's son, also continues the tradition begun by N.C. Wyeth.

The Brandywine continues its path to Wilmington, where it has long been counted upon to help fulfill the need for water for the First State's largest population center. Parks adorn its shores as the river makes its way through the city and into the Christina River, where its journey concludes.

This book is designed to accomplish multiple goals. First, the vintage postcards are designed to give readers a look at the way the area looked at the beginning of the 20th century. Most of the cards were produced before 1920, and most of them by 1910. Several newer postcards are included to give contrasting looks or to depict significant newer portions of the Brandywine's history, such as the Brandywine River Museum. The history of the Brandywine will be told in this book, along with a look at some of the characters that have given the region its character. One fascinating aspect of postcards is the message on the card. Some are mundane, some are cryptic, some are poignant, and some are funny. Some of those messages are included in the captions. Also, some myths, such as the origin of the name of Brandywine, will be discussed along with another issue—is it the Brandywine Creek or Brandywine River? Some local residents may debate the point, but no body of water with so rich a history as the Brandywine can be called by any other name than a river.

One

The Source

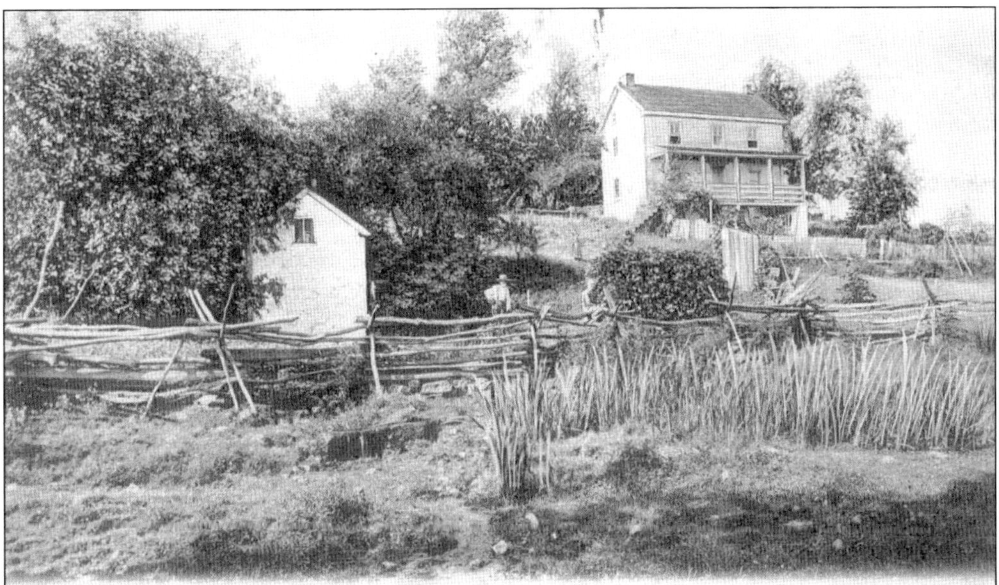

The origins of the Brandywine River begin in north-central Chester County, Pennsylvania. Two branches, one east and one west, fueled the early mills of the region. They eventually join south of West Chester, the seat of Chester County, and become one river.

The large spring, the source of the Brandywine River, is located at the foot of the Blue Ridge Mountains. The spring that begins one of the most historic rivers in the nation lies in the middle of rich farmland in the Welsh Mountain section of northern Chester County, near the village of Honey Brook. The Brandywine will be fed by a number of small river branches before joining together in the southern section of the county.

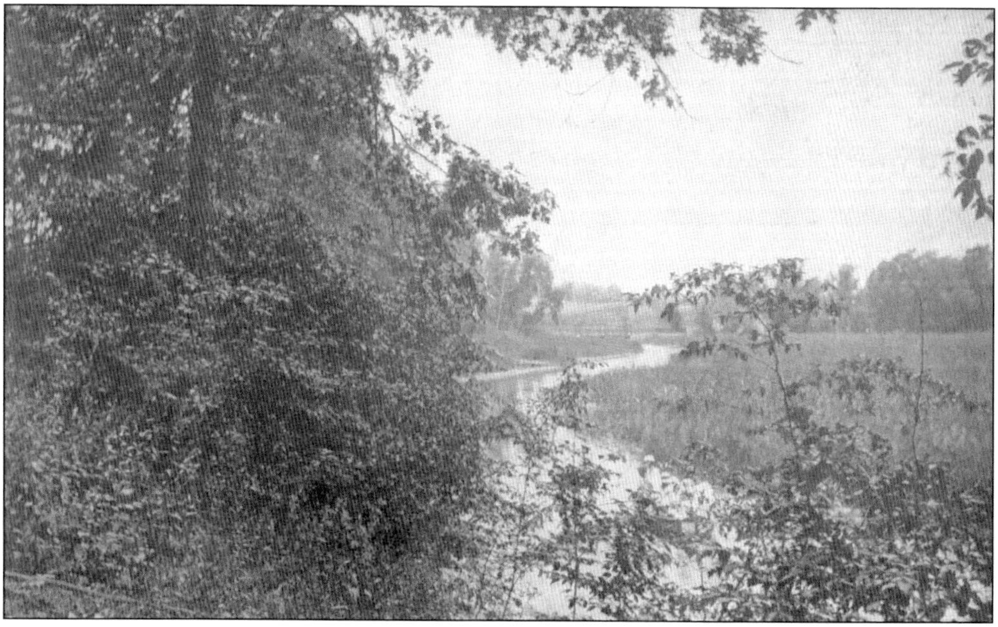

Honey Brook is just one of the many villages and towns throughout Chester County, one of the original counties settled by William Penn in November 1682, that thrives because of the rich nature of the soil and the water sources that feed the Brandywine. Honey Brook is a vibrant agriculture community. The makeup of the Honey Brook community has changed little from the early days of colonization, as farms and small family businesses continue to dominate the employment scene.

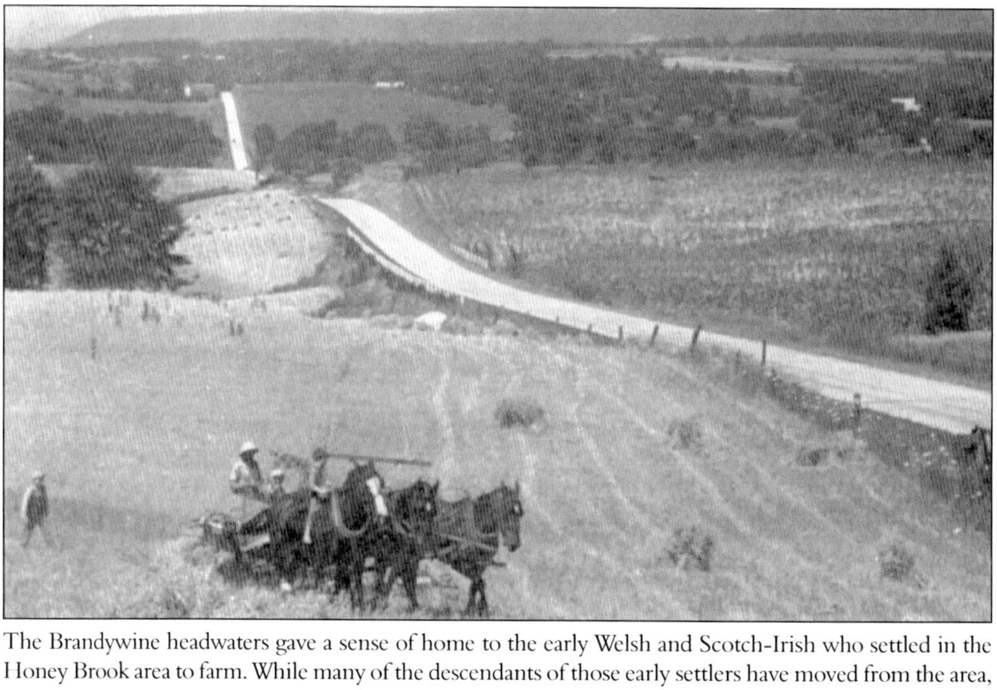

The Brandywine headwaters gave a sense of home to the early Welsh and Scotch-Irish who settled in the Honey Brook area to farm. While many of the descendants of those early settlers have moved from the area, the Amish have settled in the area to farm and live much the same way they have for many generations. In fact, the Amish farms are now proliferating all across the western sections of Chester County.

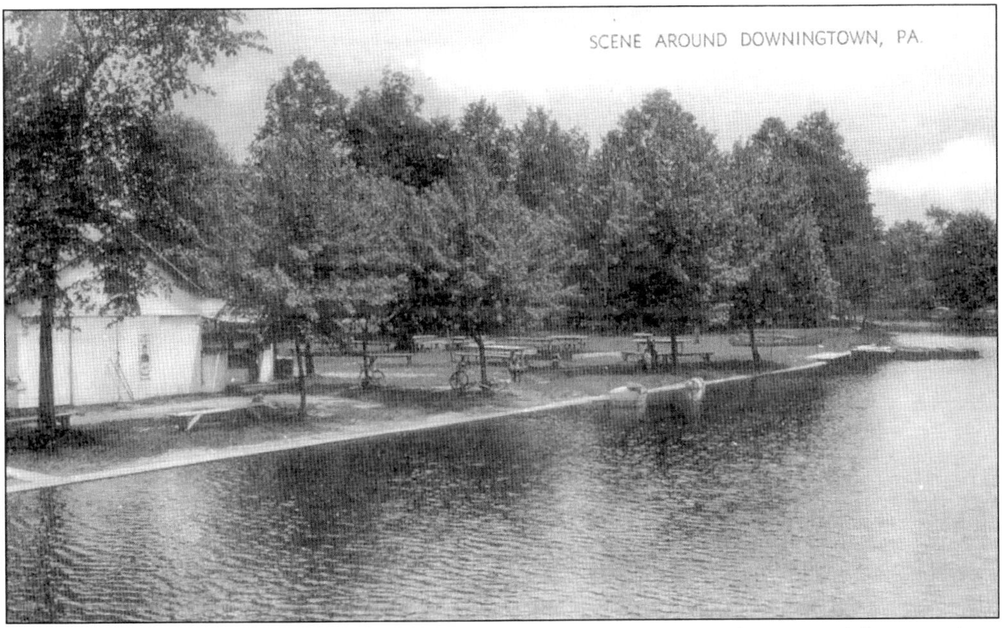

One of the greatest attributes of the Brandywine is its tranquility. The river has inspired famous writers and painters alike and has been a soothing source of peace to the generations who have stopped to enjoy its beauty. As this postcard depicts, the Brandywine is used for recreational activities. Picnics are still held on its shore, and boating takes place on the river.

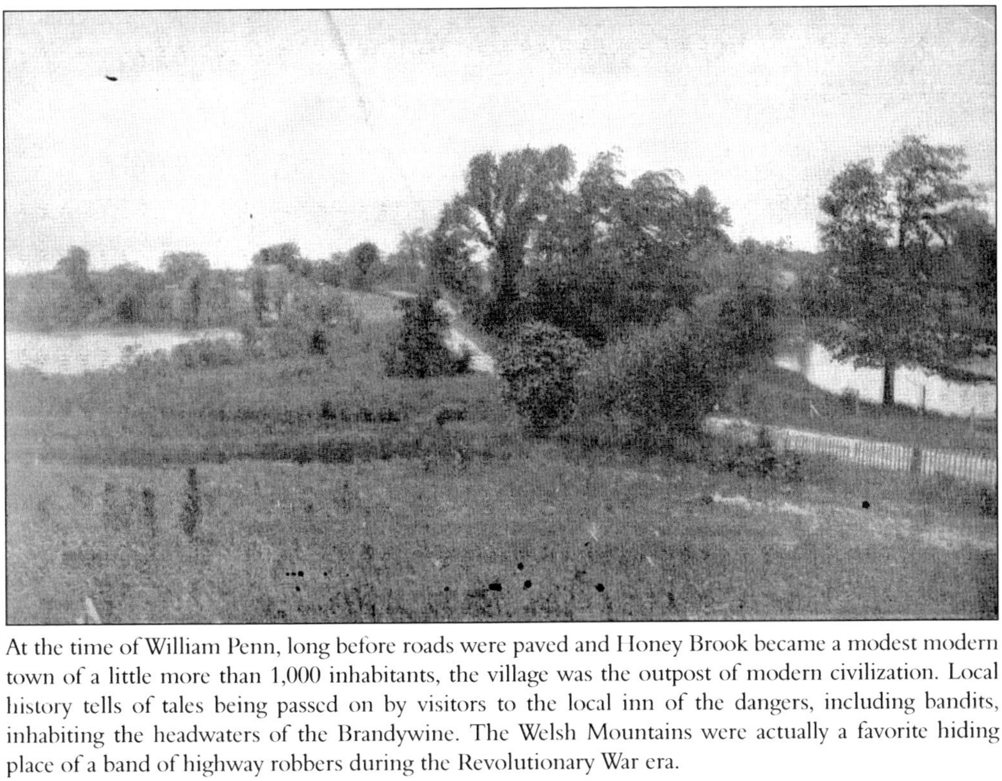

At the time of William Penn, long before roads were paved and Honey Brook became a modest modern town of a little more than 1,000 inhabitants, the village was the outpost of modern civilization. Local history tells of tales being passed on by visitors to the local inn of the dangers, including bandits, inhabiting the headwaters of the Brandywine. The Welsh Mountains were actually a favorite hiding place of a band of highway robbers during the Revolutionary War era.

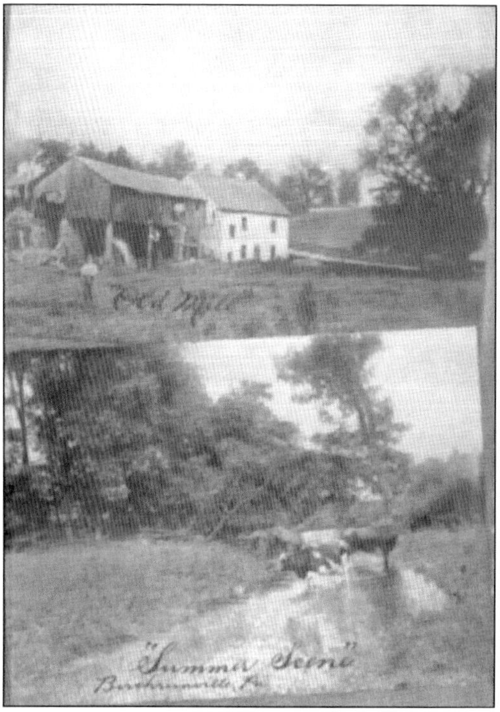

As the "summer scene" suggests in this postcard dated 1908, the Brandywine valley was a working community in the early 1900s. Farms used the Brandywine and its tributaries to feed the livestock. The mill pictured is one of many that flourished in the area because of the Brandywine. The mill fueled the local economy and contributed food to the hungry troops at Valley Forge during the long winter of 1777–1778.

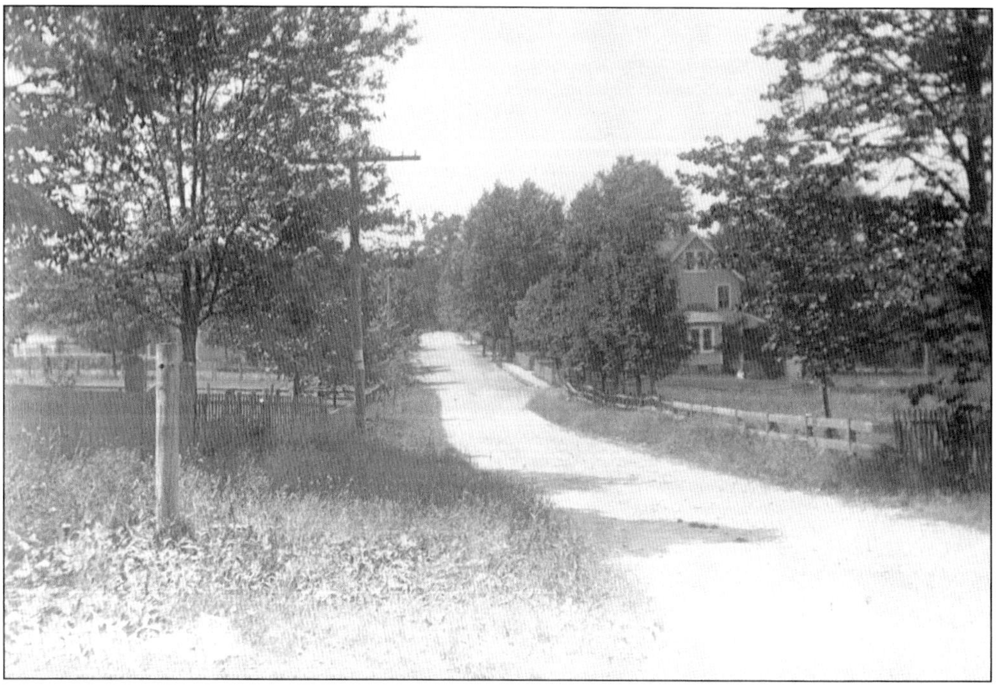

Sitting in Wallace Township, near Honey Brook, is Glenmoore. It is one of the sleepy communities that has never developed into a highly populated area, but as with all of Chester County, it is fighting sprawl. This postcard with a 1911 postmark shows the home in which the sender and her family are staying, including a baby who is fast asleep. On June 5, the sender writes, "It is quite rainy today."

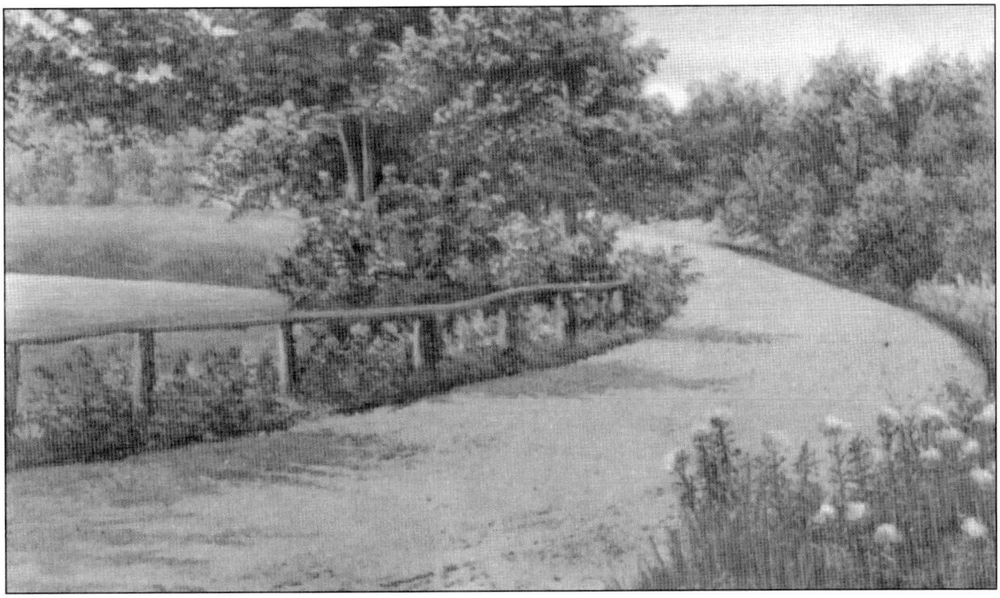

When most people think of covered bridges, they usually think of New England, but Chester County had its fair share, including some over the Brandywine. Glenmoore also had one for many years over the east branch of the Brandywine. Most of the covered bridges in the county were thought to be unsafe, and many were burned and replaced by steel and concrete bridges in the 1930s and 1940s.

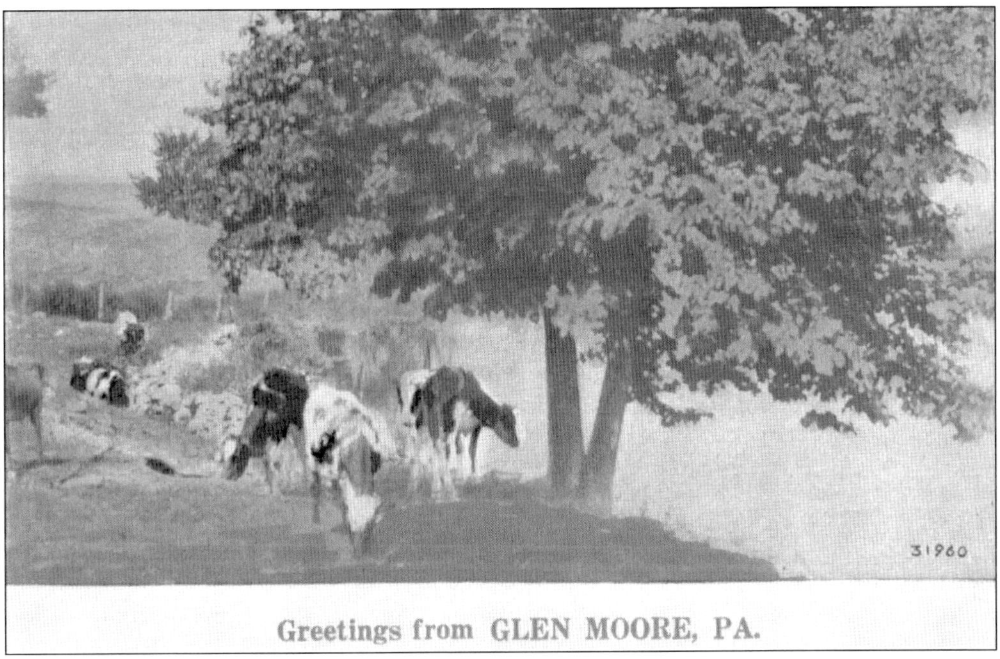

The caption of this postcard reads, "Greetings from GLEN MOORE, PA." This postcard from the White Border era (1915–1930) is a typical one. Because of the high cost of labor, inexperience, and public taste, many poor-quality cards were produced in the United States. The quality caused a number of publishers to go out of business. The white border was introduced to save on ink. Note the spelling of Glenmoore on the card.

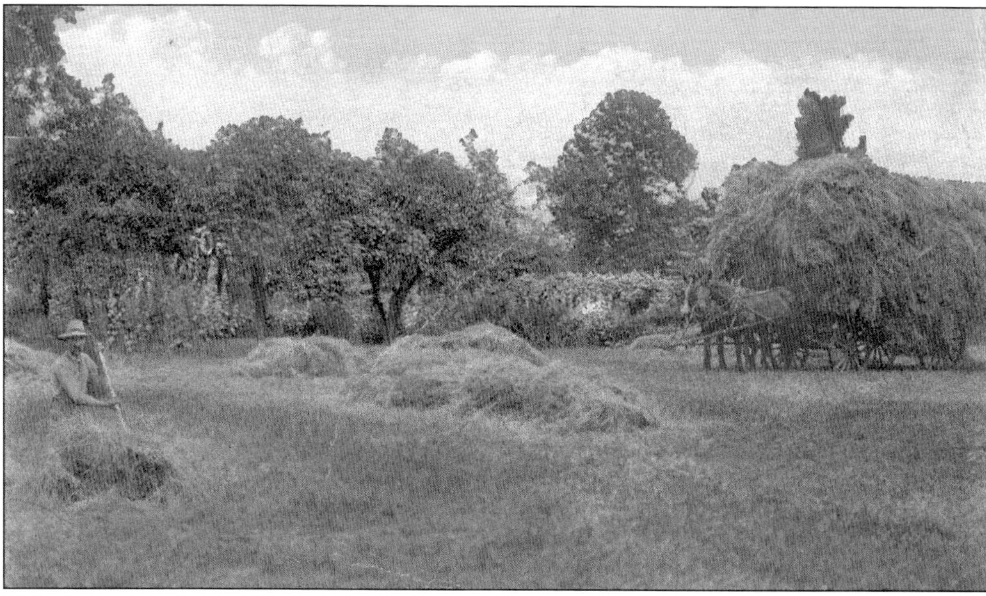

The farms of Chester County offered homes during the summer for young relatives during the Great Depression. In another White Border–era card from Glenmoore, the young writer says, "Dear father & mother: Just a card to let you know we are well and hope you are the same. H. has been working in corn and I have been hauling in as fast as I could to keep up." He also talks about eating fresh apples.

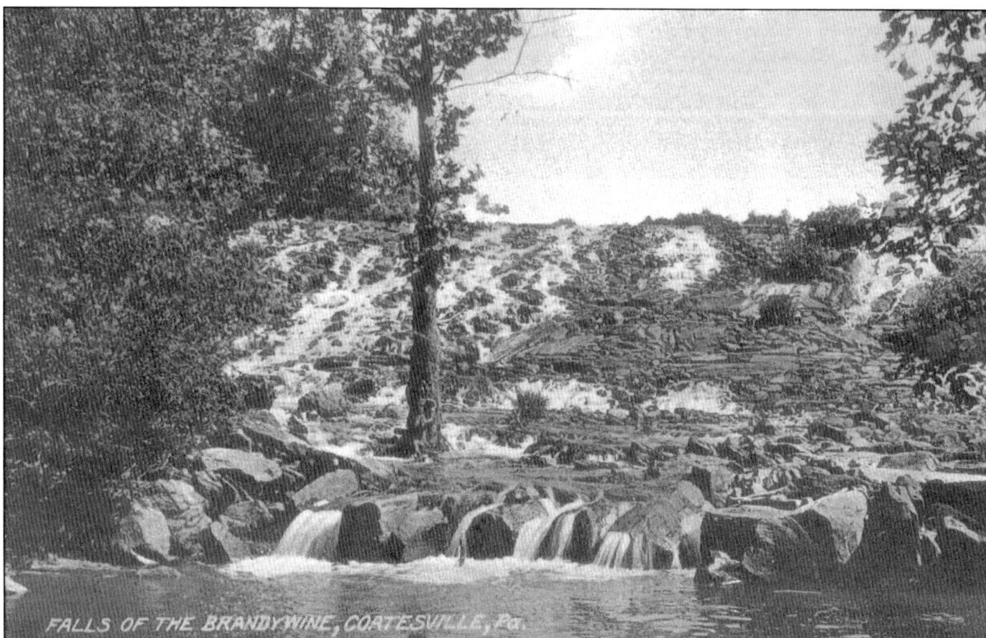

The west branch of the Brandywine, which begins as no more than a trickle in the Welsh Mountains, begins to gather strength as it heads south from Honey Brook and the Icedale area. It also picks up fresh water as the Rock Run feeds it above the city of Coatesville and Sucker Run flows from the west through Valley Township to Coatesville.

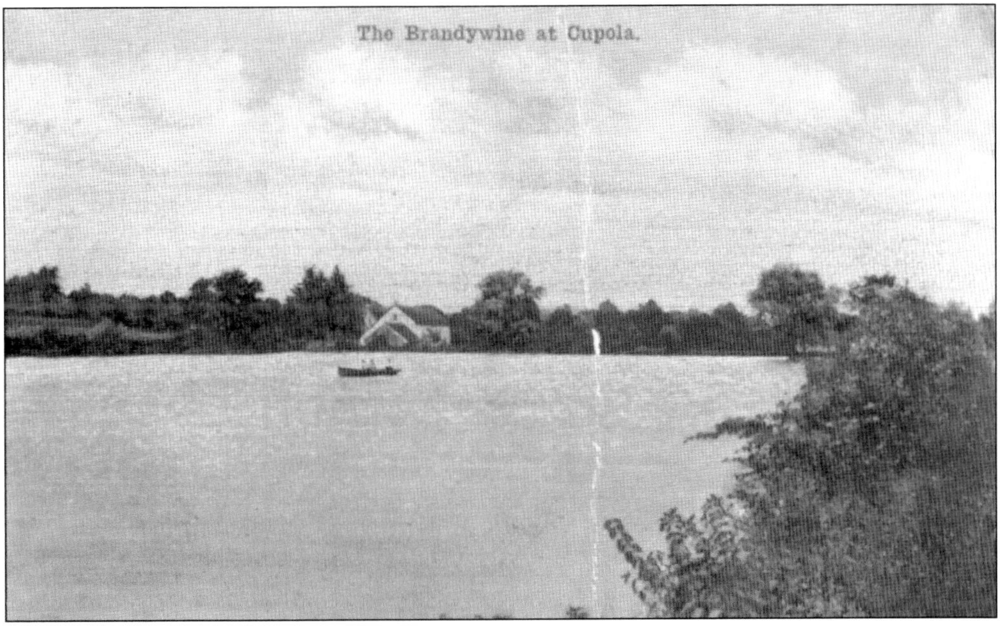

The Brandywine passes through Cupola, where a dam once held back the Brandywine in the northern region of the east branch of the river. An old gristmill on one of the properties surrounding the river was powered by the Brandywine. The mill had long since ceased functioning and had been turned into a home. The large pond made by the dam was a local favorite of young ice-skaters during the winter.

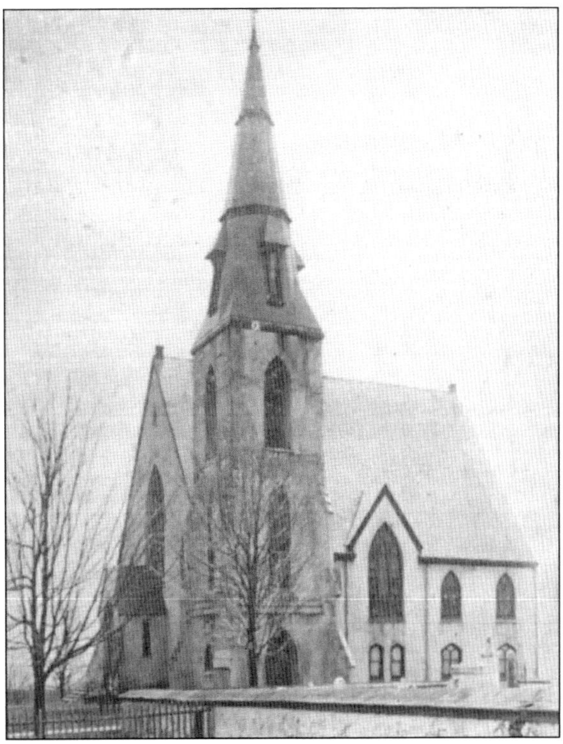

Religion was a big part of early life in Chester County, and local church congregations continue to grow today. William Penn and others who established this country knew the value of religious freedom. The Amish, Mennonites, and Quakers can be seen along various sections of the Brandywine. Presbyterian churches (like the one shown) and Baptist and other denominations prosper. Many date back to the 1800s.

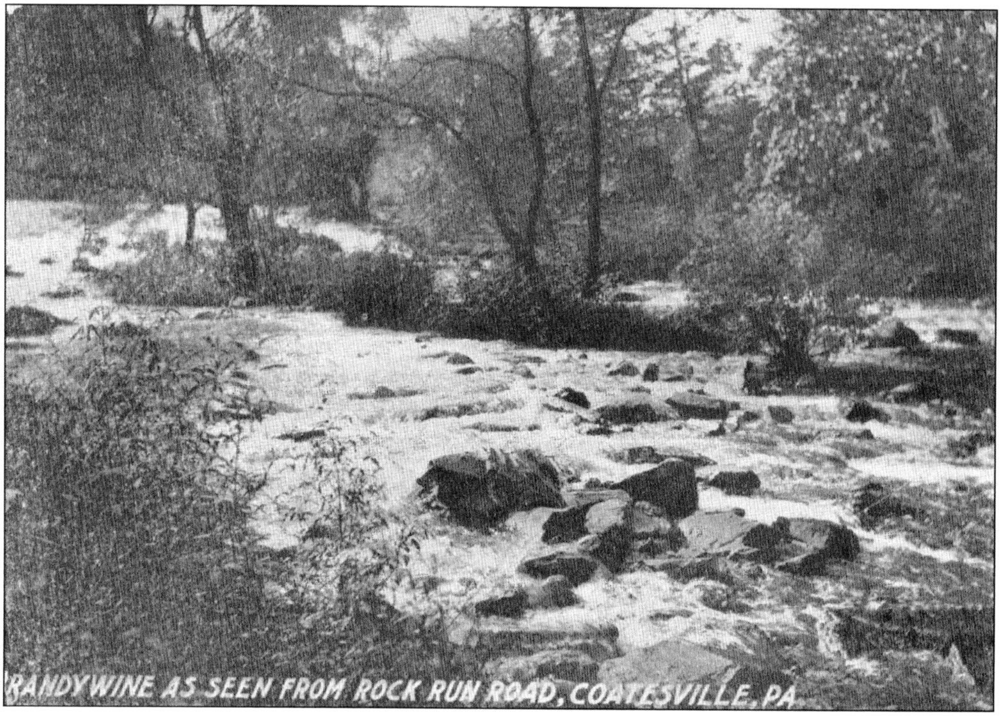

Just north of Coatesville, the Brandywine flows past the old Hibernia furnace and to the Rock Run. In the 18th century, Samuel Downing converted pig iron into bar iron in the forge. The forge was active for more than a century but is now used as a centerpiece for a Chester County park. At one point, the property contained two forges and heating furnaces, a rolling mill, a gristmill, and several houses.

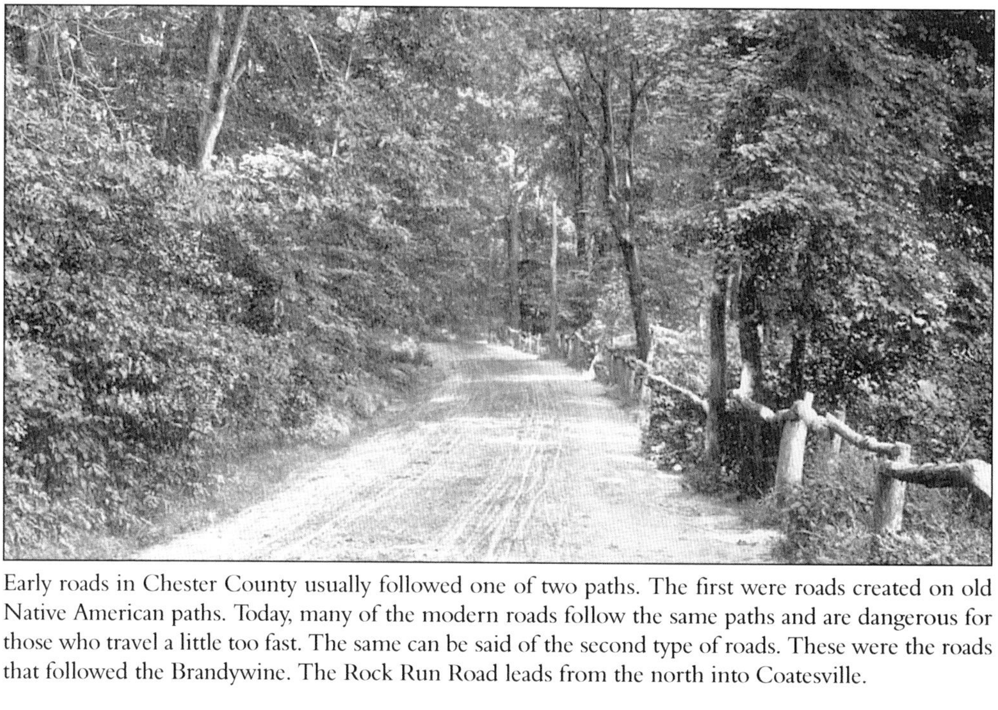

Early roads in Chester County usually followed one of two paths. The first were roads created on old Native American paths. Today, many of the modern roads follow the same paths and are dangerous for those who travel a little too fast. The same can be said of the second type of roads. These were the roads that followed the Brandywine. The Rock Run Road leads from the north into Coatesville.

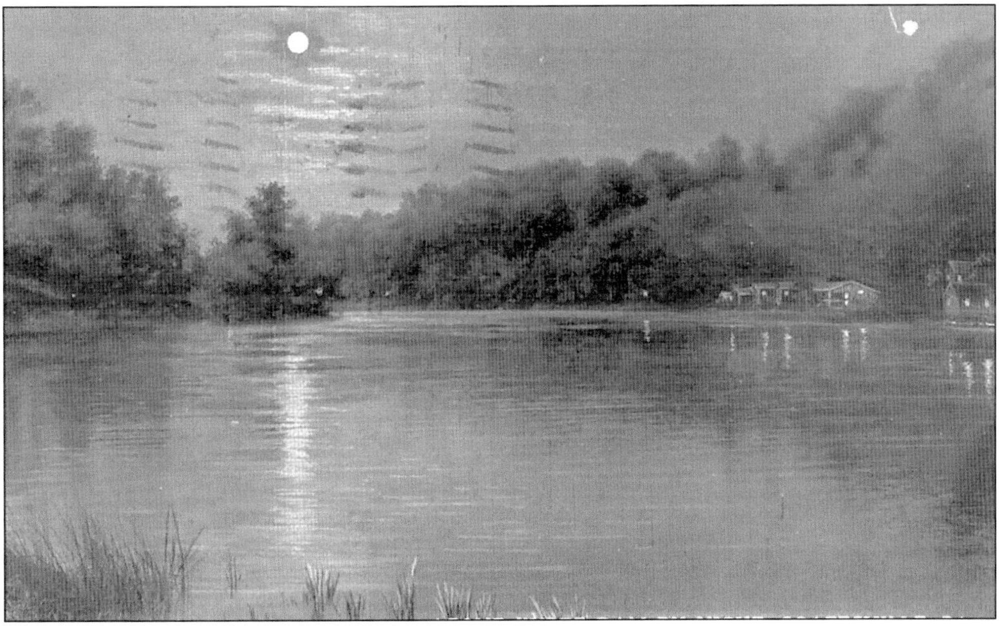

Coatesville is not known as a tourist destination, but many families stayed at cottages on the Brandywine and its tributaries near the city. A woman who lived on Strode Avenue in 1913 used this card of Kurtz's Dam to admonish a friend for not writing. "Are you cross or don't you want to write, or what is the reason you don't answer. When are you coming over. Please write soon. Your Friend, Mabel. Don't forget to write." She included her own address on the card.

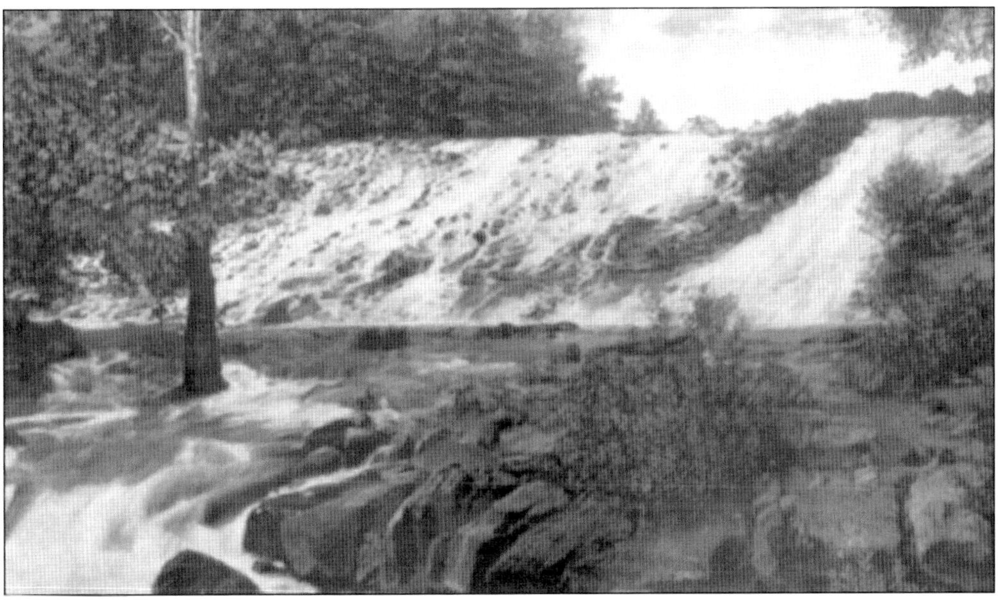

This postcard with a daylight view of Kurtz's Dam has a very different message written on it than the one the Coatesville woman penned to her friend. In fact, this postcard (the postmark is blurred, but a 1¢ stamp is attached, indicating the early 1900s) has a short message: "Arrived home safe and will send pictures later. Horace." The card was sent to a "Miss Katherine in Morrisville, Penna." The use of postcards as a note to announce safe arrivals was common in the early 1900s.

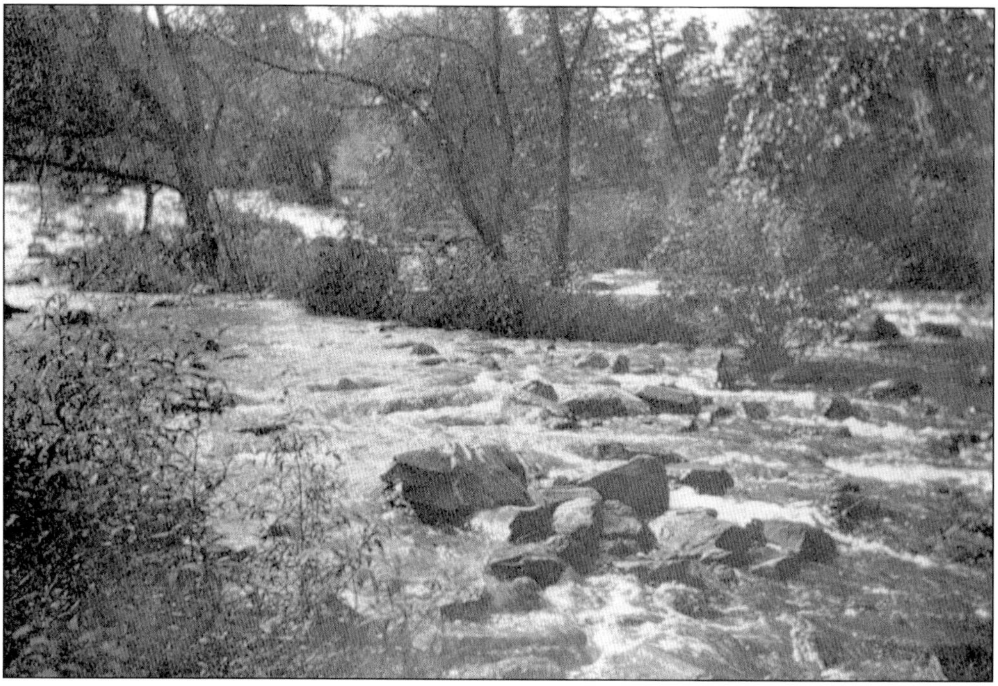

This scene on the Brandywine, north of Coatesville, can still be enjoyed today. While most of Chester County, especially along the southern region of the Brandywine, fights sprawl and a growing population, Coatesville's population has remained stagnant. The lack of increased population actually is a plus for the Brandywine, as the river remains unspoiled and can still be used for recreation.

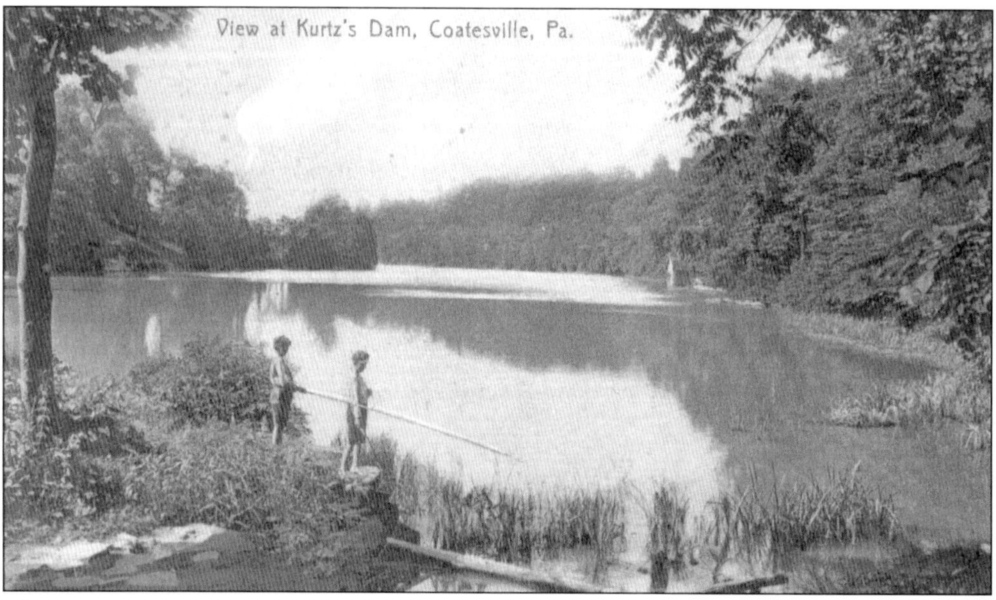

The caption of this 1907 postcard says, "View at Kurtz's Dam, Coatesville, Pa." The depiction of two youngsters at play at the dam looks like a scene from a Norman Rockwell painting. At first glance, the boys appear to be fishing. Only one of them has a pole, however, and it appears to be much longer than a fishing rod. They are both barefoot. The cabins at the dam can be seen in the background.

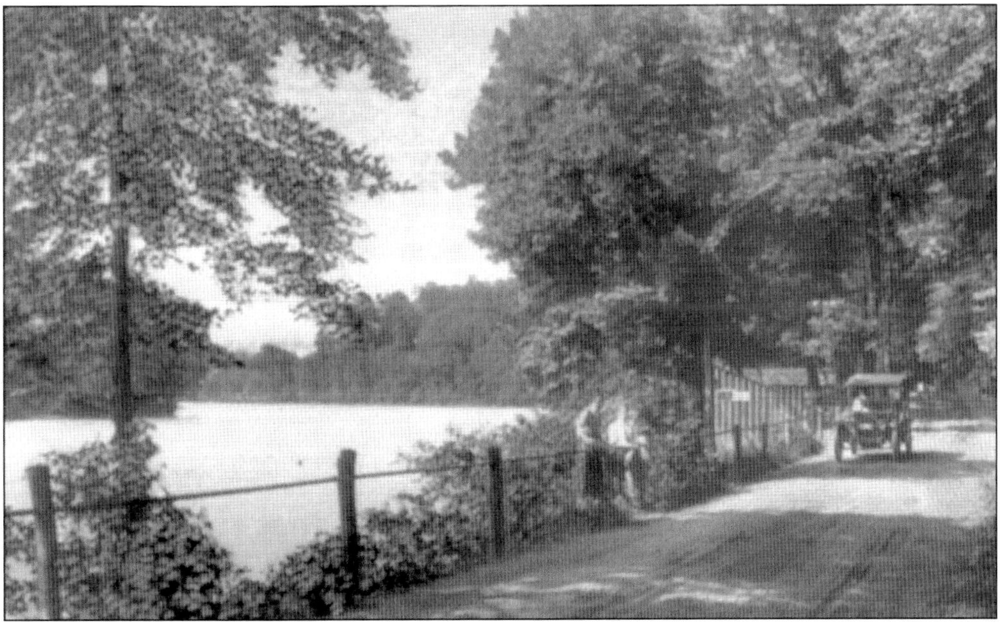

One of the joys of postcards is seeing how things have changed. Postcards also show items that no longer exist. In this card of "Kurtz's Dam Boat Club and Drive, Coatesville, Pa.," an early automobile is depicted along with some residents, maybe waiting for a ride. Their clothing definitely has a style that is not seen today. Also, few modern-day residents of Coatesville remember the boat club.

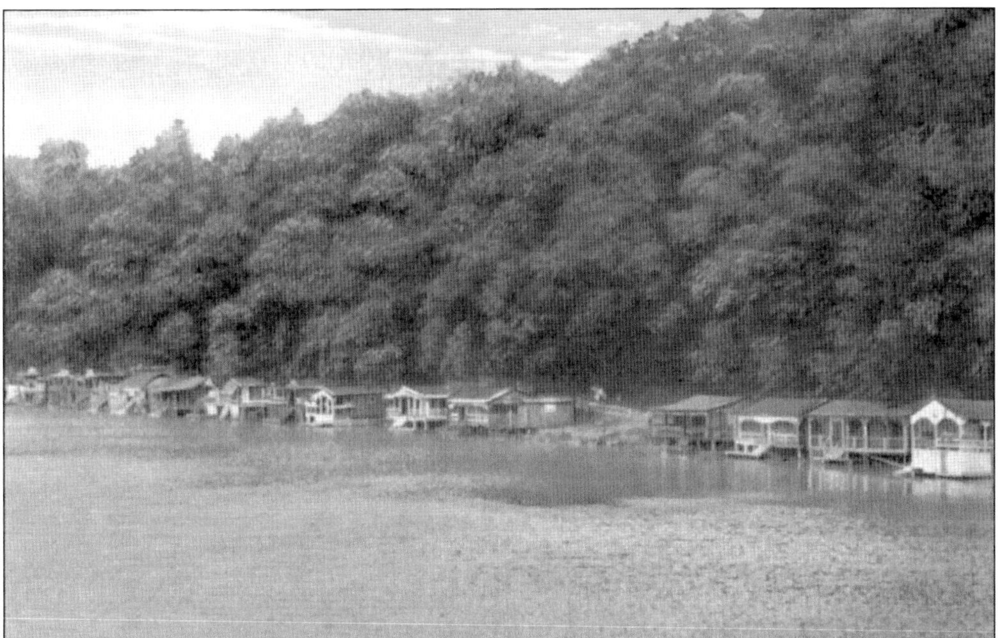

Speaking of things that no longer exist, the cottages depicted in this scene on Kurtz's Dam and the dam itself are only memories. Kurtz's Dam formed a reservoir beside Rock Run, which was used as a summer retreat with boathouses along its shores. While the small village of Rock Run has survived, only the Brandywine flows as a reminder of a bygone day of the city of Coatesville.

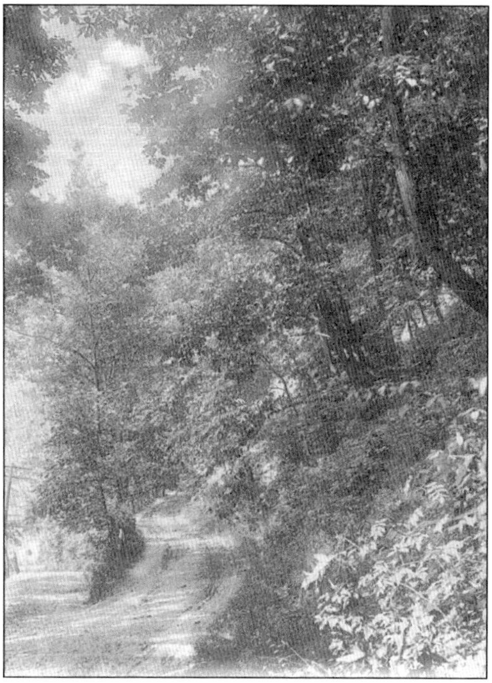

The road leading through Rock Run, along the Brandywine, and into Coatesville still carries travelers today, but the road has been paved and modernized. The village has not prospered over the years, and all of the industry (along with the dam and the recreation) has left Rock Run. Rock Run has become another victim of the fall of the manufacturing industry that has claimed several communities in the northern regions of Chester County.

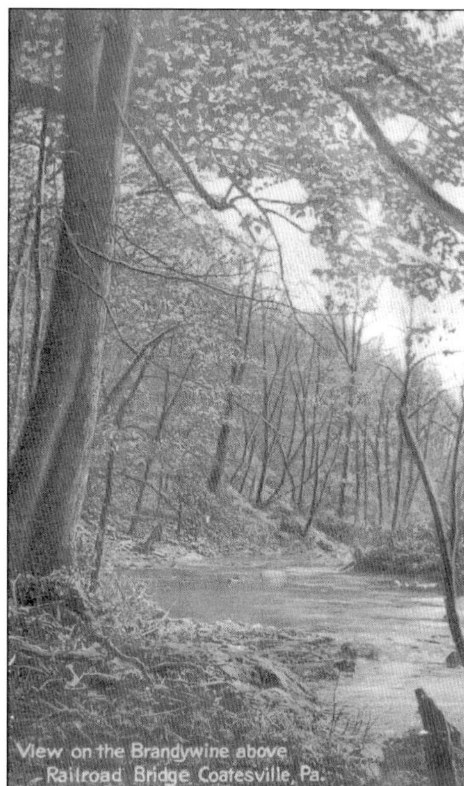

This is a "view on the Brandywine above Railroad Bridge, Coatesville, Pa." As the west branch of the Brandywine departs the Rock Run region, it has only a short trip to the scene of its next major location where the steel industry built what is known as the Steel City. Rebecca Lukens, a pioneering woman entrepreneur of the 19th century, helped build Lukens Steel Company into a major corporation. The note on this card with a 1909 postmark states, "The scenery of Chester County is so beautiful."

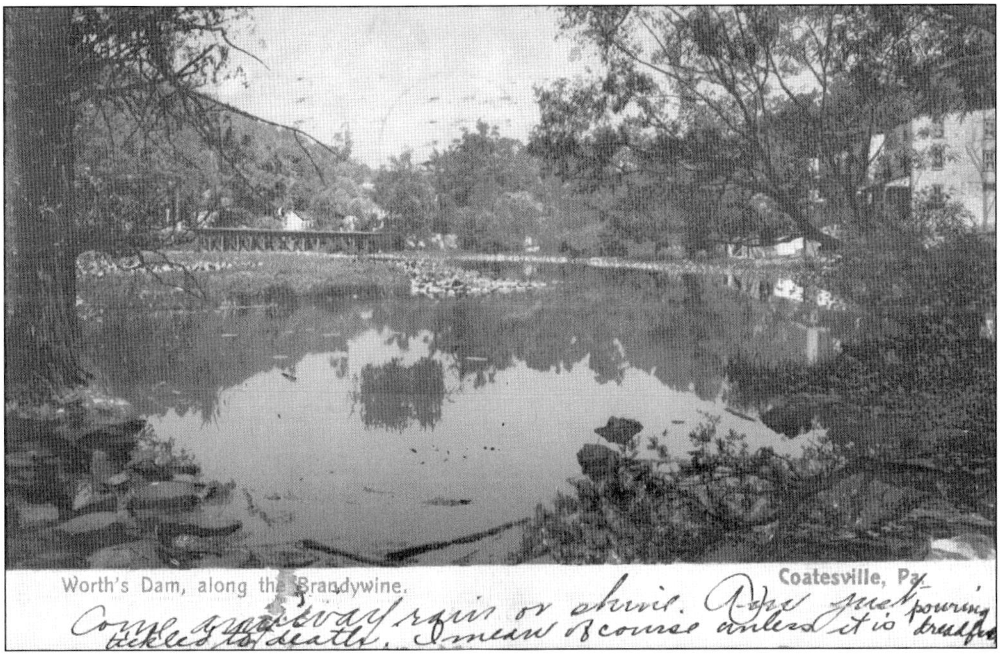

Another dam along the Brandywine near Coatesville was Worth's Dam. Several residences are seen to the right of the dam. To visit or not to visit is the question on this card (postmarked 1907) to a Wilmington woman. Postcards had many uses, including invitations to gatherings. "Come anyway rain or shine. Ann just tickled to death. I mean of course unless it is pouring dreadfully."

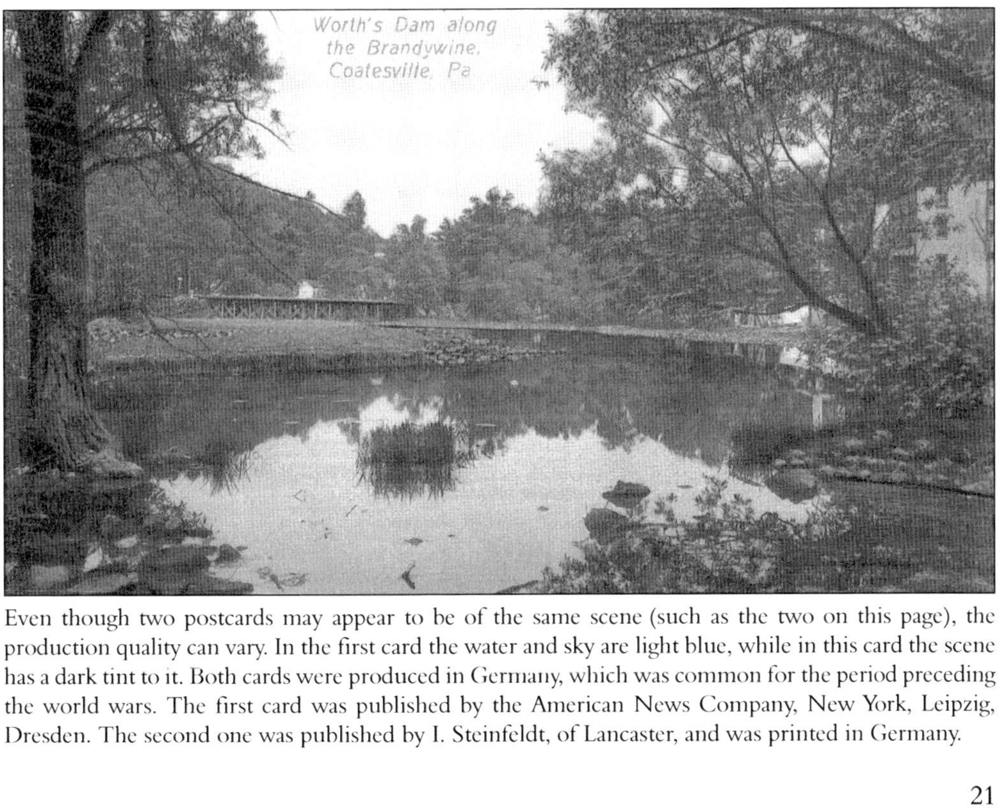

Even though two postcards may appear to be of the same scene (such as the two on this page), the production quality can vary. In the first card the water and sky are light blue, while in this card the scene has a dark tint to it. Both cards were produced in Germany, which was common for the period preceding the world wars. The first card was published by the American News Company, New York, Leipzig, Dresden. The second one was published by I. Steinfeldt, of Lancaster, and was printed in Germany.

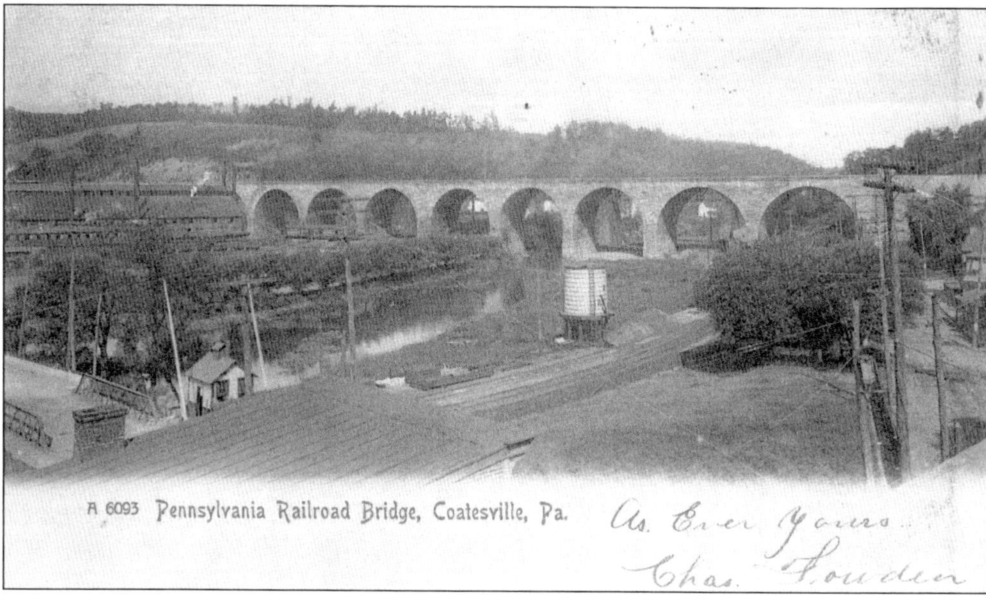

The west branch of the Brandywine enters the city of Coatesville under the Pennsylvania Railroad Bridge, or High Bridge. Seen in the postcard are a water tower and other equipment needed for the freight trains that traveled to and from the Lukens Steel Company. The scene is from a postcard dated 1905. Colorized cards of the same scene appeared the following year.

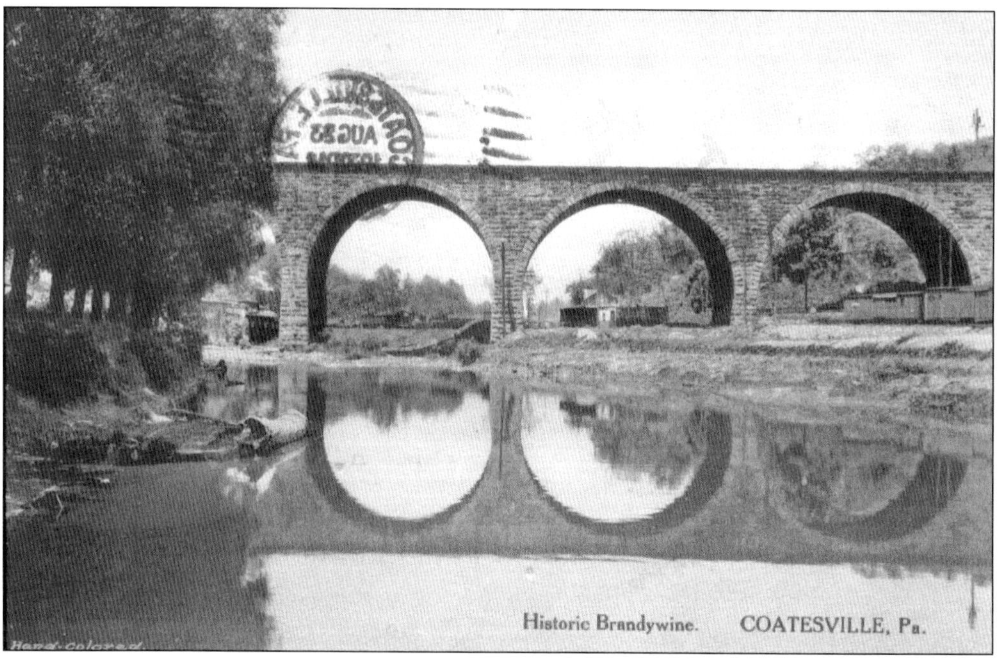

"Historic Brandywine. COATESVILLE, Pa." is the title of this card. Indeed, the Brandywine is historic for many reasons, as is noted in this book. The postmark on the card is August 23, 1916, and on the card it is noted that the scene is hand colored. Besides the bridge and the Brandywine, trains are depicted. The writer is not enjoying the summer in Coatesville, as he informs a family member that he is "alright but don't enjoy this warm weather very much."

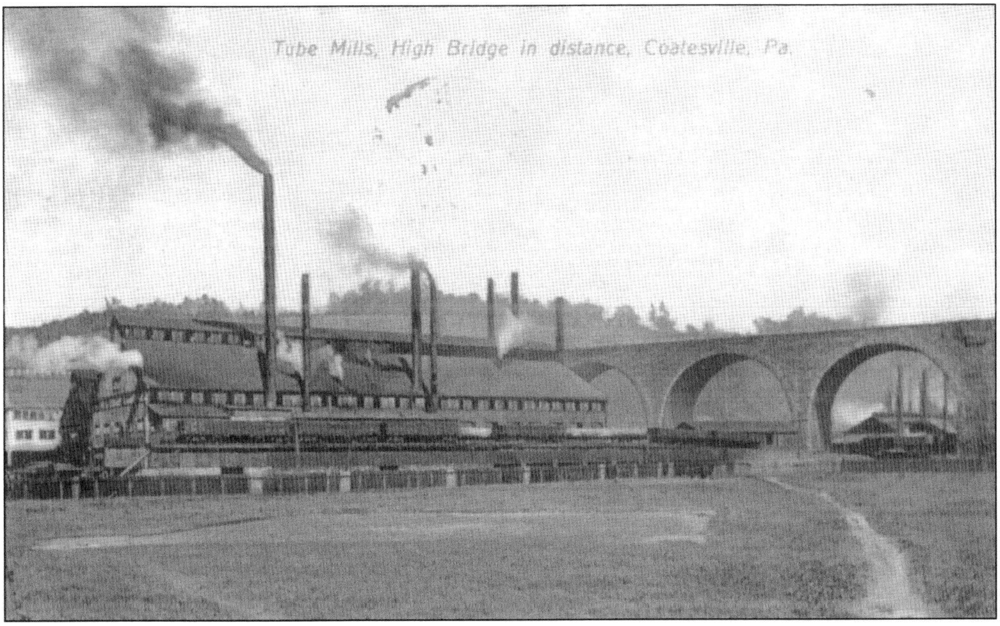

Shown here are the "Tube Mills. High Bridge in distance, Coatesville, Pa." The scene on this card shows a glimpse of the city's steel mill. Coatesville and another town to its west, Parkesburg, became busy areas of Chester County during the early 1900s because of manufacturing. Both towns have now fallen on hard times, as the Lukens Steel Company has drastically cut employment.

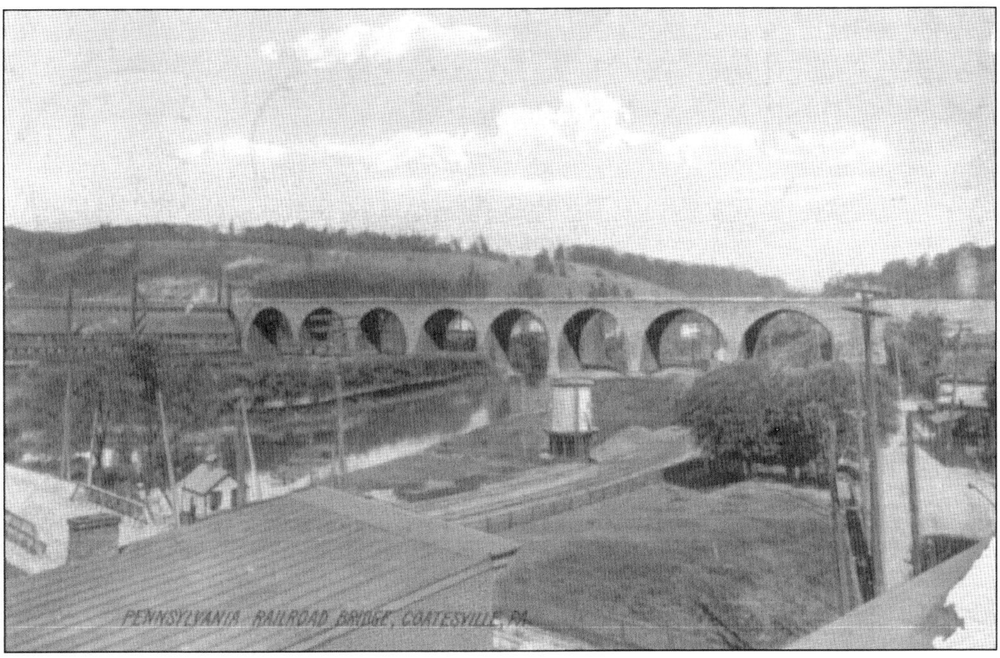

The Brandywine Iron Works was established in the early 1800s. The ironworks became Lukens Steel Company and is now part of Bethlehem Steel Company. At one point in history, Lukens was a leader in specialty plate steel, and its products were used in military equipment during the world wars. It was a major national industry. The Brandywine flows through the city and under the High Bridge.

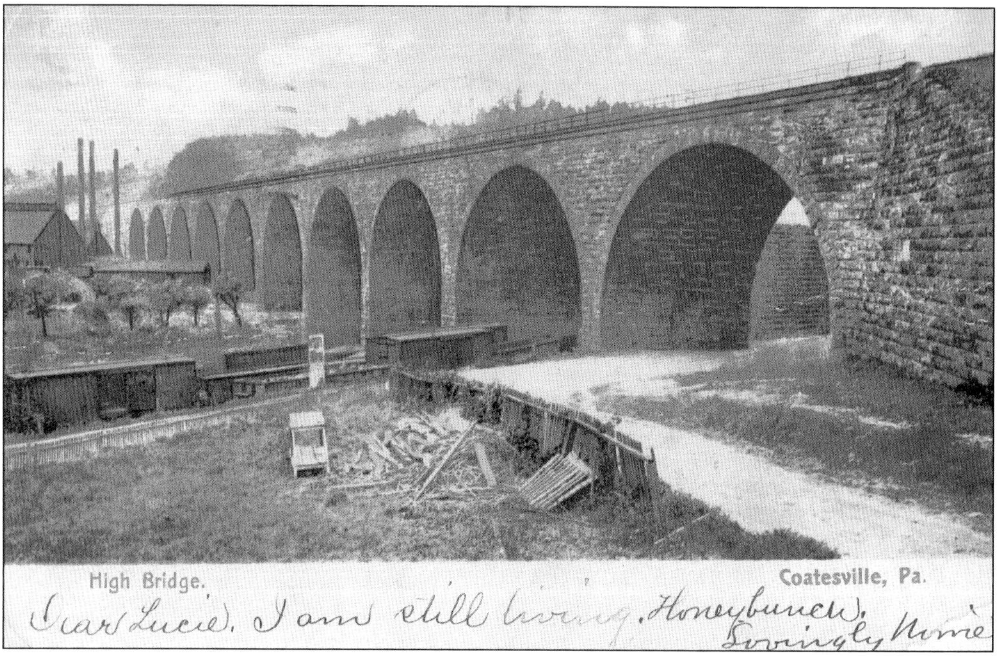

Rebecca Pennock, whose father was an ironmaster, married Charles Lloyd Lukens. Charles Lukens soon took over the operation of the mill. After his death in 1825, Rebecca Lukens took over running the ironworks, an unheard-of job for a woman of that era. With the help of a neighboring ironmaster in Hibernia, who supplied bar iron, Lukens began to prosper.

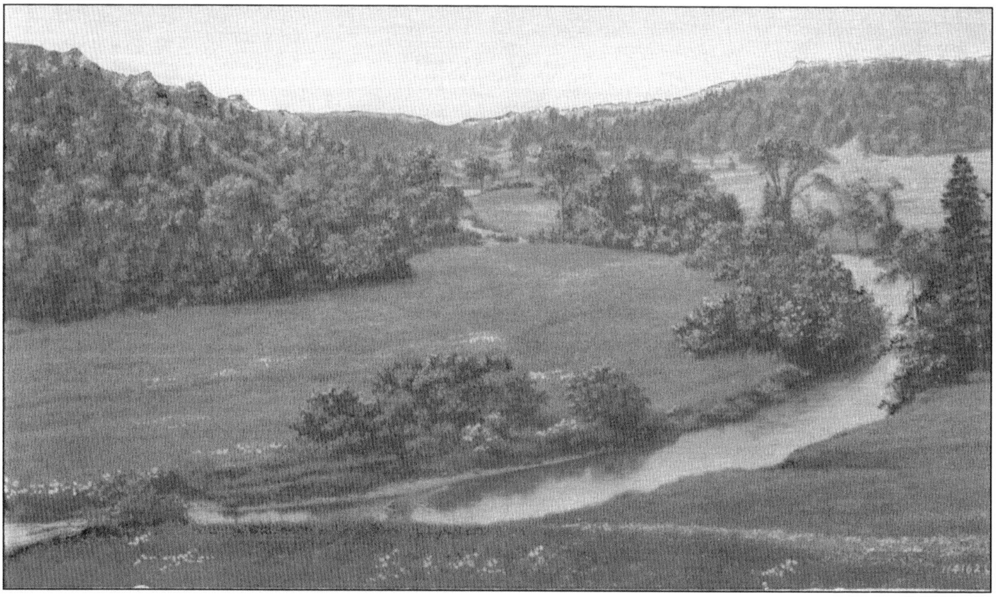

The west branch of the Brandywine winds through the steel mill, departs Coatesville, and passes through the small village of Modena, which was the location of material supply companies for Lukens Steel. In this postcard, a father writes to his daughter in Bridgeton, New Jersey, and assures her he will be home soon. He also reports that the roads in the area were awful and that there was "a big car upset right in front of our house last night. I helped pull the man out but he wasn't hurt."

The east branch of the Brandywine winds its way from Glenmoore to what is now Marsh Creek State Park. The park contains a lake made from tributaries of the Brandywine. The Struble Trail now follows the river and borders Uwchlan Township. This area contained many early American mills. The sender uses this postcard as a thank-you card for sending thread.

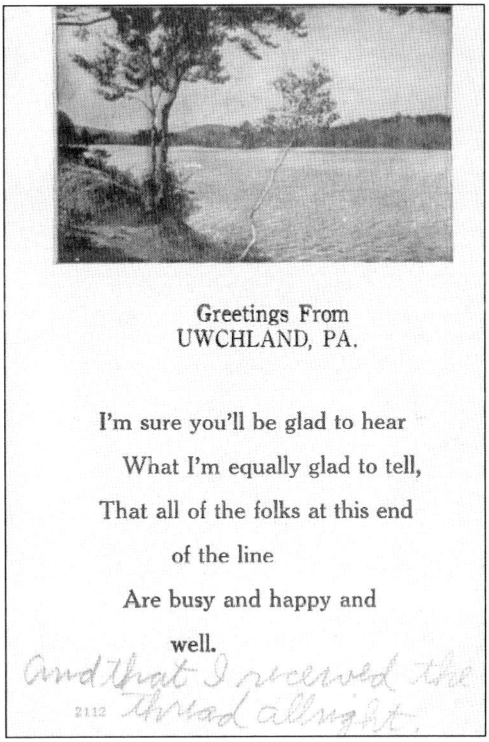

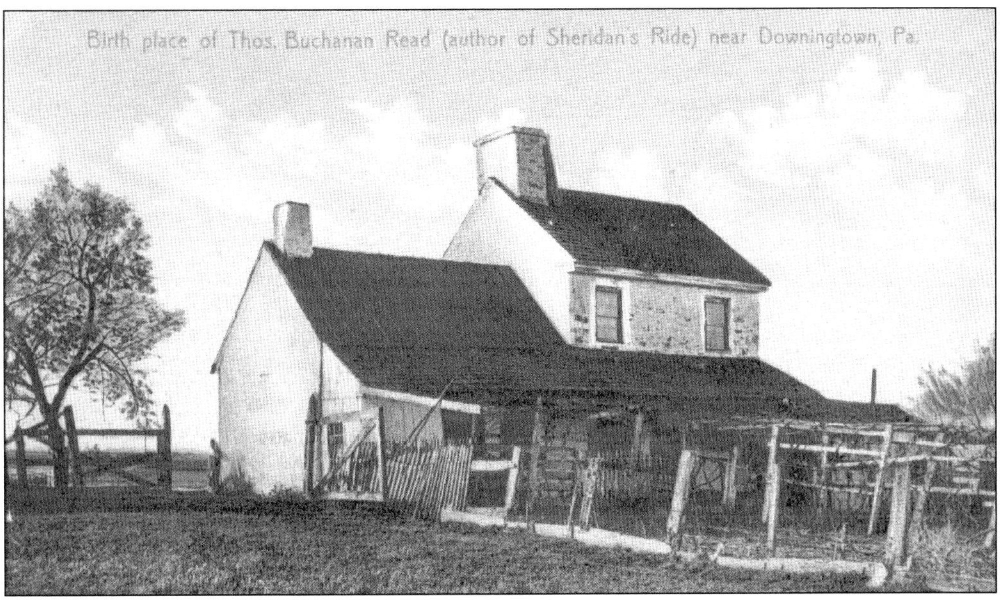

The Brandywine has inspired many writers over the years. Bayard Taylor and Thomas Buchanan Read were two of the most notable 19th-century writers who were influenced by the river. In East Brandywine at Corner Ketch is the 1822 birthplace of Read, known as a poet, painter, and patriot. His poem "Sheridan's Ride," written during the Civil War, was consistently used in schools for many years. His other famous poem, on Italian beauty, was titled "Drifting," which began, "My soul to-day / Is far away / Sailing the Vesuvian Bay."

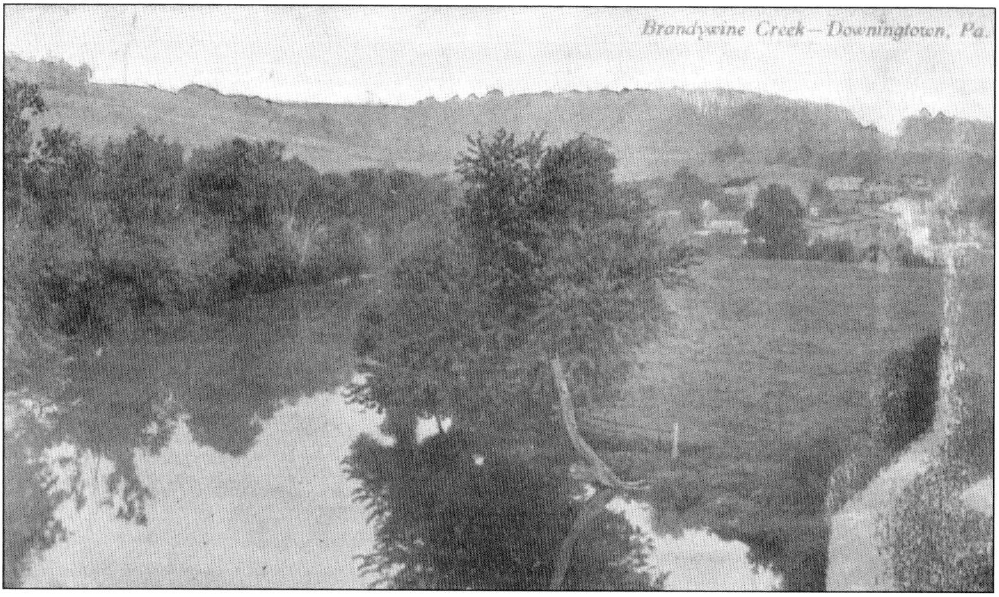

The east branch of the Brandywine gains strength as it approaches Downingtown and passes Marsh Creek and the 535-acre man-made lake that was formed in 1969. Wilmer W. MacElree wrote about the area in his 1912 book *Down the Eastern and up the Black Brandywine.* The term black Brandywine came from the swamp water that formed in the area. The writer of this card, for some reason, wrote her message upside down.

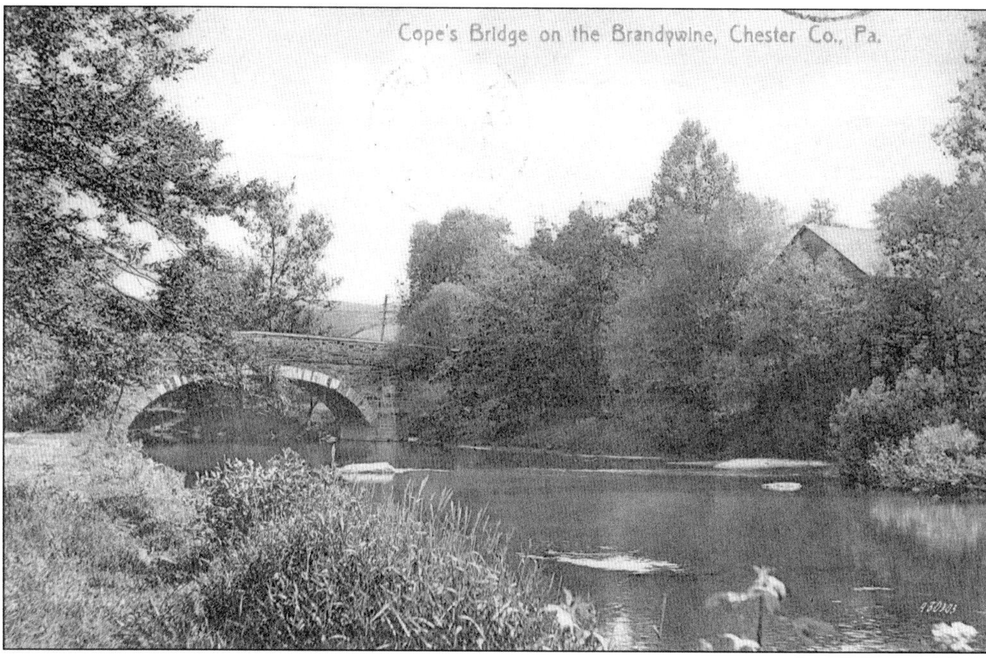

The Brandywine above Downingtown is an area where Chester County residents and others gather for recreation. An RV park sits along the river just south of Lyndell where the river is used to pass many pleasant summer days. The opening day of trout season in Pennsylvania will always find standing room only at the best spots along the Brandywine in this area.

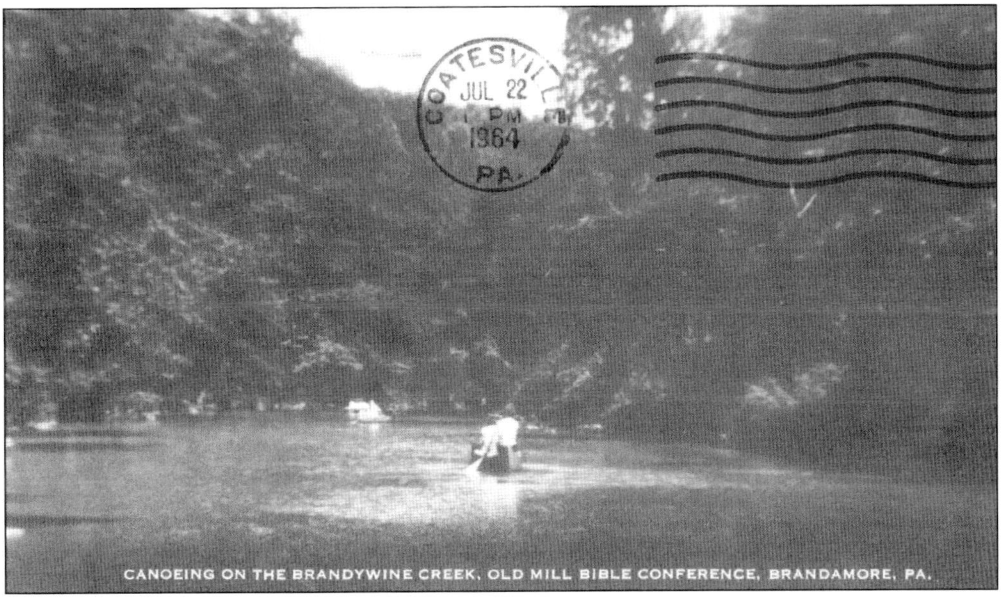

This is an old mill that was once used to grind grain stands on the west branch of the Brandywine just south of Icedale. The mill operated until World War I. In 1933, a Philadelphia Presbyterian church purchased Brandamore mill and constructed a retreat called Old Mill Bible Conference. Pictured in the postcard is a group canoeing on the Brandywine at the camp. The inscription reads, "It's very nice here, I like it. Joey."

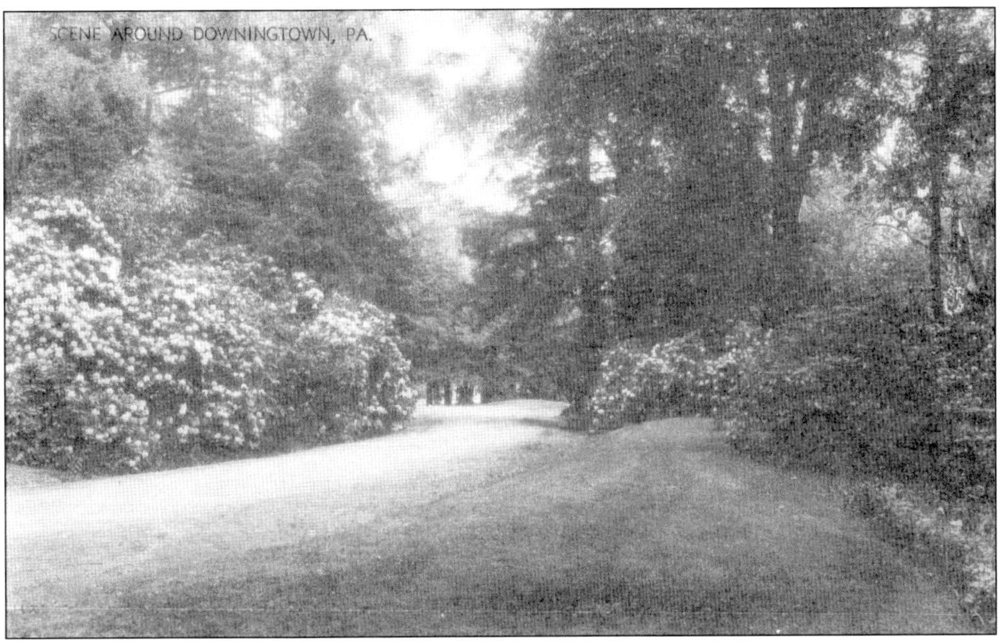

The Brandywine continues its path south from Lyndell. The Struble Trail—a recreational running, walking, and hiking path named for a Chester County conservationist—follows the river as it makes its way into the borough of Downingtown. The Brandywine helped fuel the industrial town noted for many years for its paper mills. As with most of the industrialized county, those industries are declining.

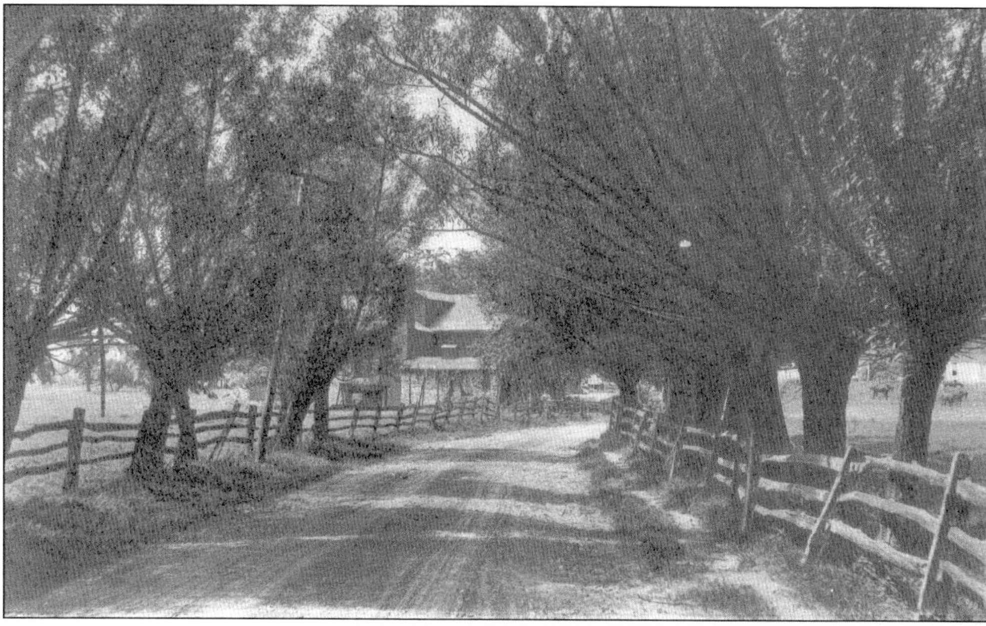

Kerr's Mill sits on the Brandywine near Downingtown. There were many such mills in the area. During the harsh winter of 1777–1778, Gen. George Washington relied on the mills to feed his troops during the Philadelphia campaign that started with the Battle of Brandywine near Chadds Ford. Washington's troops would disable the mills by taking the millstone if they felt the British were going to capture a mill.

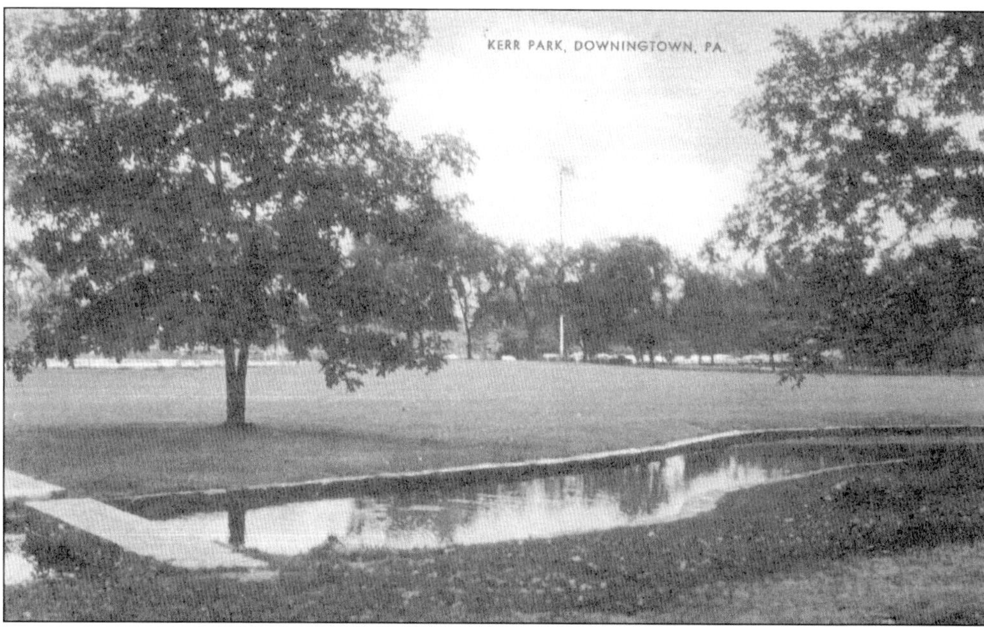

Chester County, one of the three original counties founded by William Penn, has a proud history. The ancestors of the Brandywine's early settlers can be found throughout the area. As the Struble Trail is named for Bob Struble, Kerr Park in Downingtown is named after the Kerr family. The Brandywine runs on its border and is used as the base for a long-running community celebration on the Fourth of July.

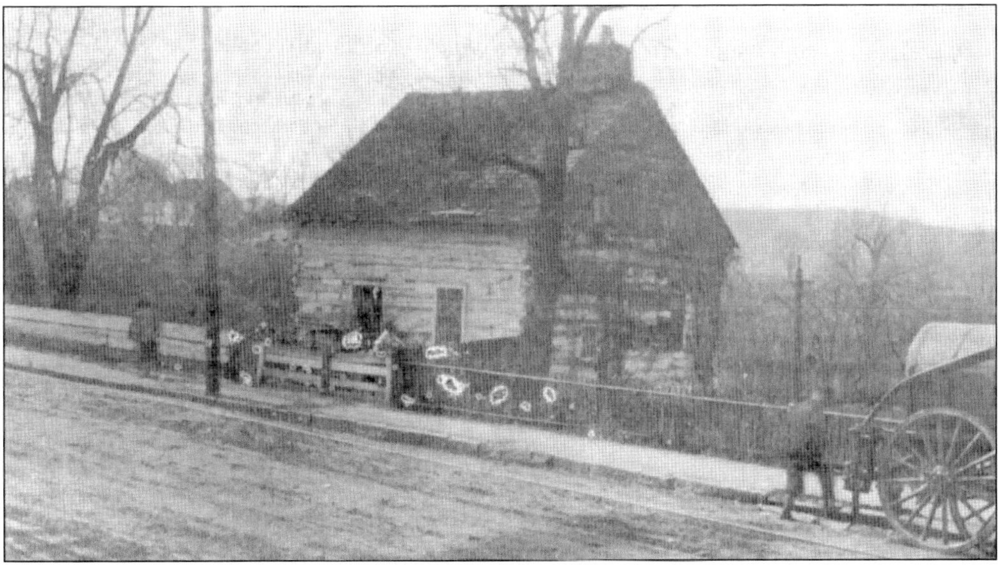

Downingtown was a favorite stop for travelers on the Great Turnpike, which connected Philadelphia with communities to the west. Along the road were taverns for both the individual travelers and those who transported crops and livestock. The oldest house in the borough still stands. The building once housed the Downing family, for whom the borough was named. The house sits within a few yards of the Brandywine and is shown as it looked in the early 1900s.

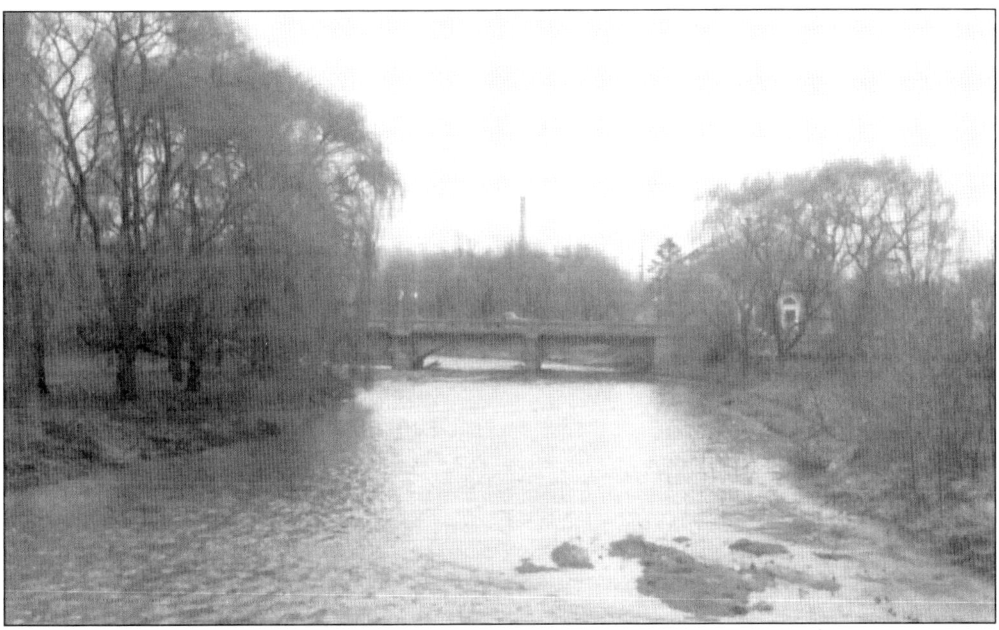

The east branch of the Brandywine runs past Kerr Park and the old log house and under the Lancaster Avenue Bridge. The road is known as Lancaster Avenue in Downingtown. In other sections of Pennsylvania, it is the Lincoln Highway. Also known as Route 30, it was once a road that was heavily traveled and was one of the most important roads in the United States.

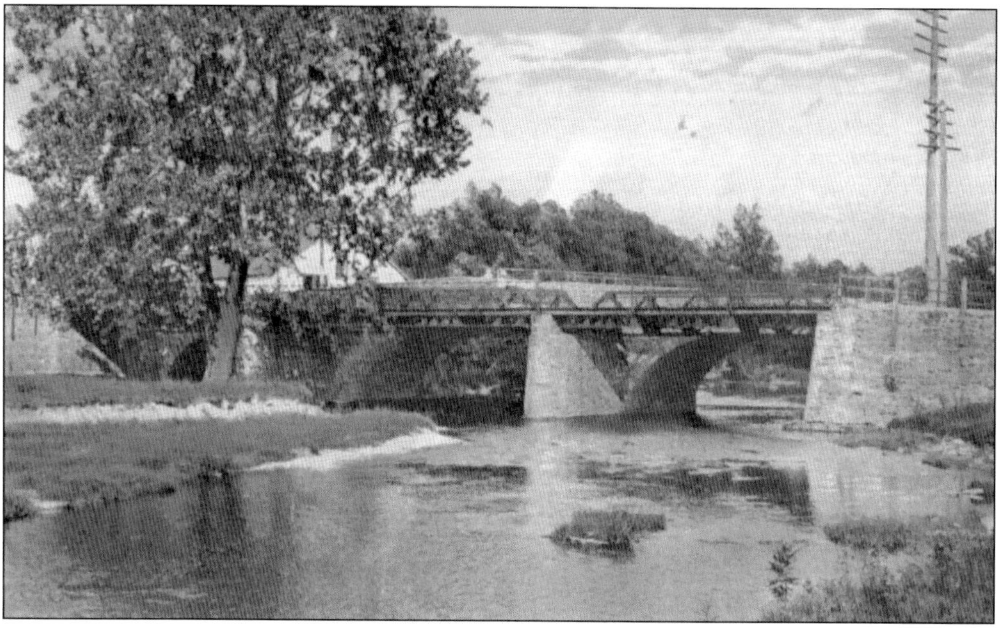

Not all of the postcard companies were accurate in their description of cards. In this postcard of the old stone bridge, the caption says, "Bridge across Brandywine Creek on Lincoln Highway, Downingtown, Pa." The designations of Lincoln Highway and Lancaster Avenue are sometimes switched. The card was published by the Henderson Advertising Company of Johnstown, which is on the opposite side of Pennsylvania from Downingtown.

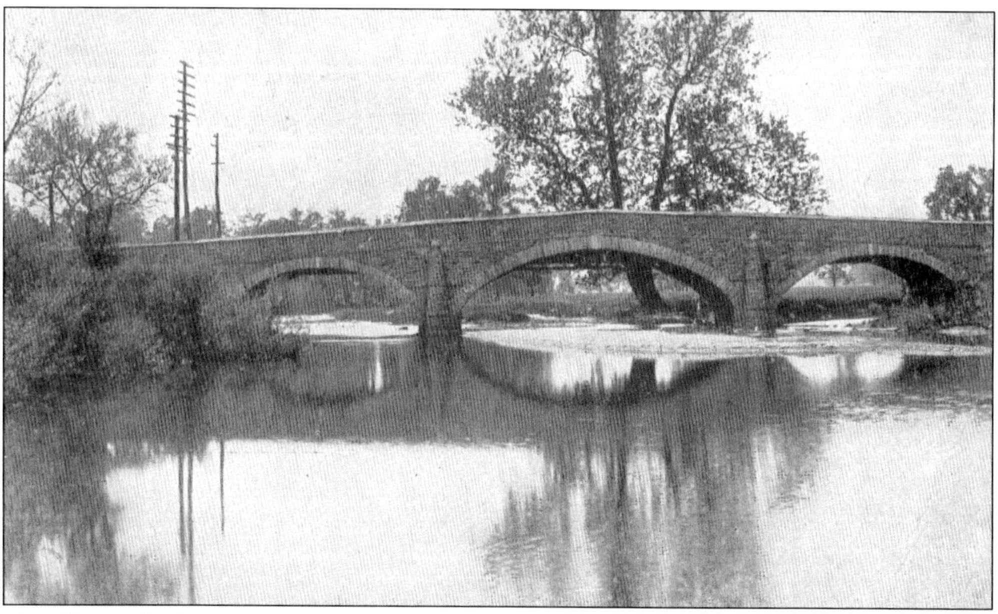

The old stone bridge over Lancaster Avenue was built in 1801 and is shown in this postcard, which is postmarked 1907. The Brandywine has been known to flood at this point in Downingtown for many years, but improvements have controlled the problem to some extent. Downingtown officials constructed their new borough hall just to the east of the east branch of the Brandywine near the bridge.

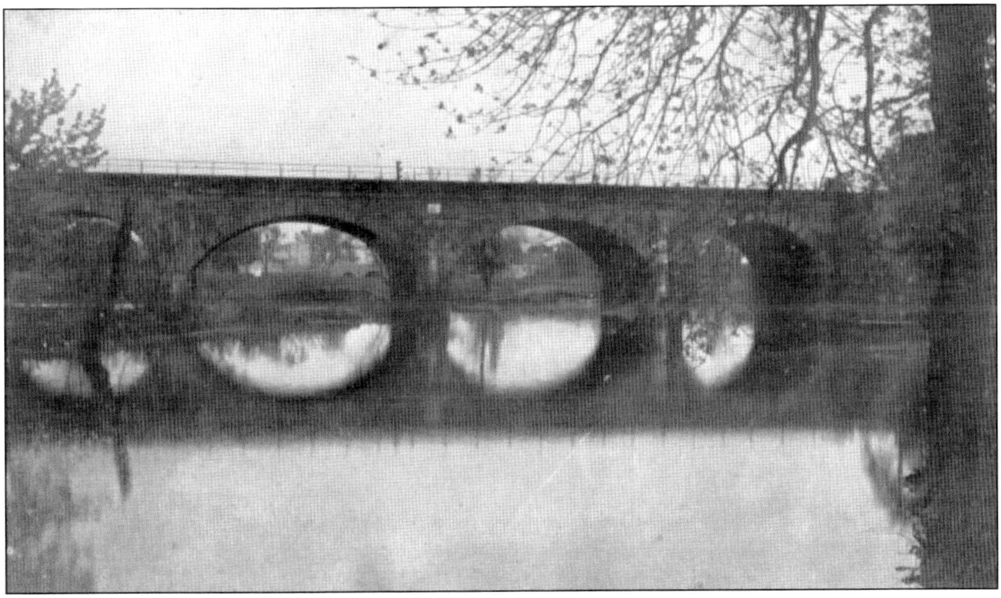

This postcard shows the "Pennsylvania Railroad Bridge over the Brandywine at Downingtown, Pa." The railroad played an important part in the development of Chester County. The Philadelphia Main Line, the area made famous by wealthy families from the city who made their summer homes in the suburbs, developed along the same railroad line that continues to Downingtown. Freight trains and passenger trains, now carrying commuters to work in Philadelphia, continue to run through the borough.

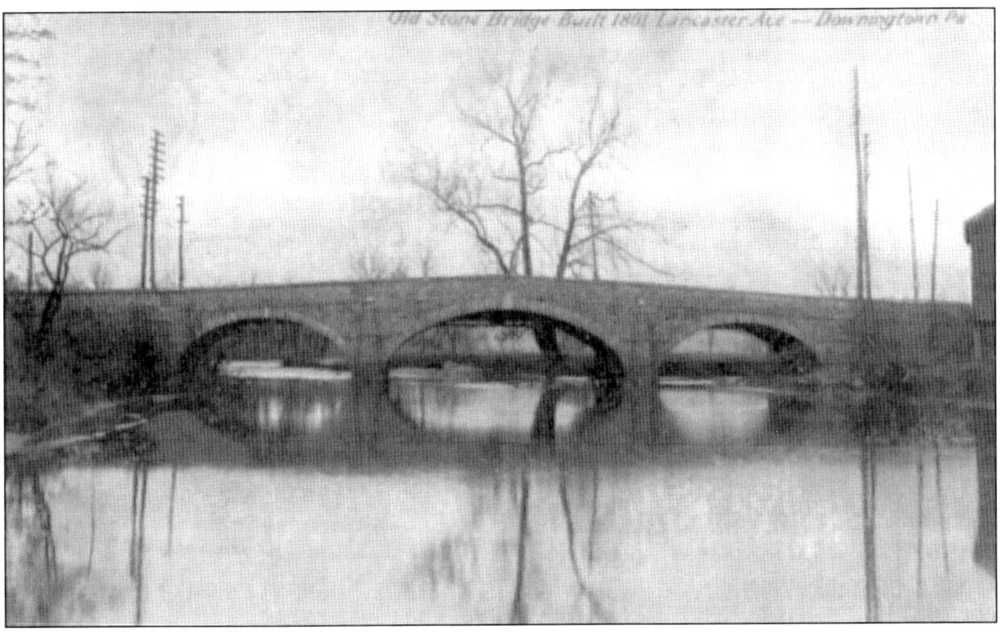

Many of the postcards in this book have been used for thank-you notes and invitations to parties. The sender of this *c.* 1911 postcard communicated the train schedule to a friend living in Lancaster County, which is to the west of Downingtown. "Maggie phoned to the Chester Valley depot this morning, the trains leave at 6:40; 11 and 5:13. We will have to go at 11 for you can't get down in time for the 6:40 and the 5:13 is too late."

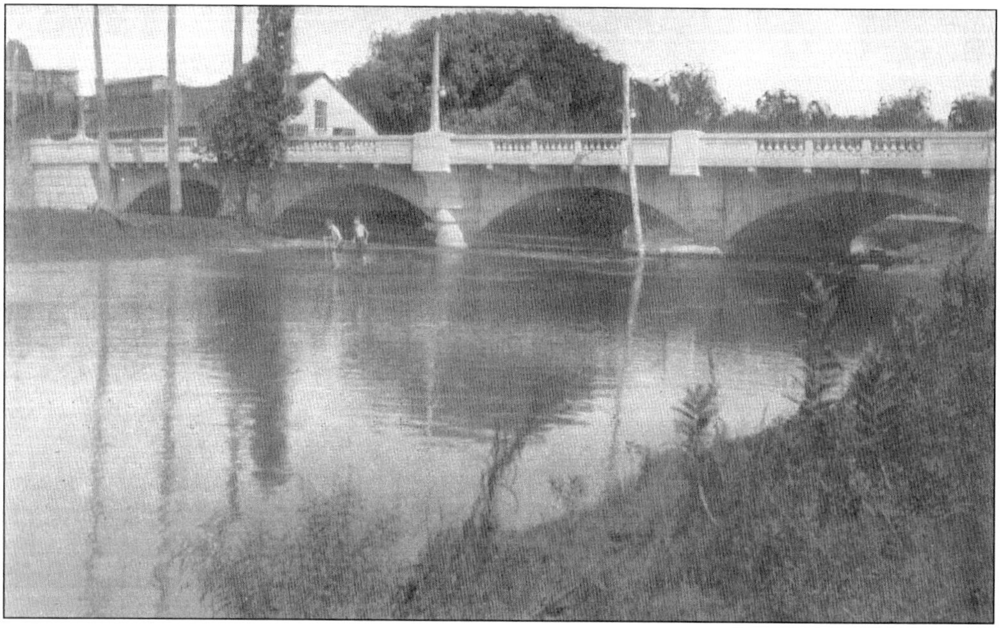

The Brandywine was the drawing card for paper mills in Downingtown. In 1840, the Davey Paper Company was the first to set up operation in the borough. The process used by paper mills at the time caused the discharge of by-products into the Brandywine. As production processes improved and people became concerned about the environment, the pollution stopped and the health of the Brandywine improved.

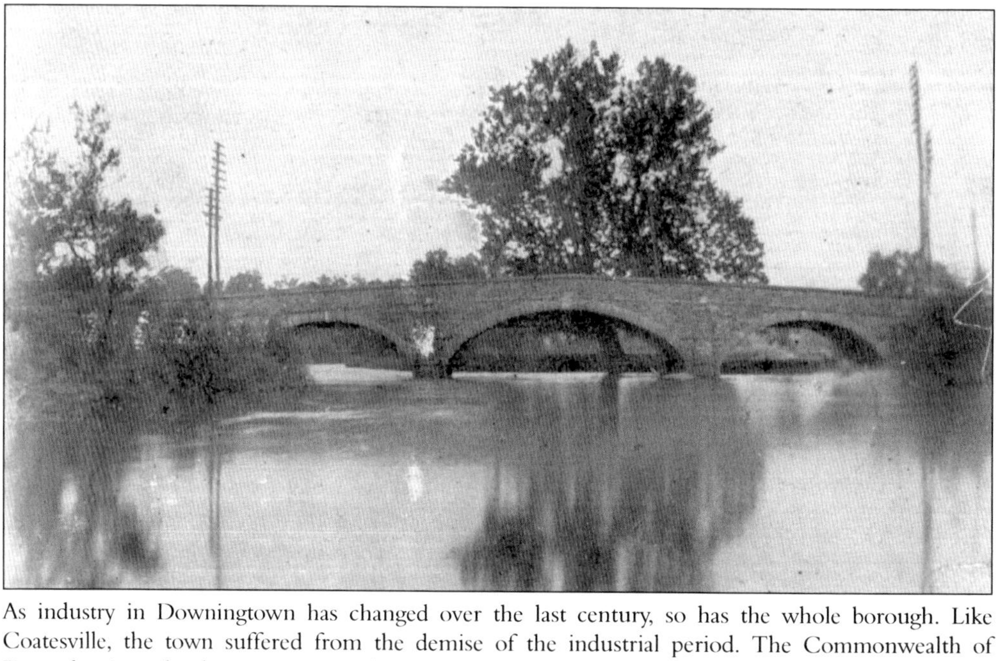

As industry in Downingtown has changed over the last century, so has the whole borough. Like Coatesville, the town suffered from the demise of the industrial period. The Commonwealth of Pennsylvania and other governmental agencies have developed programs to bring new businesses into Downingtown and build residential construction projects. The one thing that has not changed in Downingtown is the east branch of the Brandywine.

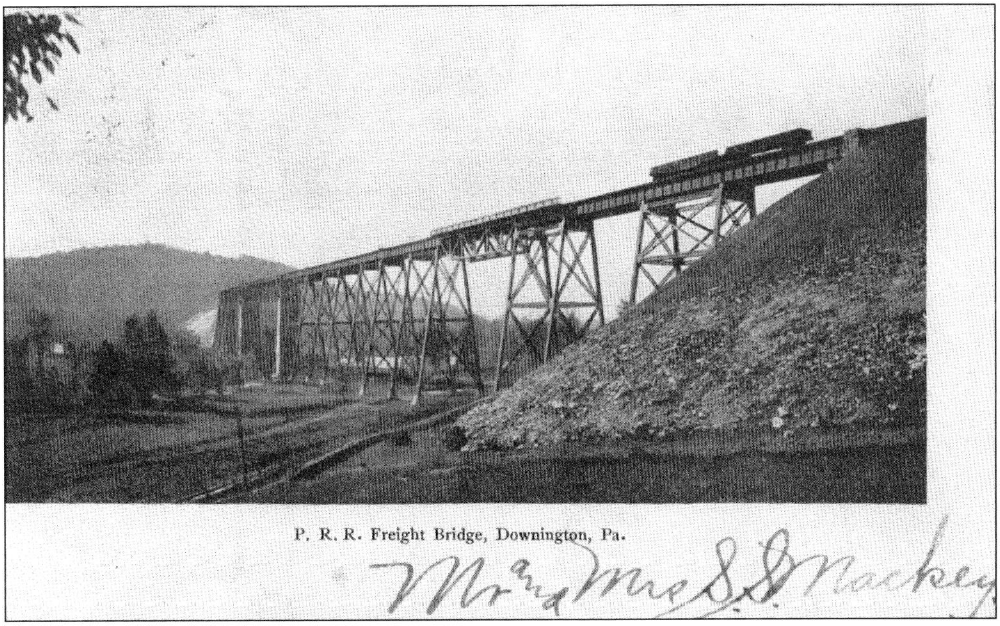

Below Downingtown an iron railroad trestle was erected in the early 1900s to carry freight above the Brandywine. This card, postmarked 1906, contains an early view of the Pennsylvania Railroad Freight Bridge. The bridge still stands today and clearly marks the border of the town. The busy Route 322, which connects Downingtown and West Chester, runs next to the east branch of the Brandywine and also under the freight bridge.

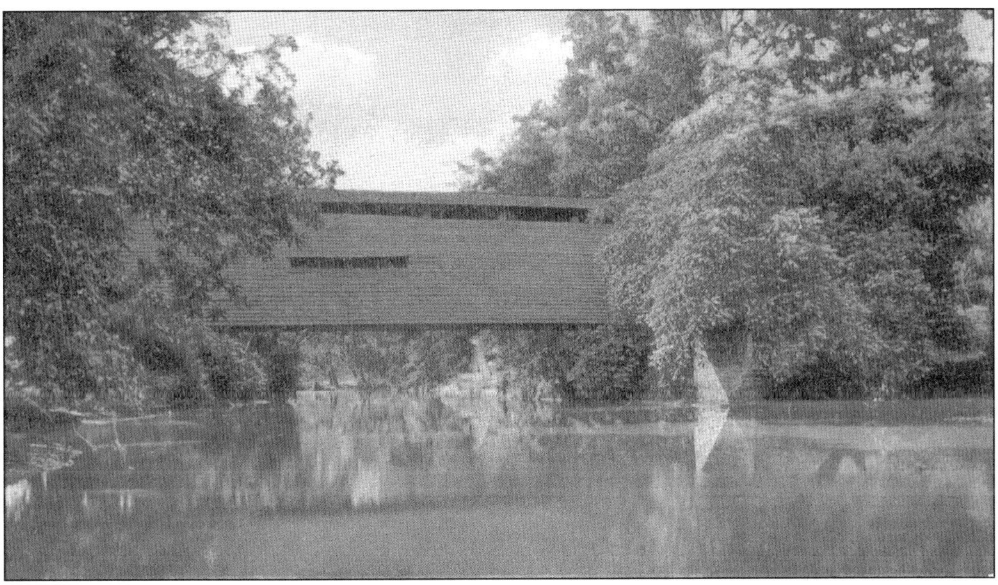

Seen here is "Sugars Bridge, on the Brandywine, near West Chester, Pa." As the Brandywine departs Downingtown, the river comes to the last remaining covered bridge over the east branch. This bridge, known as Gibson's Bridge, crosses at Harmony Hill Road. At one time, 11 covered bridges spanned the east branch of the Brandywine. Time, weather, and safety issues have all caused the covered bridges to pass into history.

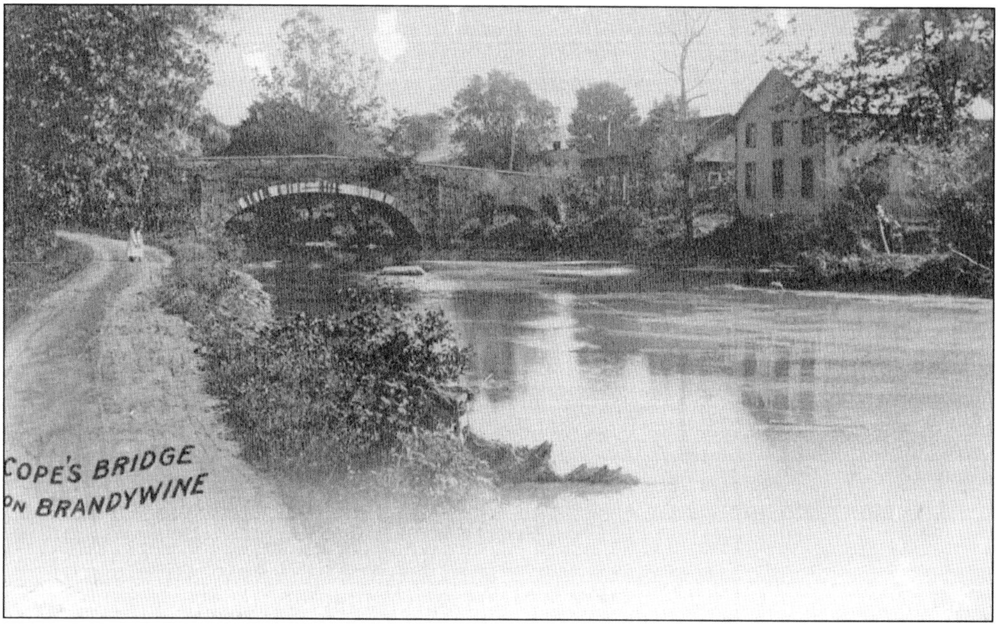

While most of the covered bridges are no longer with us, plenty of other types of bridges span the Brandywine. Cope's Bridge covers the Brandywine just outside of West Chester to the west of the borough. West Chester is the seat of Chester County, and many residents use Strasburg Road to reach the borough. The west branch of the Brandywine also encounters the Strasburg Road.

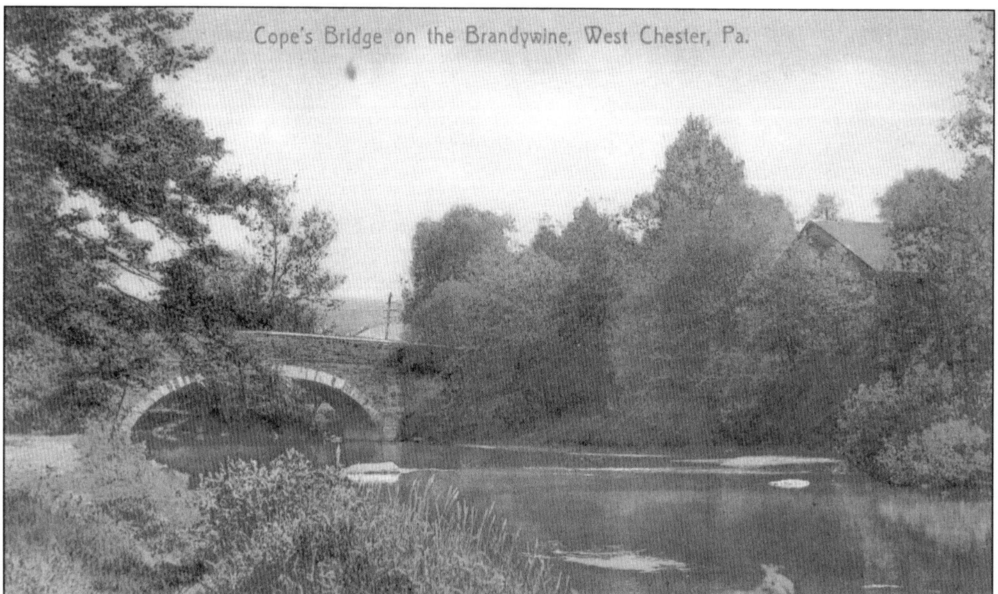

The area surrounding "Cope's Bridge on the Brandywine, West Chester, Pa." was home to many Native Americans, including the Lenapes. The Brandywine, south of West Chester, runs through the community that is now known as Lenape. The area has a rich history that predates the colonials. The gentle Brandywine and the beauty of the Chester County countryside have spawned many romantic tales that may or may not be true.

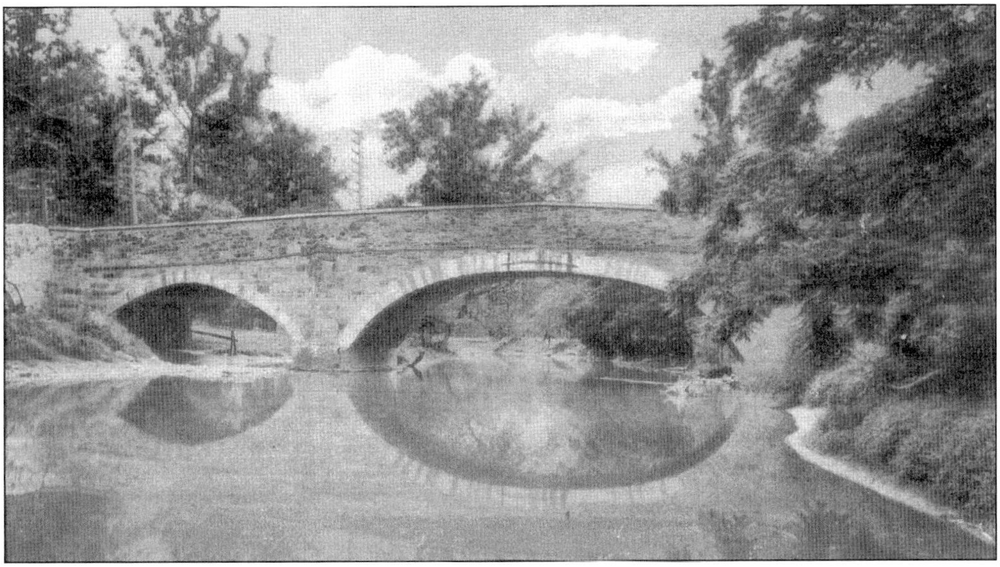

This postcard is titled "Cope's Bridge on the Brandywine, near West Chester, Pa." One of the area's legends involves a rock that some say was named for a legendary Native American maiden. One point past Cope's Bridge, the river veers to the east. The Brandywine bends around a granite cliff that is known as Deborah's Rock. The story behind the naming of the rock has been debated for many generations.

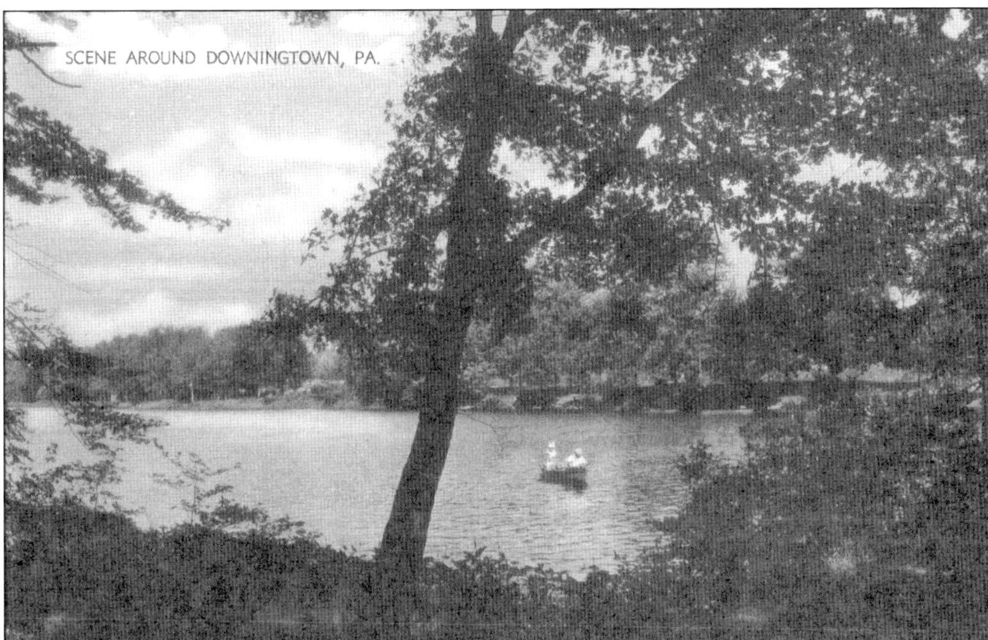

One story has Deborah remaining in Chester County when her tribe departed. A settler's son who was taken with Deborah tried to seize her one moonlit night, and she broke away and fled down a path. That path ended at the rock over the Brandywine. Her choice was dishonor at the hands of the young settler or death. Deborah plunged to her death in the Brandywine.

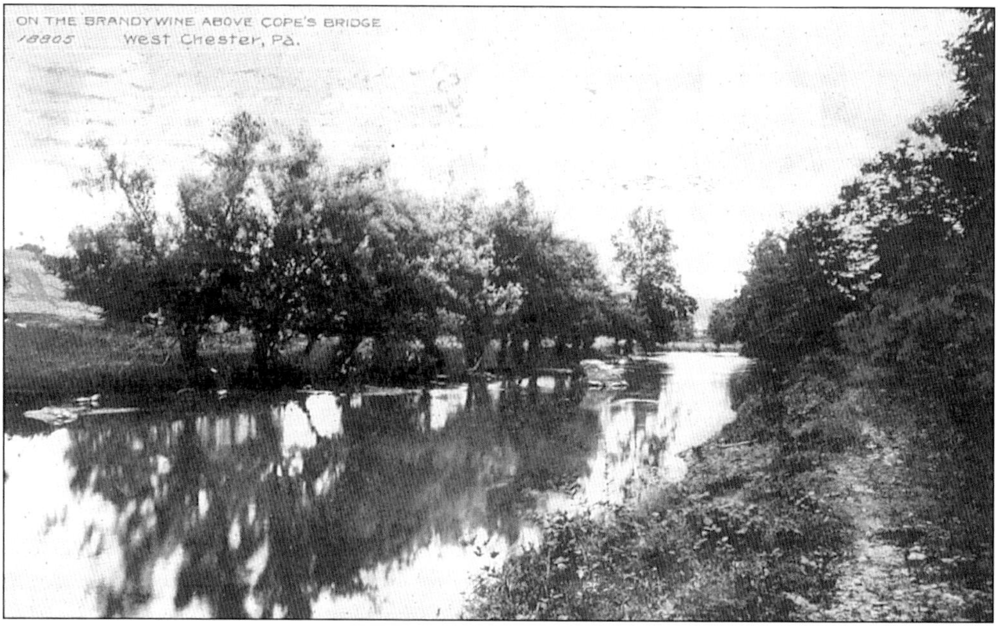

Another legend tells of a young princess named Deborah, the daughter of a Nanticoke chief, being courted by two braves. Her true love, Wawaset, was the son of a chief of an opposing hostile tribe. After Wawaset was killed by Deborah's other suitor, Kaucke, Deborah went to the rock and plunged to her death. While the tales are interesting, many people believe the rock was named for Deborah Taylor, who lived close to the Brandywine and Deborah's Rock.

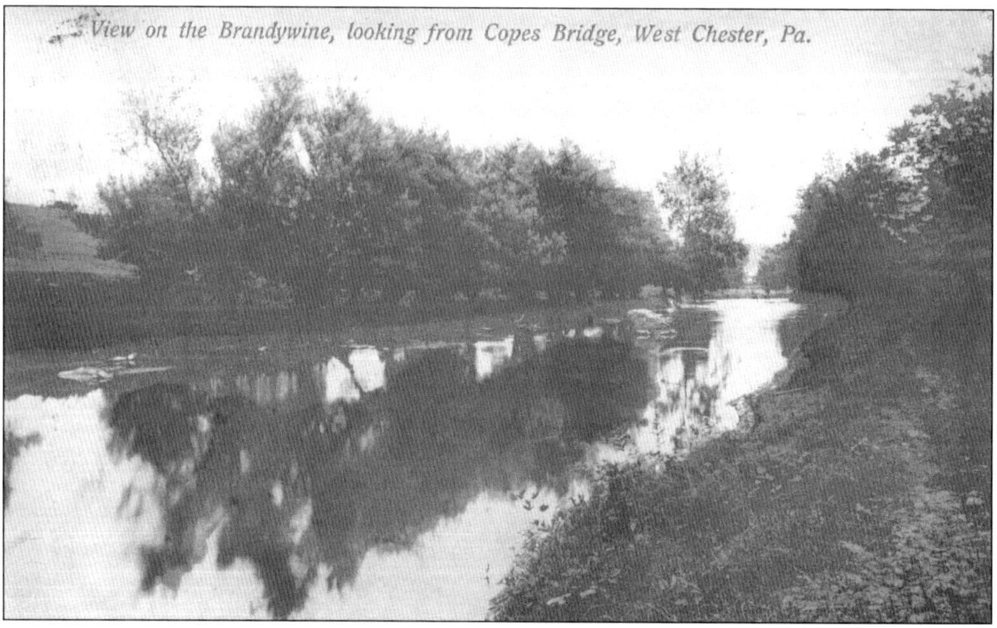

This is a "view on the Brandywine, looking from Copes Bridge, West Chester, Pa." Legends may be debatable, but the beauty of the Brandywine is not. This card, postmarked in 1909, has the following note: "This may give you some ideas of this beautiful place in which I am having a lovely time. I'd love to be able to paint this."

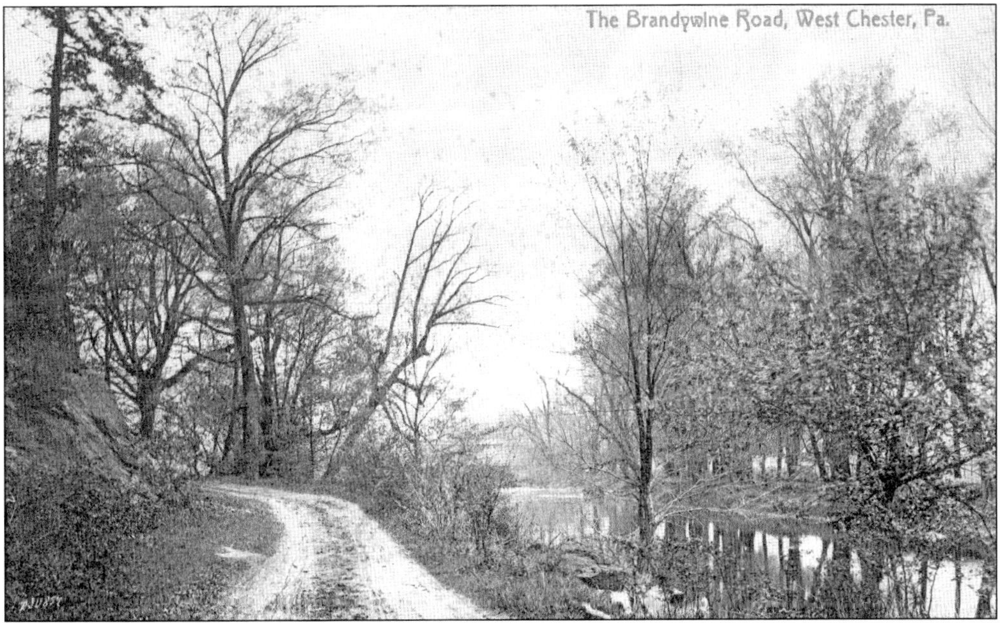

Seen here is "the Brandywine Road, West Chester, Pa." As the Strasburg Road was the main route to West Chester from the west, the Brandywine Road was one of the byways to the county seat from the north, especially in the Downingtown region. Here the road runs along the tree-lined banks of the east branch of the Brandywine. Even though Chester County has many different sections, West Chester is the focal point for the government and many social events.

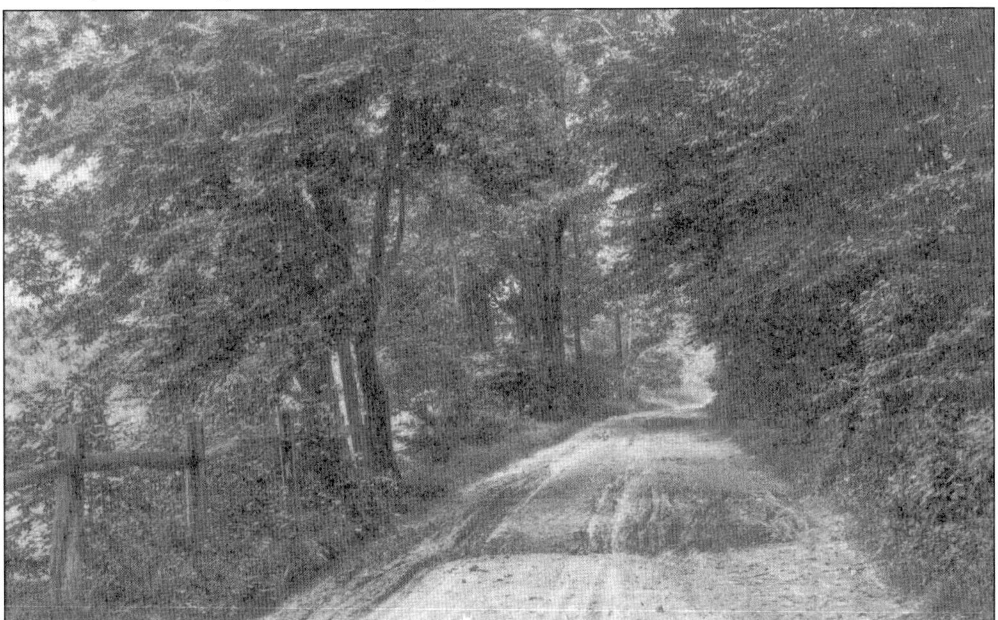

This postcard depicts "the Brandywine road, Downingtown to West Chester, Pa." The card was mailed in West Chester in August 1908 and was published by S.J. Parker & Sons of West Chester. Many regional postcards of the era were published by the Parker firm. This one is No. 150 of a series and was made in Germany, where many postcards were produced for this country.

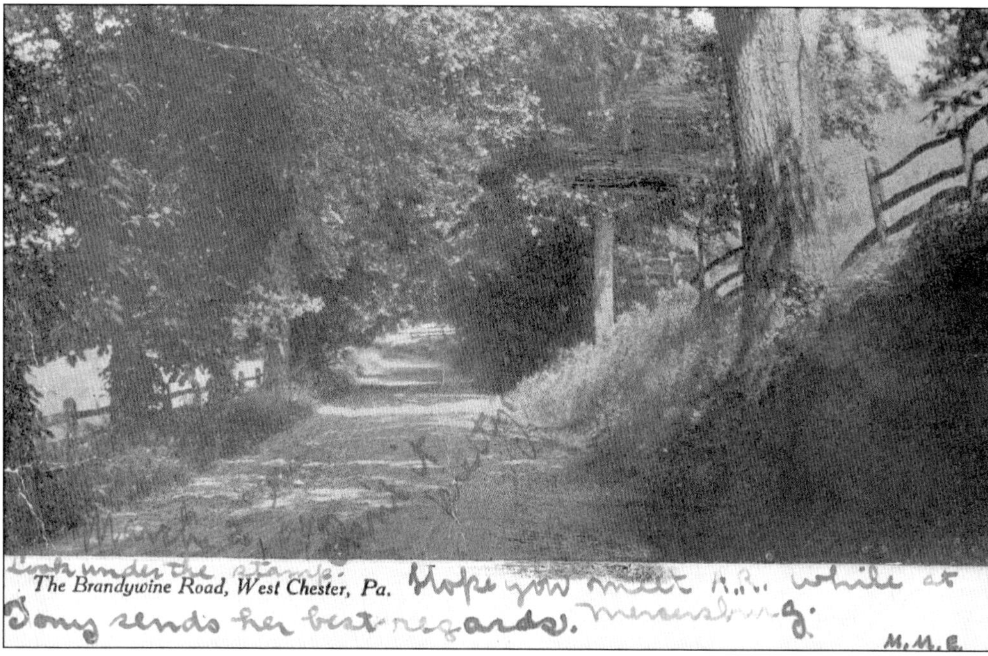

The scenes around West Chester on the Brandywine Road have many of the same qualities as depicted in these cards, both postmarked in 1907. There are dirt roads, wooden fences, trees, and the unpaved Brandywine Road. The card below depicts "the Brandywine Road (West Branch), West Chester, Pa." This is another of the S.J. Parker & Son cards made in Germany, but in a different series. For it to be the west branch, the road would have to be the current Strasburg Road leading to West Chester.

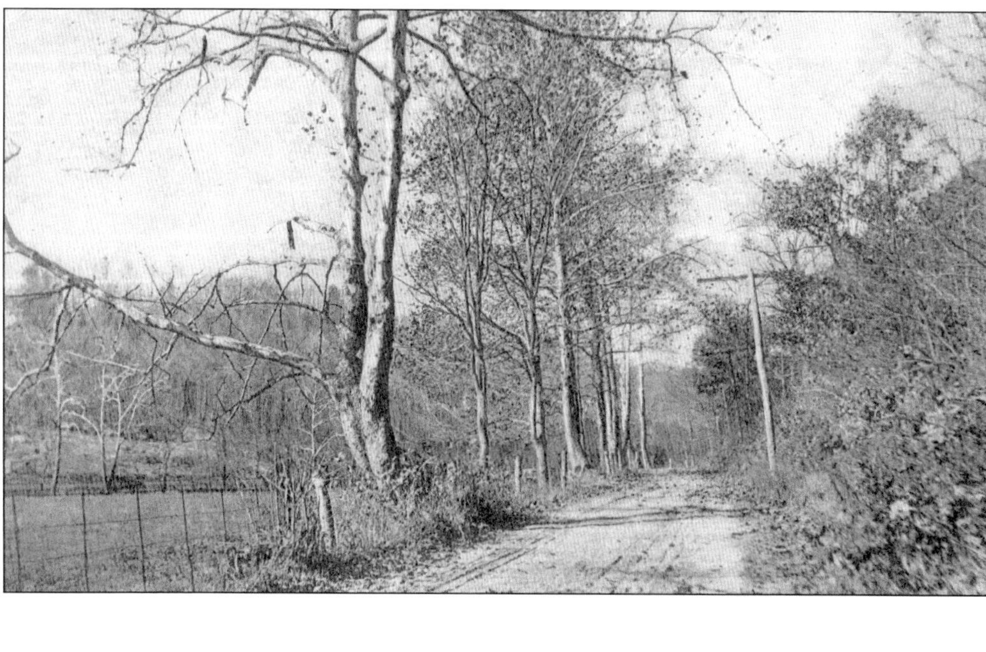

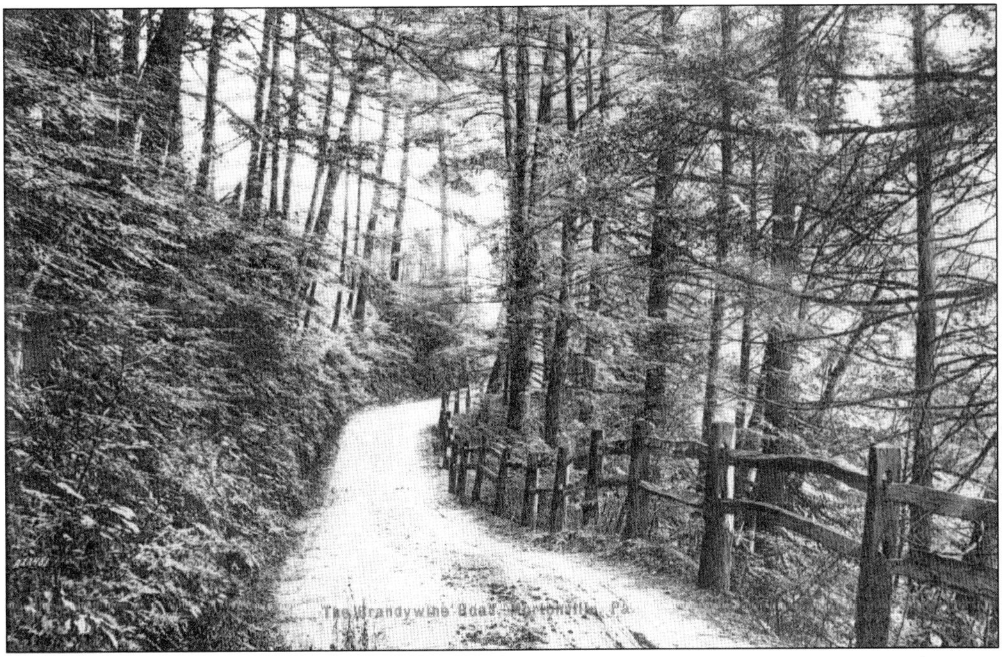

Seen here is "the Brandywine Road, Mortonville, Pa." This section of the road definitely runs between the two branches of the Brandywine. The west branch comes from the Coatesville and Modena section and flows to Mortonville, where another old stone bridge connects the two shores. This card, sent in 1907, asks about the "chapel program for Thursday night." The postcard was the e-mail of the 19th century.

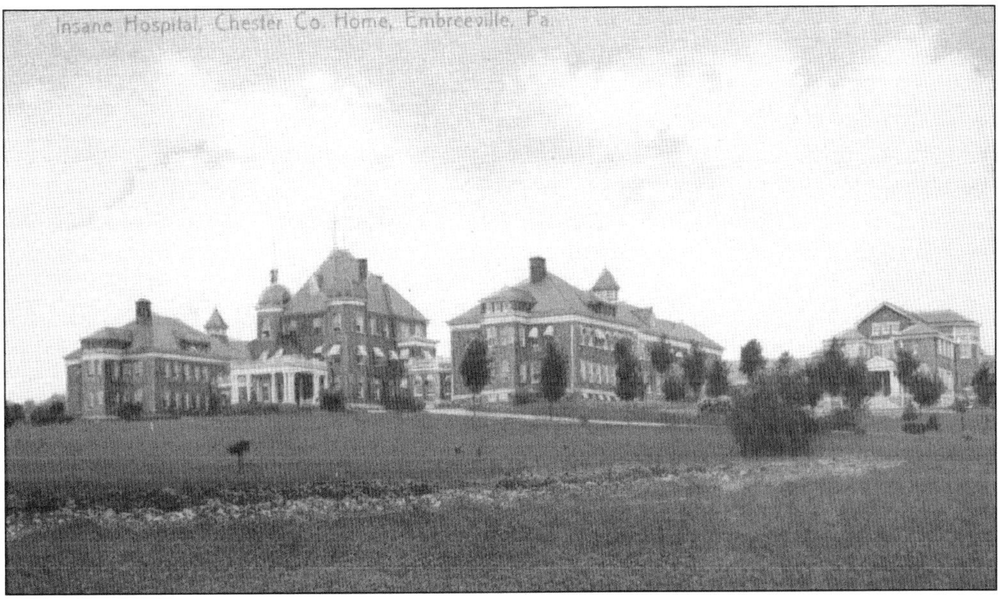

One of the most interesting set of buildings along the Strasburg section of the Brandywine Road was the "Insane Hospital, Chester Co. Home, Embreeville, Pa." The buildings housed the mentally ill for many years and were later used as a treatment center for troubled youths and a state police barracks. This postcard is No. 323 of the S.J. Parker & Son series.

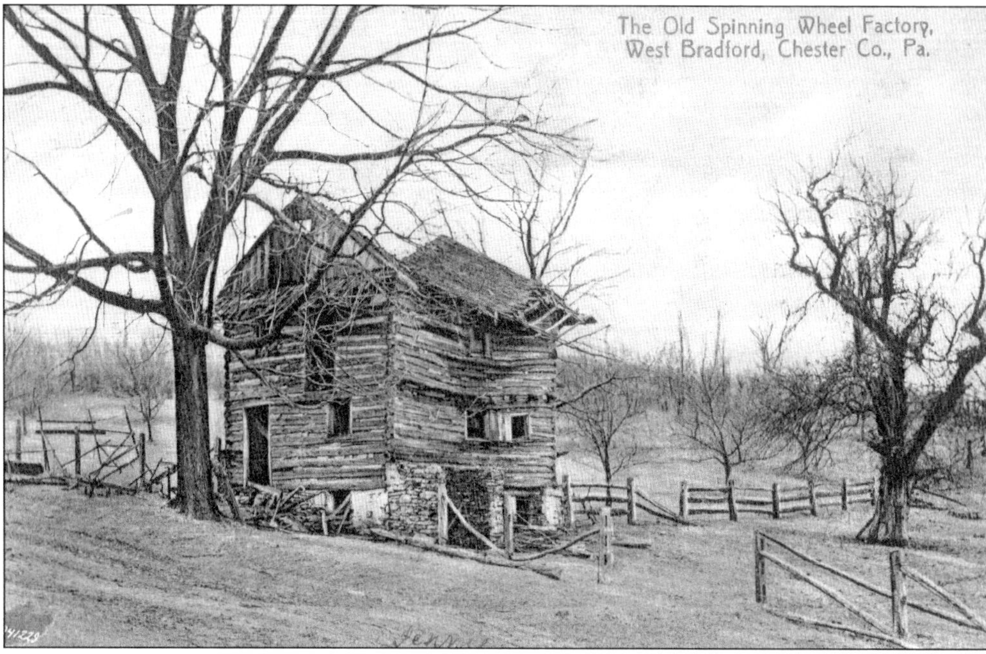

This postcard is titled "The Old Spinning Wheel Factory, West Bradford, Chester Co., Pa." The Brandywine supplied power to many of the mills of the early days of Chester County and the Brandywine region spawned a number of other industries. Between the two branches of the Brandywine sits West Bradford Township. The factory depicted in this postcard by S.J. Parker & Son, No. 115 in the series, no longer exists.

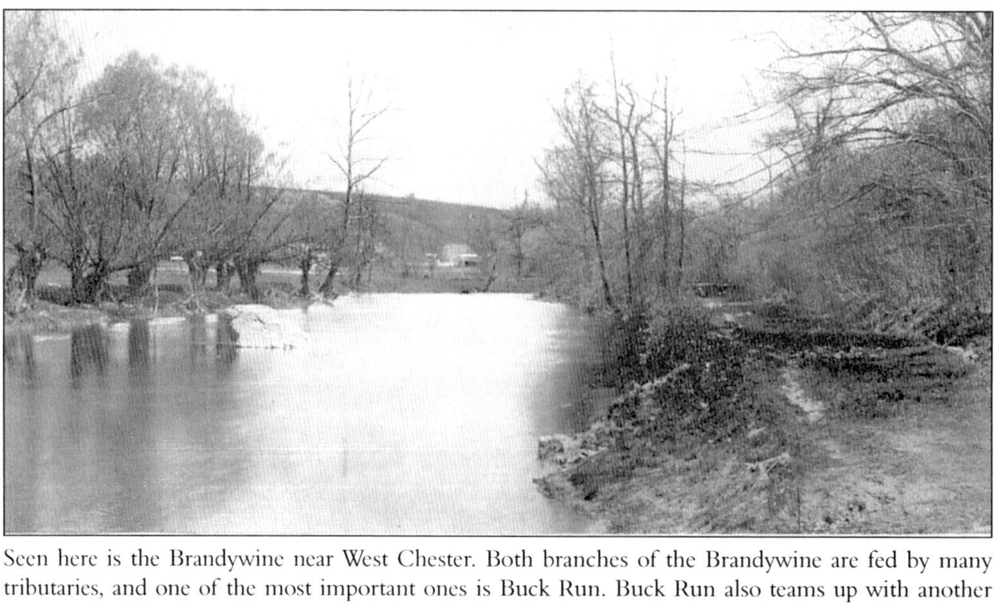

Seen here is the Brandywine near West Chester. Both branches of the Brandywine are fed by many tributaries, and one of the most important ones is Buck Run. Buck Run also teams up with another stream called Doe Run. The water feeds into the Brandywine near Modena and helps swell the river as it gains strength for its run into Delaware and its connection with the Christina River.

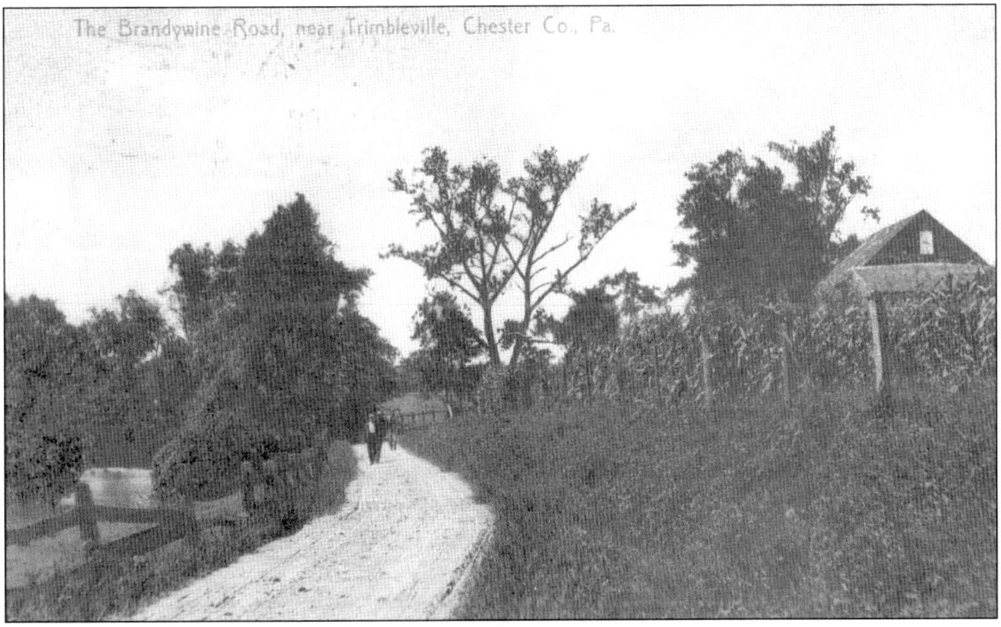

Shown here is "the Brandywine Road, near Trimbleville, Chester Co., Pa." The Brandywine, seen to the left of this card behind the wooden fence, helped to grow crops on many farms in Chester County. Several men are seen walking down Brandywine Road in this S.J. Parker & Son card, No. 155 in the series, postmarked in 1910. The message on the card is brief and to the point: "With Love."

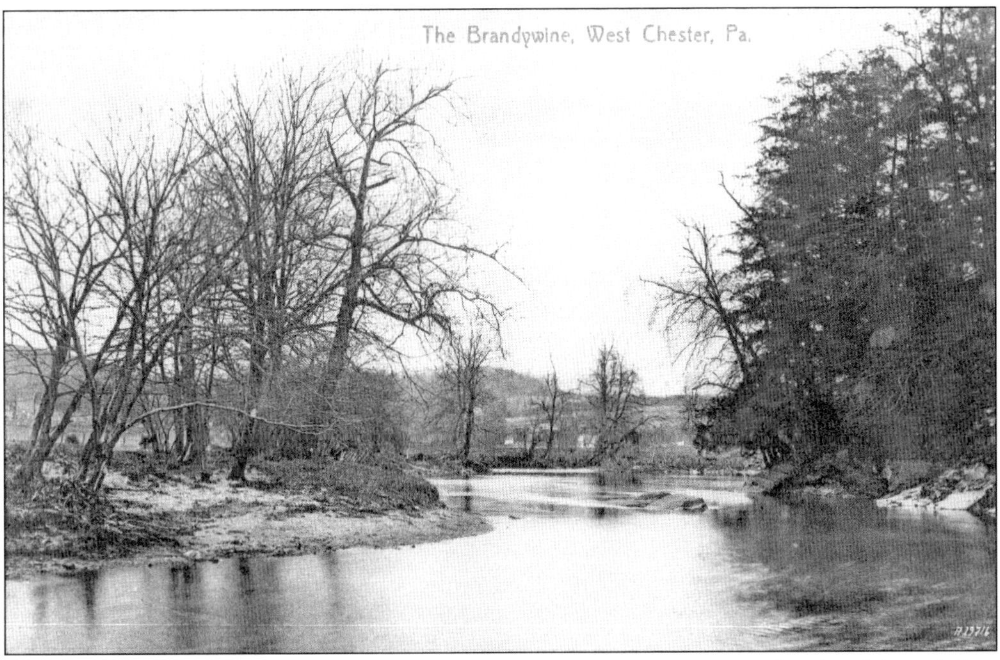

Chester County, as with most of the early settlements of the country, was agricultural and depended on the crops grown in the nearby fields for the inhabitants to survive. Even though many of the farms of the early 20th century have disappeared due to development, Chester County is still one of the leading agriculture communities in the Commonwealth of Pennsylvania.

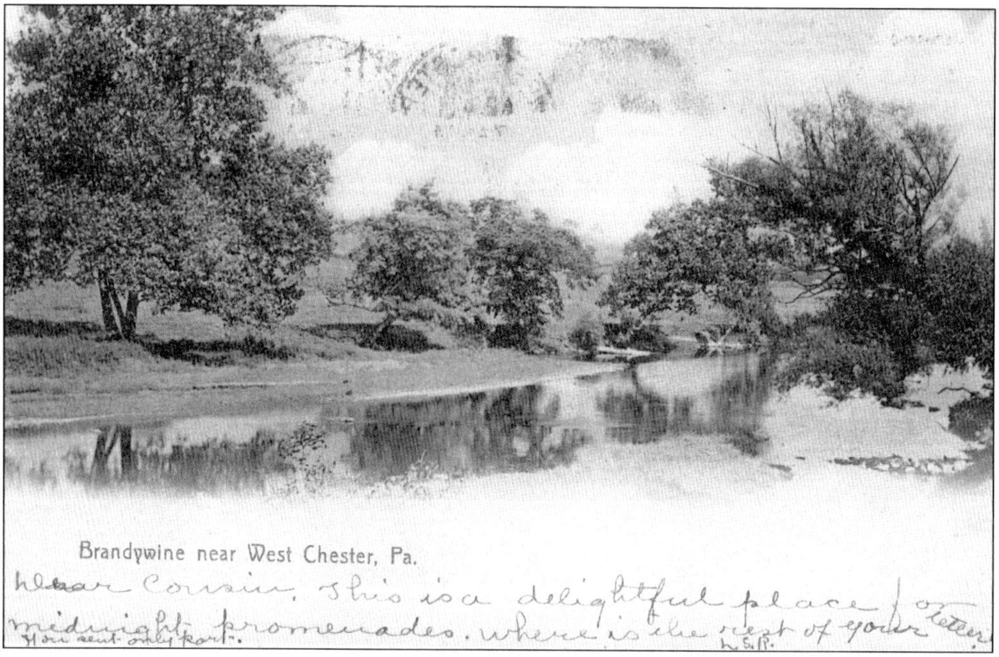

The Brandywine has inspired many writers and romantics. In the card above, "Brandywine near West Chester, Pa.," and the one below, "The Barrens, West Chester, Pa.," two different types of scenes can be discovered within a short distance. The sender of the card that shows the river says, "Dear Cousin, This is a delightful place for midnight promenades, where is the rest of your letter? You sent only part." The postmark on the card is April 11, 1906. The Barrens postcard is undated. Both of the cards on this page are S.J. Parker & Son cards, but neither is of the numbered series.

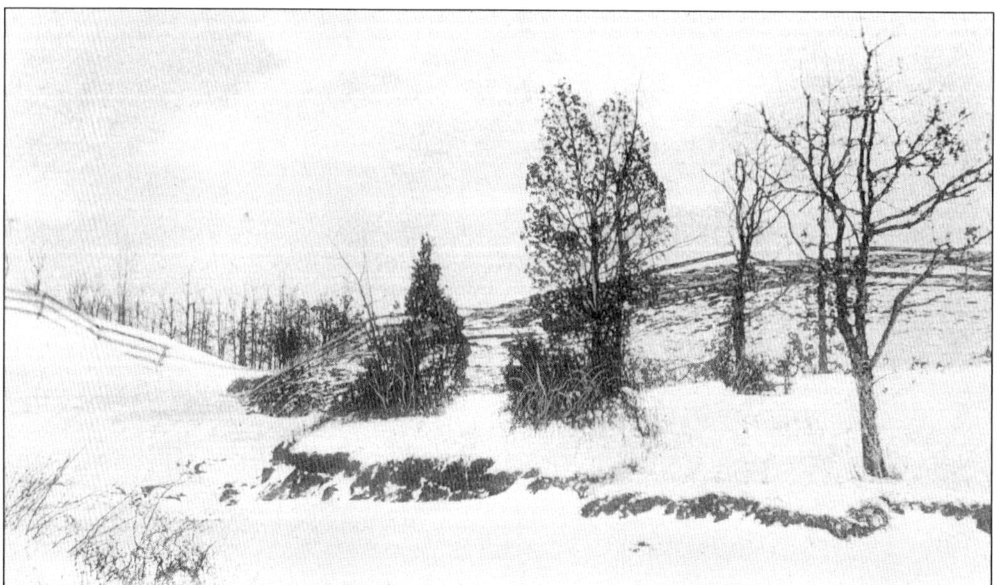

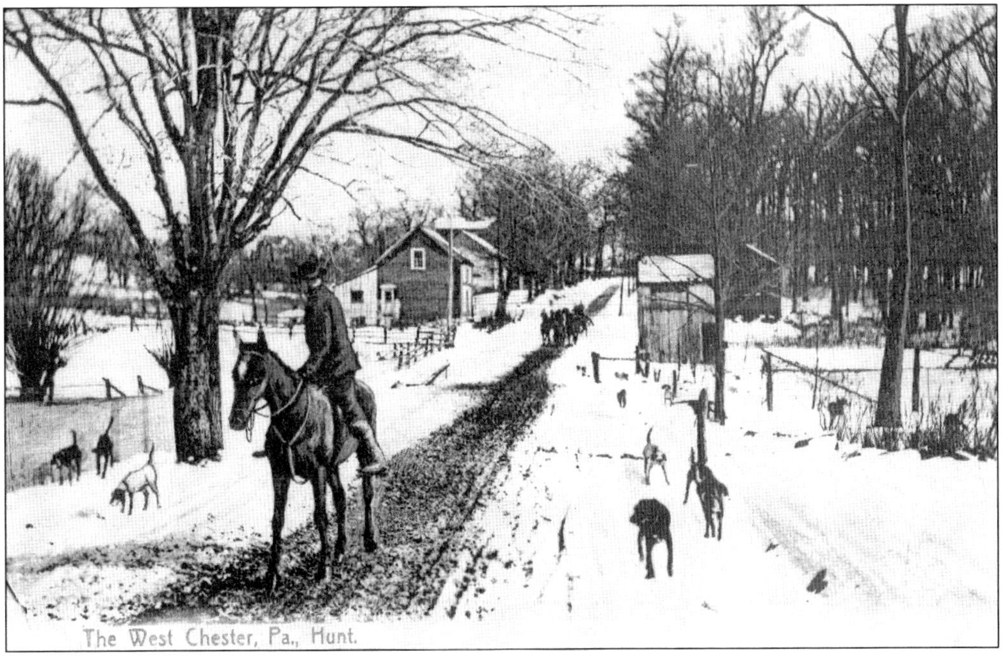

One of the attractions of Chester County is the fox hunt. Several famous hunts take place along the banks of the Brandywine. While some have been discontinued, other hunting competitions are being challenged because land ownership has changed and because of the increasing concern for animal rights. In the card above, the hunt is proceeding west of West Chester toward the Brandywine. The card below depicts "the Mather Hunt, Chester Co., Pa." Both cards are of the S.J. Parker & Son series made in Germany. The card above is No. 100 and the card below is No. 118.

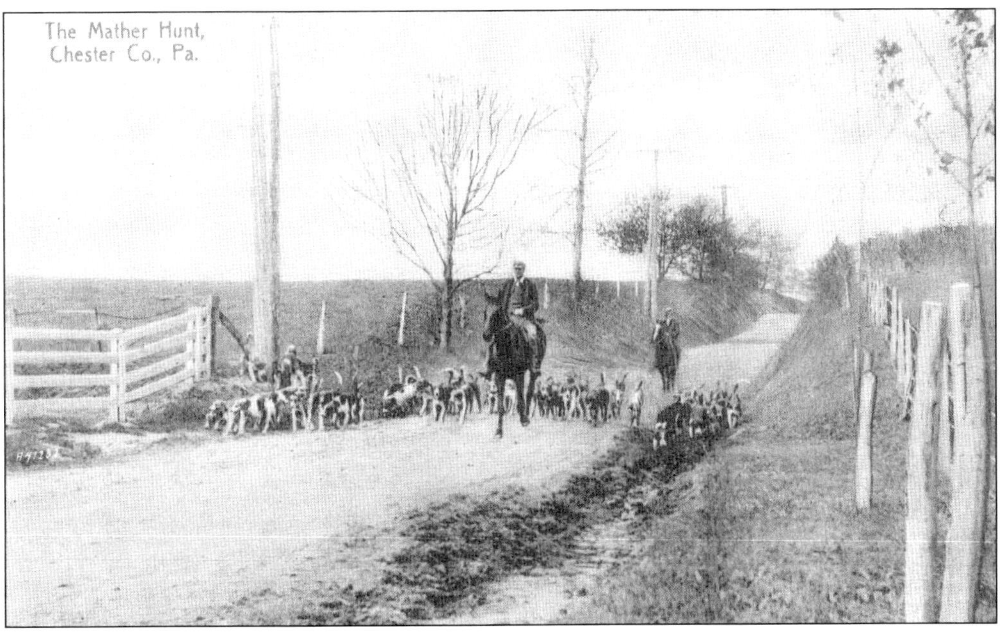

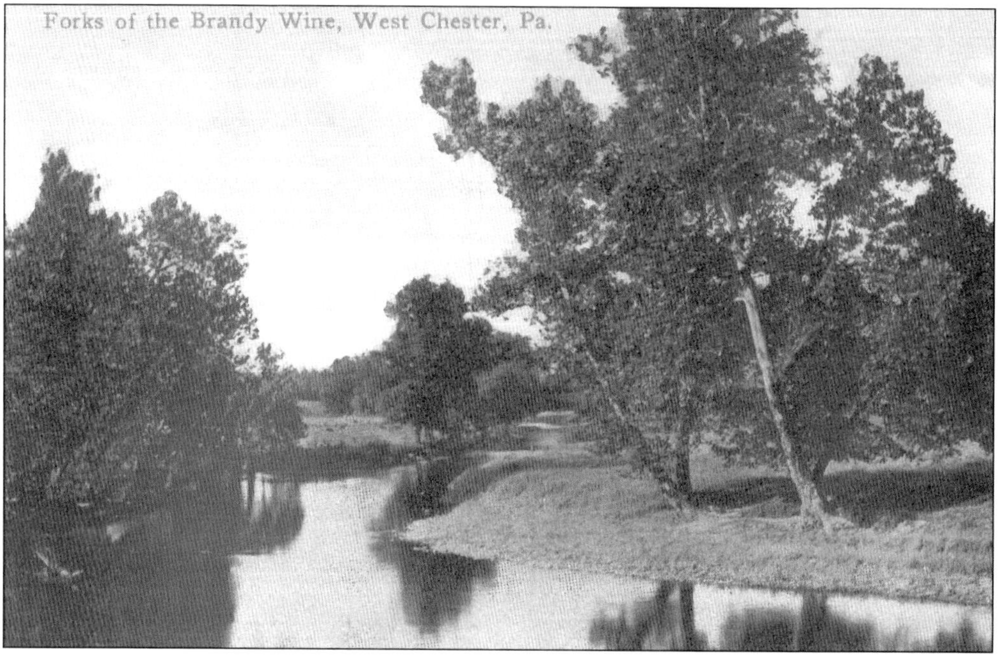

This card is titled "Forks of the Brandy Wine, West Chester, Pa." It is clear by the spelling of Brandywine that the typesetter was not familiar with the area, even though the card (No. 30073) was published in West Chester by P.F. Fath. There are several possible origins of the name for Brandywine, which will be discussed later in this book. As with Deborah's Rock, some of the theories are more fanciful than others.

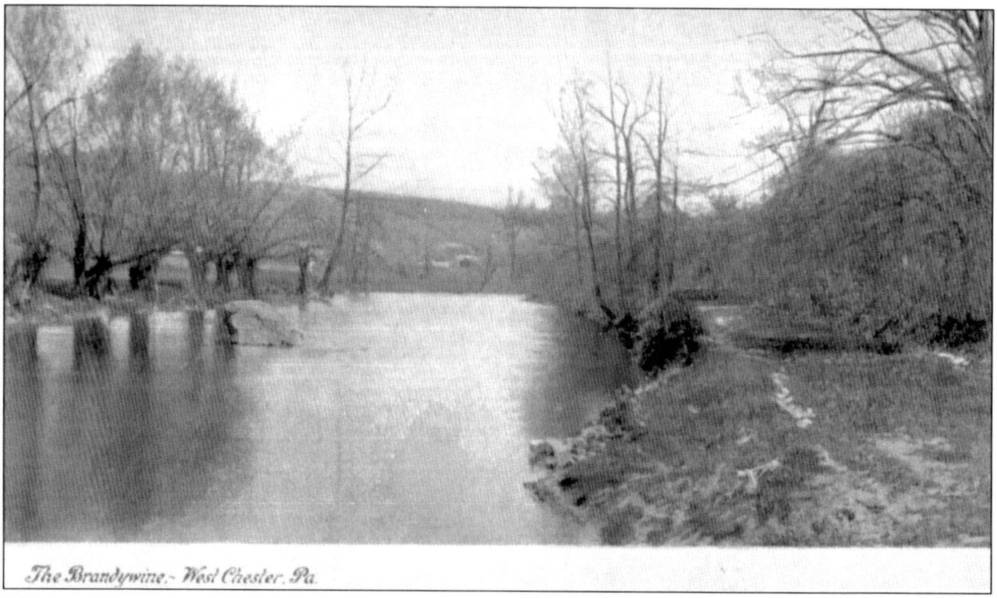

The Brandywine has served many purposes over the years, and recreation is one of the foremost uses. West Chester hosted many schools and academies, and students flocked to the river for recreation, especially downriver at Lenape. One of the leading schools, West Chester Normal School, has changed names; it is now West Chester University.

Two

Two Branches Become One

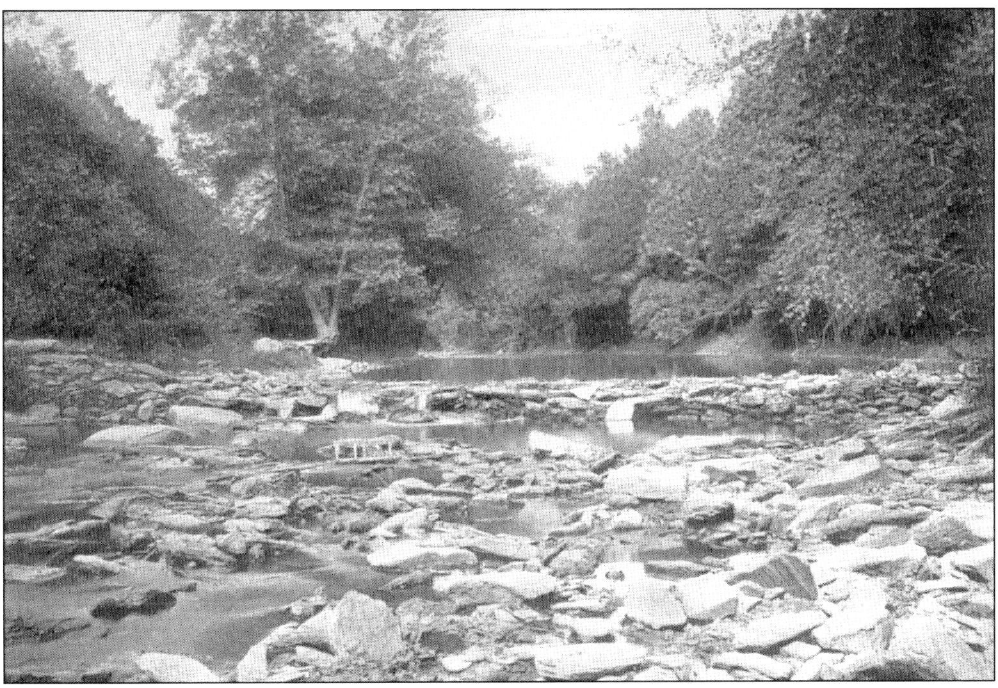

The east and west branches of the Brandywine become one where the Battle of Brandywine took place on September 11, 1777. This area was also the site of the Stargazers' Stone, used by Mason and Dixon to locate Pennsylvania's boundary. This area also hosts the Brandywine River Museum and Longwood Gardens, two major cultural institutions. The area surrounding the region where the east branch meets the west branch of the Brandywine is rich in beauty and history. This card was produced in Maine and printed in Germany.

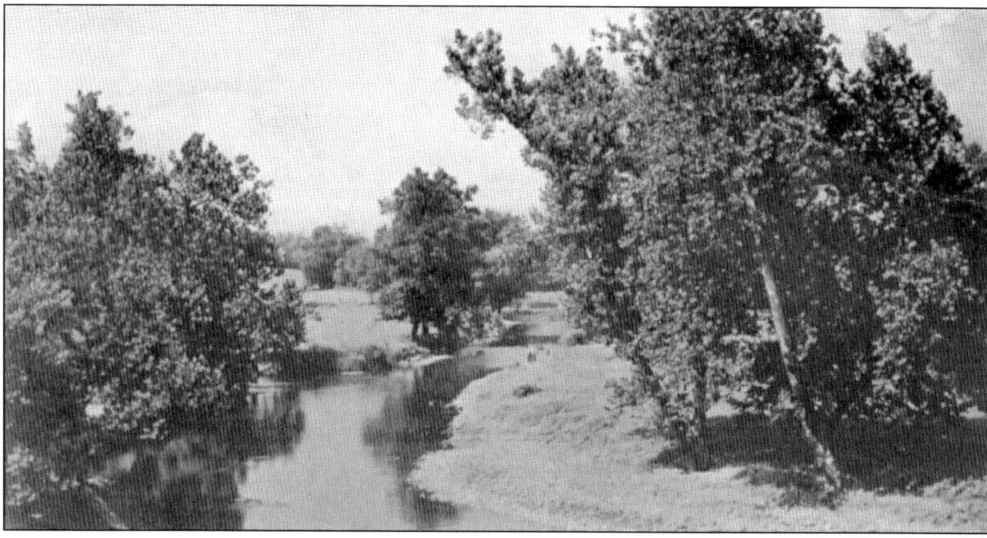

Seen here are the "forks of the Brandywine near West Chester, Pa." This area is one of the last settlements by the Lenapes in Chester County. Even though they had peaceful relations with the colonists for many years, the Native Americans voluntarily moved from their camps along the river shortly after the French and Indian War. The Lenapes headed toward where Pennsylvania borders Ohio. They later settled in the Oklahoma area.

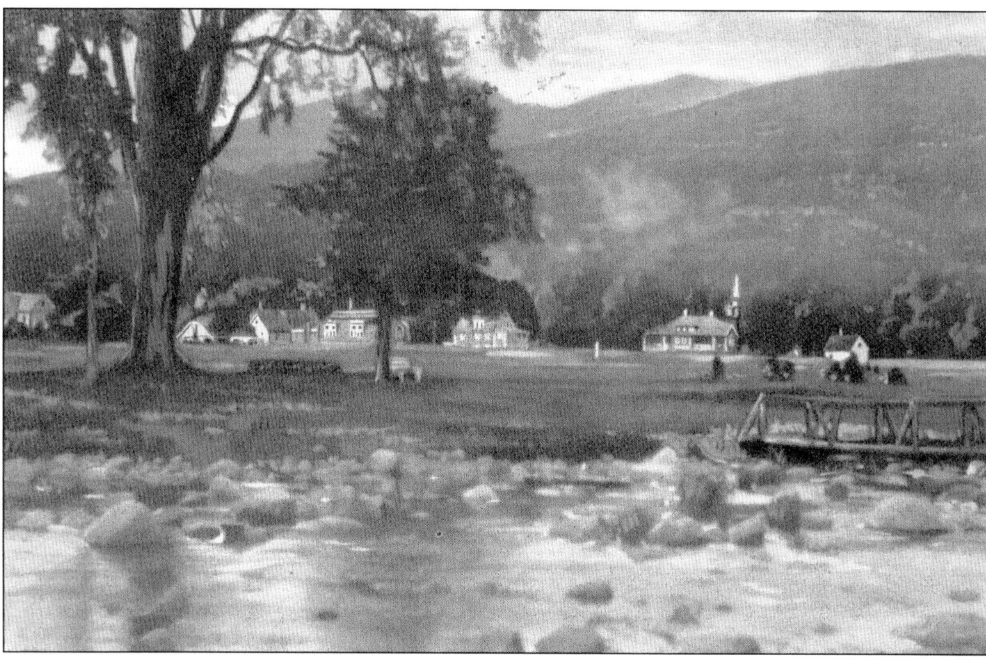

This hand-painted scene resembling the area of Lenape was sent from West Chester in 1948. This was the Linen era of postcards, which showcased a new printing process that used bright dyes for coloring and resulted in a linenlike finish. The sender of the card appears to be a boss who is on a vacation. "Having a great time here—getting a much needed rest. Call on the folks at the office if you need anything."

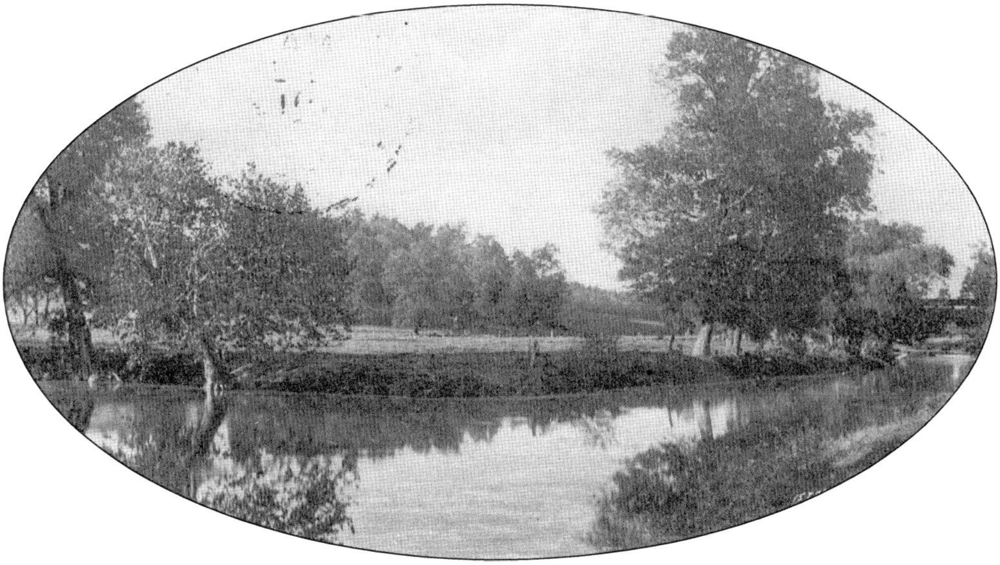

Even before the peaceful Quakers established communities along the Brandywine, the area that is now called Lenape was a gathering spot in the summer. The Lenni-Lenape Indians shared the water with other tribes who came to the spot for the fantastic fishing that was available. They also grew maize (corn), which was planted in rows near the banks of the Brandywine. The Native Americans called the Brandywine River the Wawasan.

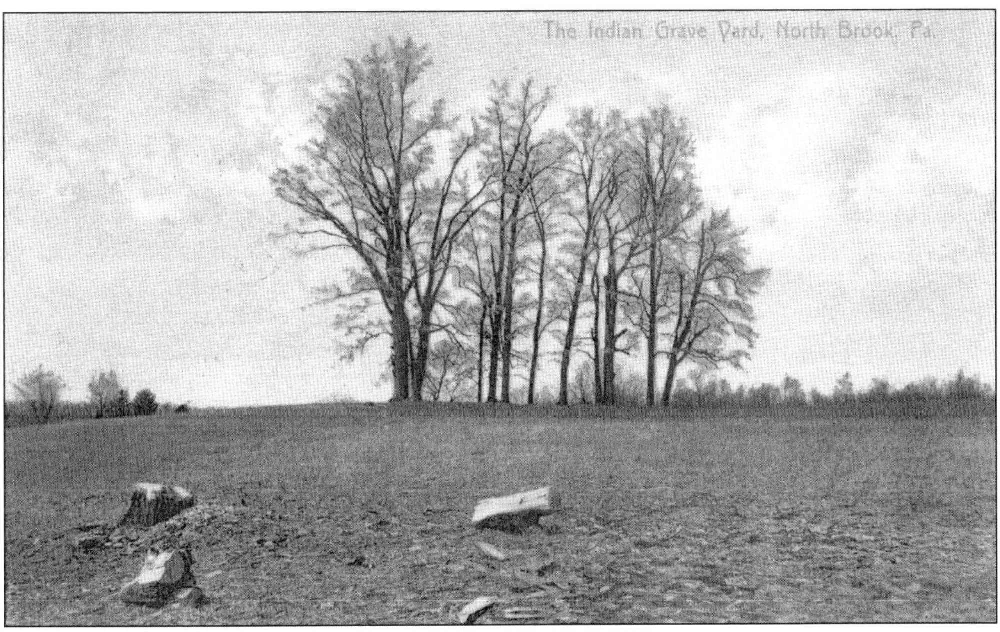

Shown here is "the Indian Grave Yard, North Brook, Pa." Because the Lenni-Lenape lived on the land for generations, the area is rife with artifacts. With the excavation of the soil for the building of modern homes, many relics are still being uncovered. The same goes for the Brandywine Battlefield land, where homeowners have, at times, had to evict relic hunters with metal detectors from their land.

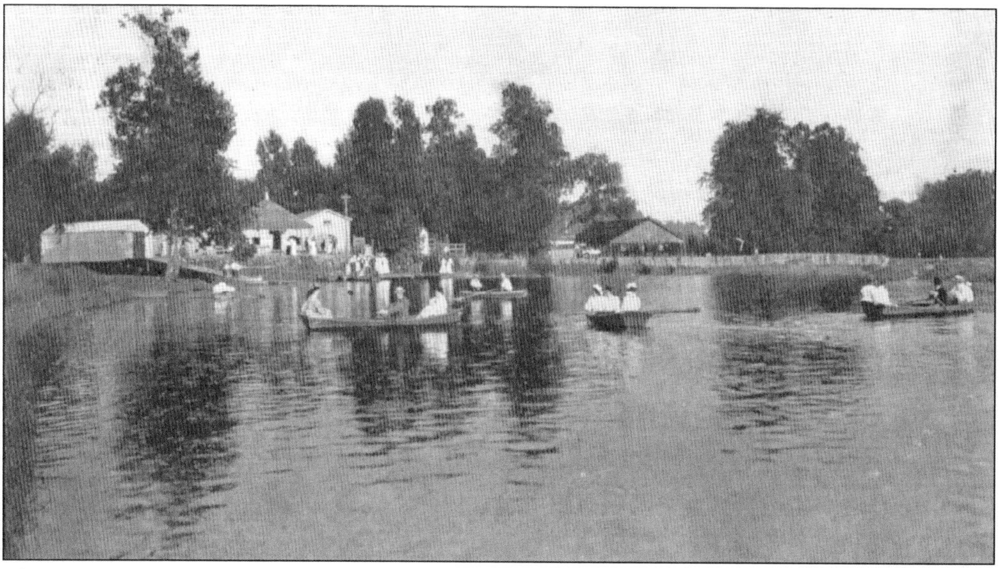

This postcard is titled "Brandywine at Lenape Park." During the late 19th century and all of the 20th century, Lenape had fields and parks used for recreation on hot summer days. Canoeing has always been a popular activity. In this card with a 1907 postmark, Frances writes, "Dear Margaret, I wish you were with me." This card was published by A. Henry of 18 North Church Street, West Chester, another publisher of many cards.

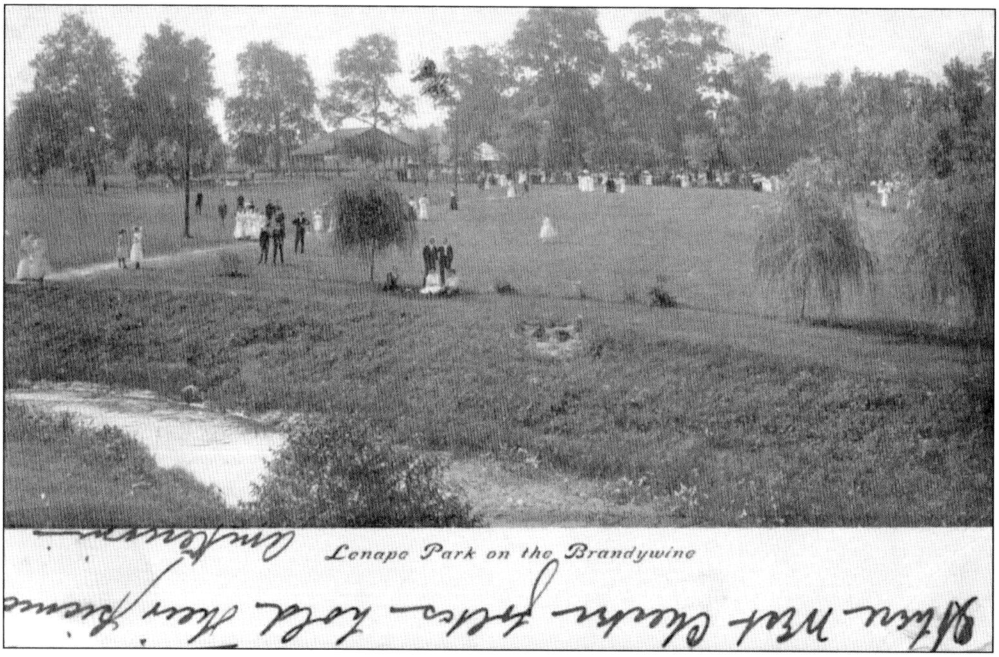

Seen here is the "Lenape Park on the Brandywine." Lenape is a short ride by horse, trolley, or car, depending on the era, from West Chester. The amusement park provided the first jobs for many area residents who later became successful business owners. Picnics and music went hand-in-hand during the outings and attracted many visitors, as this card by A. Henry of West Chester (postmarked 1907) shows. Amusement rides were added in the 20th century.

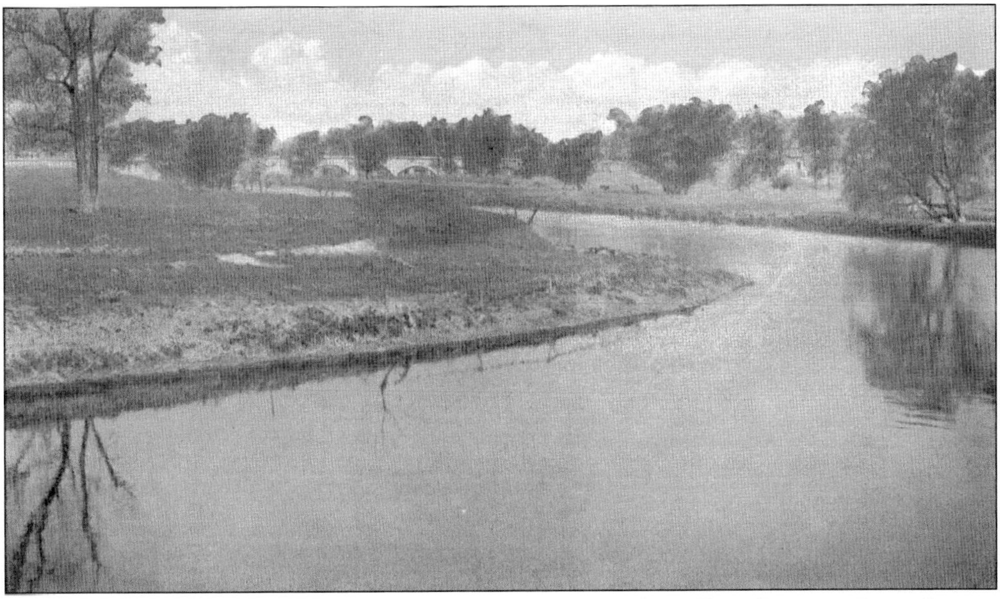

"Brandywine at Lenape, Pa." is the title of this postcard. During the 1870s, a Pocopson farmer began a public picnic ground along the Brandywine, a half mile below Lenape. The trains would bring people from Wilmington, Coatesville, and as far away as Reading. It is estimated that as many as 1,000 people would gather for socializing and games. In the later days of the amusement park, a merry-go-round and roller coaster were two of the main attractions.

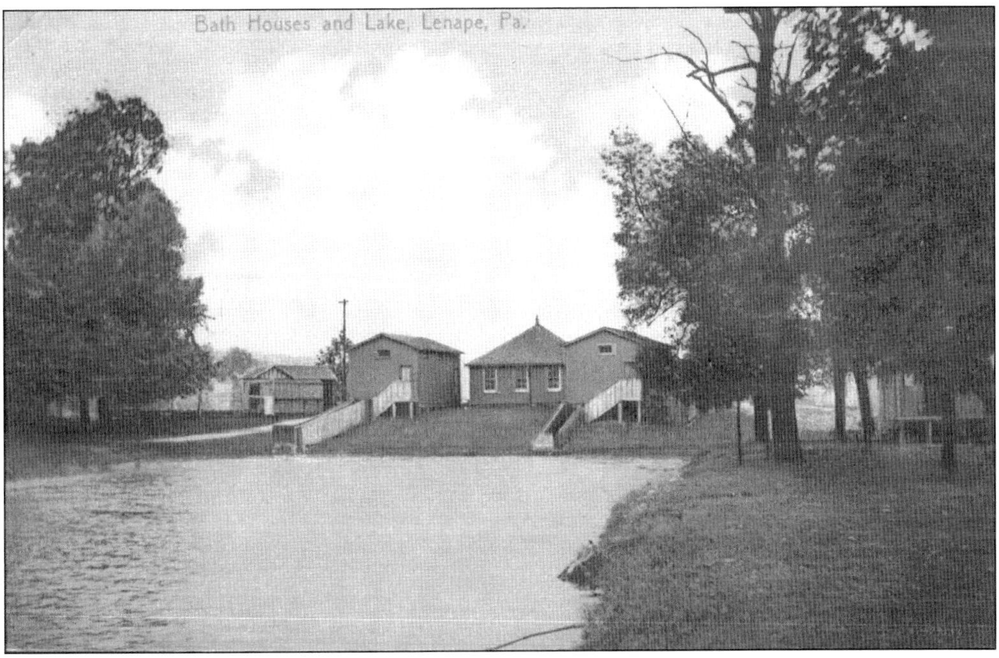

This postcard is titled "Bath Houses and Lake, Lenape, Pa." The Brandywine provided access to bathing and fishing for those who did not want to participate in the land sports of tennis, baseball, and even cricket. There was also another water diversion for a brief period. At one time, a small steam-powered excursion boat named the *Minnehaha* would charge passengers 10¢ each for a brief cruise on the river.

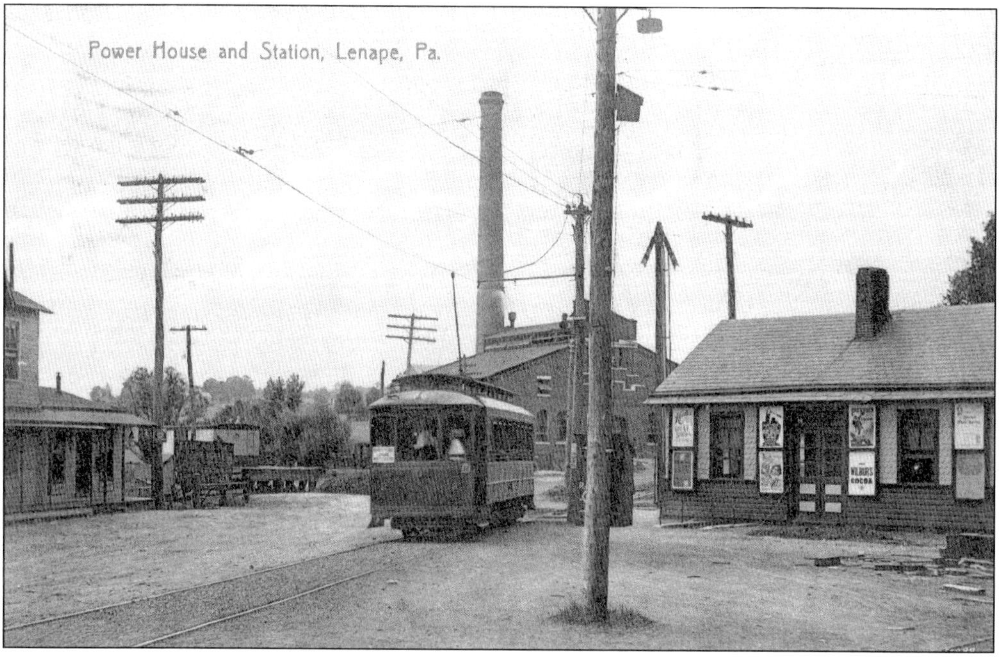

Besides recreation, Lenape also housed a forge where a factory, located next to an inn, made parts for steam generation. The streetcar, as seen in this postcard, was used to transport riders to and from West Chester. The card, postmarked 1908, is No. 142 of the S.J. Parker & Son series. The writer of the card said he has a day off from work and came to Lenape to spend the day.

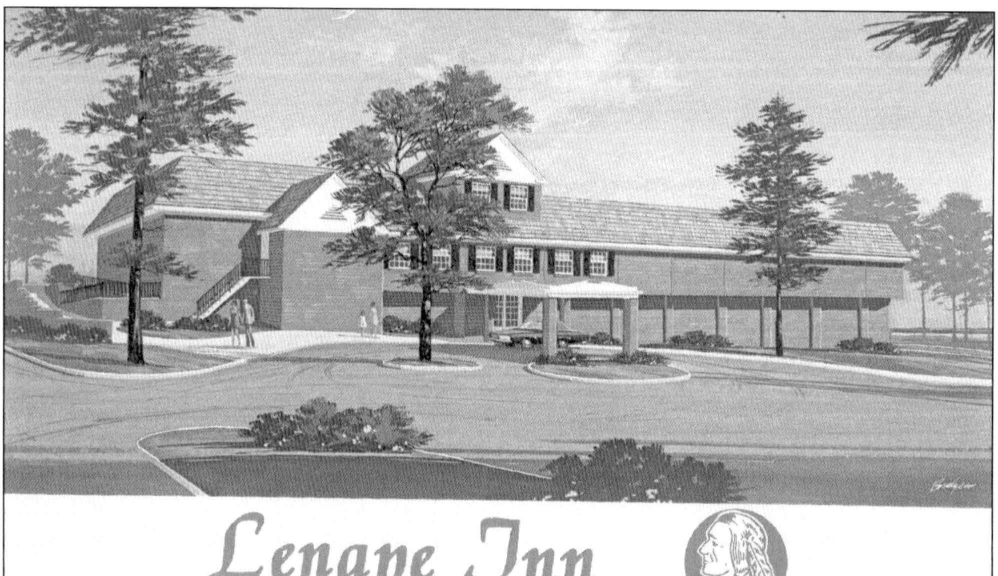

"Lenape Inn on the Historic Brandywine," reads the back of the card. The inn's name has changed, but it continues to serve as a restaurant and still offers a great view of the Brandywine. Ducks also seem to like this spot on the Brandywine. The inn is located on the west bank, across from the Brandywine Park. A narrow, two-lane bridge over the Brandywine connects the two banks.

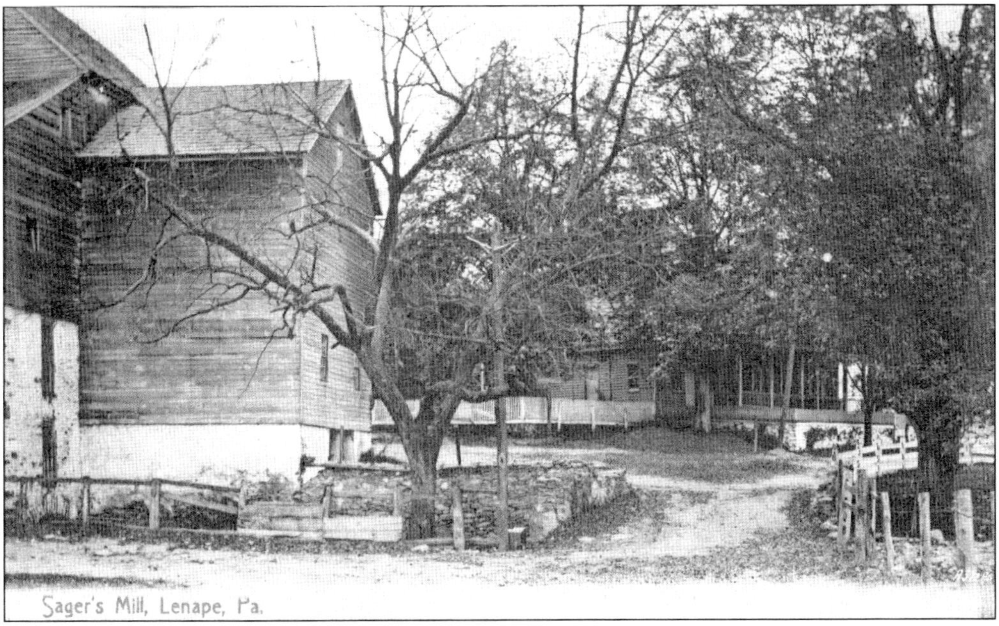

This is "Sager's Mill, Lenape, Pa." Around Lenape the Brandywine drops. The river offered power for the mills that helped make Chester County prosper in the beginning years. The power generated made the Brandywine more productive than many larger rivers. At one point, the Brandywine was called "the Creek of a Hundred Mills" because of the great number of waterwheels at work every day.

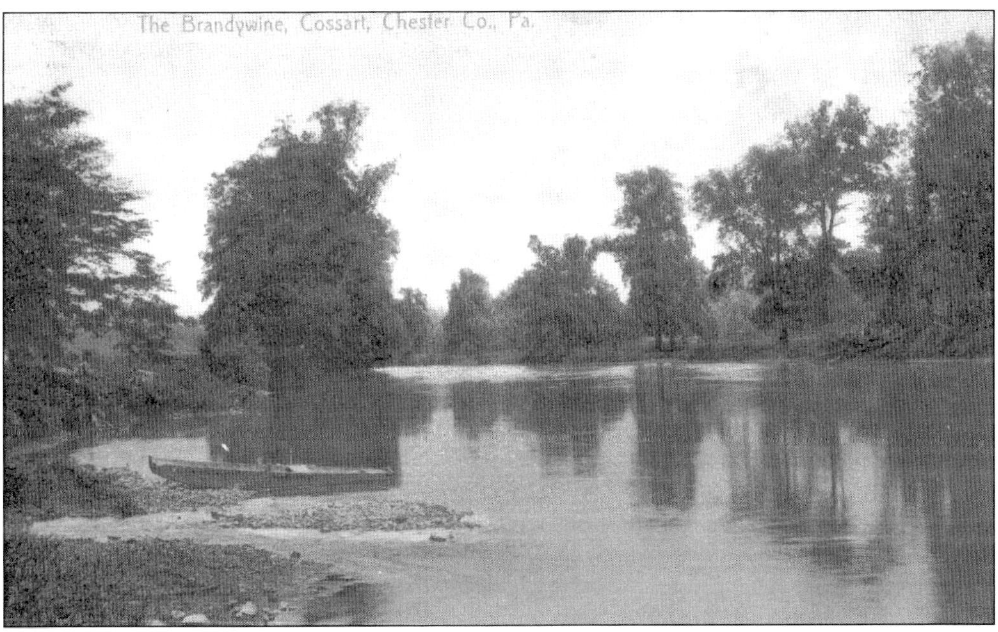

Seen here is "the Brandywine, Cossart, Chester Co., Pa." When industry began to enter the Brandywine around Lenape, railroads were built. As the tracks were laid, a number of small towns became stops along the rails. Cossart, Chadds Ford Junction, Pocopson, and Wawaset were some of the stops along the railroad. The railroad still offers minimal service, but the importance of these towns as railroad stops has decreased.

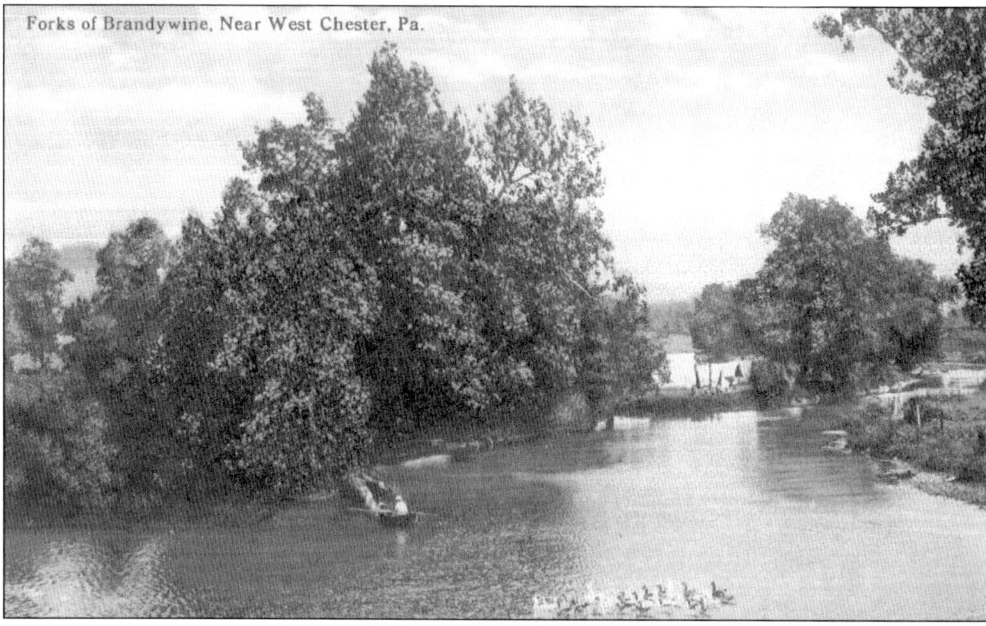

Postcards of the Brandywine near Lenape have been popular over the years, and sometimes the basic scene is shown in postcards published by two different companies with some little changes. The postcard titled "Forks of Brandywine, Near West Chester, Pa." has a canoeist along the riverbank with a camp along the banks near the right of the card and a flock of ducks in the foreground. The card below is from the later White Border era and has a postmark of 1921. Its caption, "Forks of the Brandywine, Near West Chester, Pa.," is at the bottom of the card. The scene is cropped tighter on the left, and the ducks are missing.

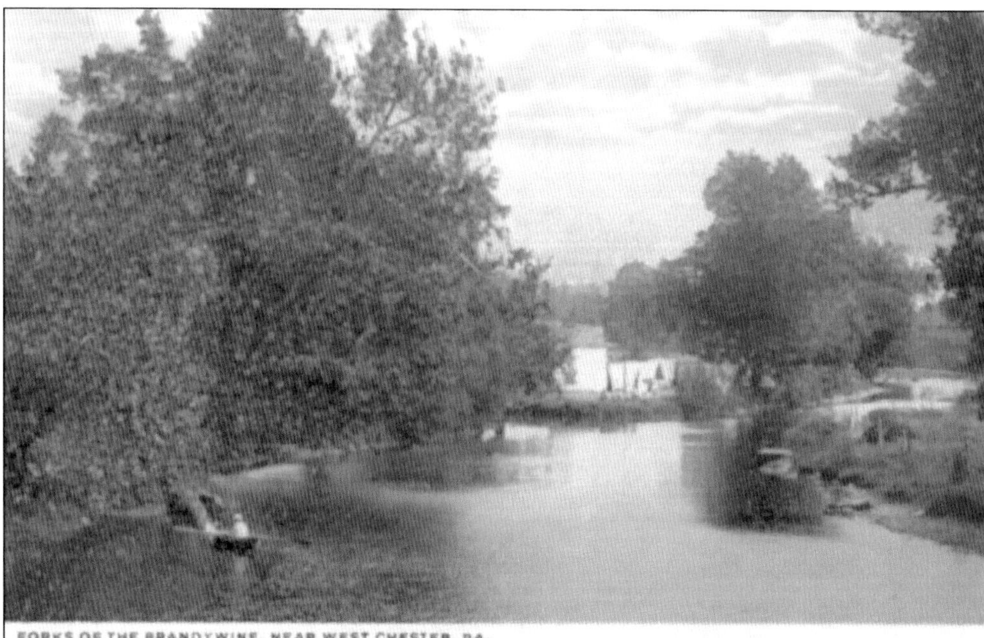

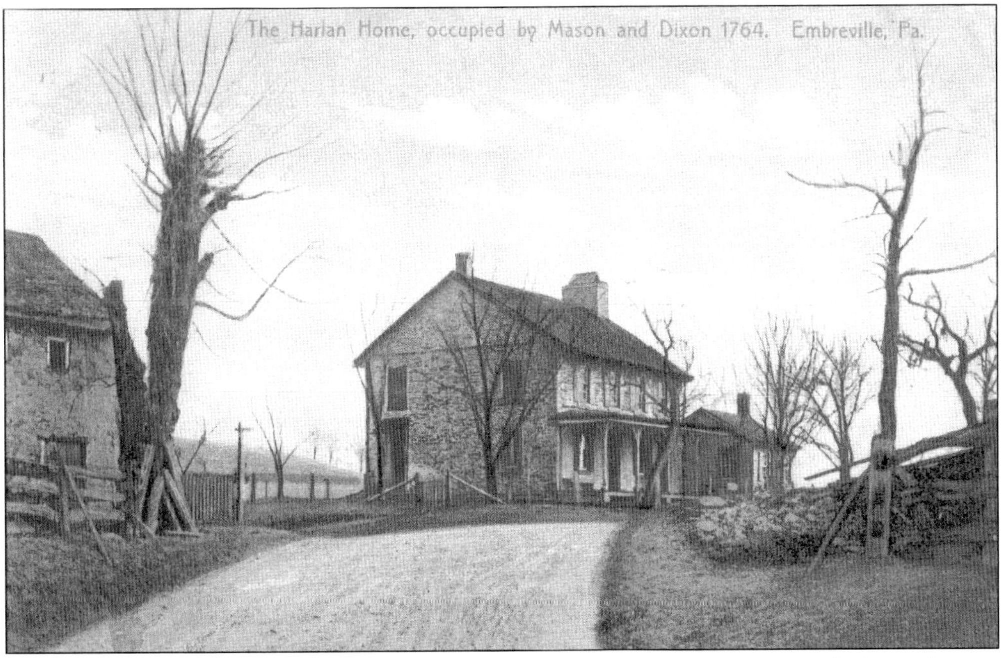

Two English surveyors were commissioned in the mid-1700s to use astronomical observations to determine the boundary between Maryland and Pennsylvania. Later, the Mason-Dixon line was used to clearly divide slave and free states during the Civil War. The card above depicts "the Harlan Home, occupied by Mason and Dixon 1764, Embreeville, Pa." The Brandywine runs past Embreeville. The card below, "Star Gazers Stone set by Mason and Dixon 1764, Embreeville, Pa.," shows the stone (still standing in Newlin Township) that was used to fix the boundary. The cards are part of the S.J. Parker & Son series. The card above is No. 324, and the card below is No. 263.

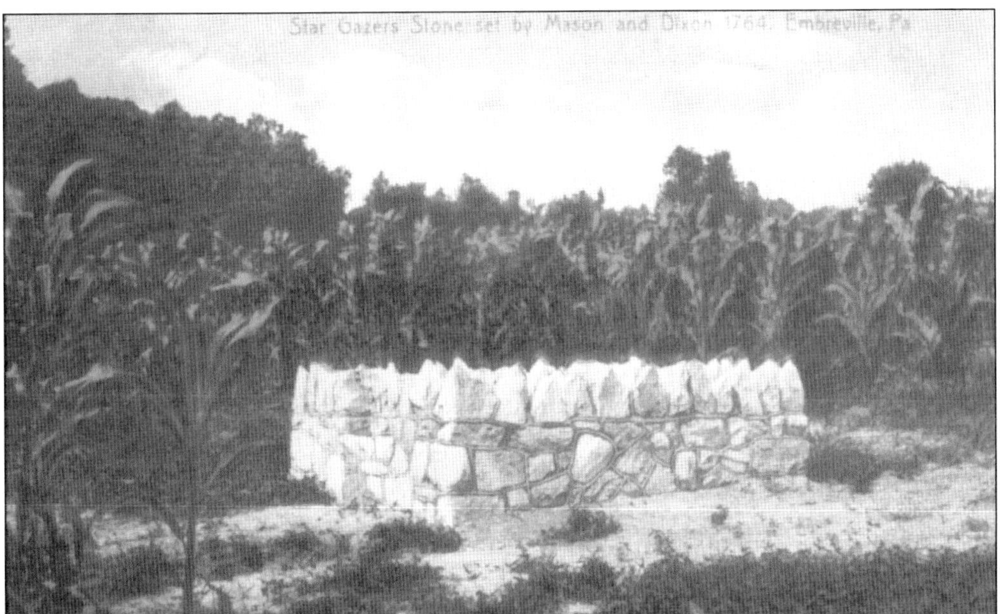

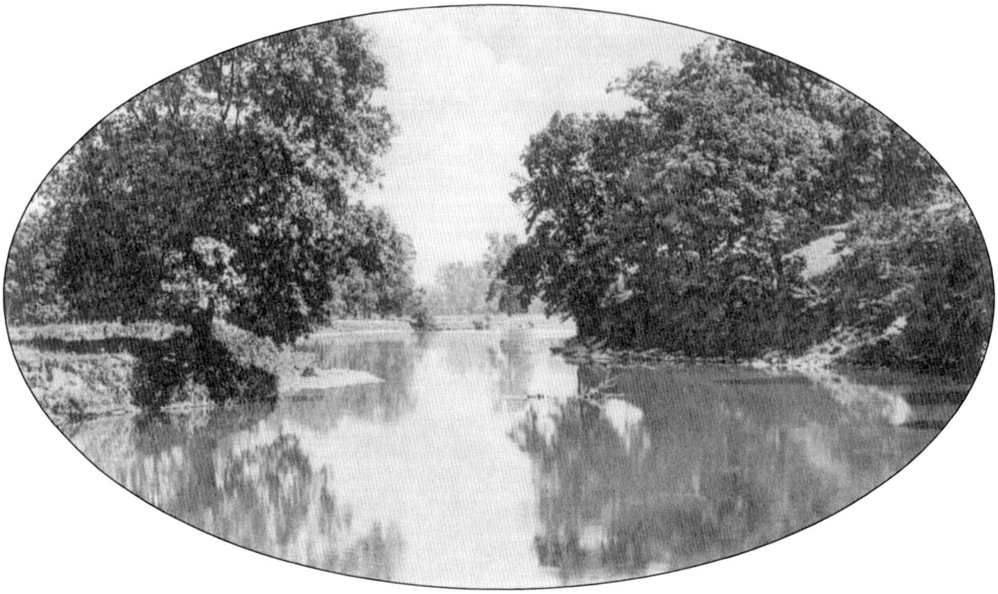

The Brandywine at Pocopson marks the northern area of the land that saw one of the major battles of the American Revolution, the Battle of Brandywine. The river would play a major role in the conflict that pitted Gen. George Washington against the British in a battle that would decide if Philadelphia, the capital of the upstart American nation, would escape being captured by the British.

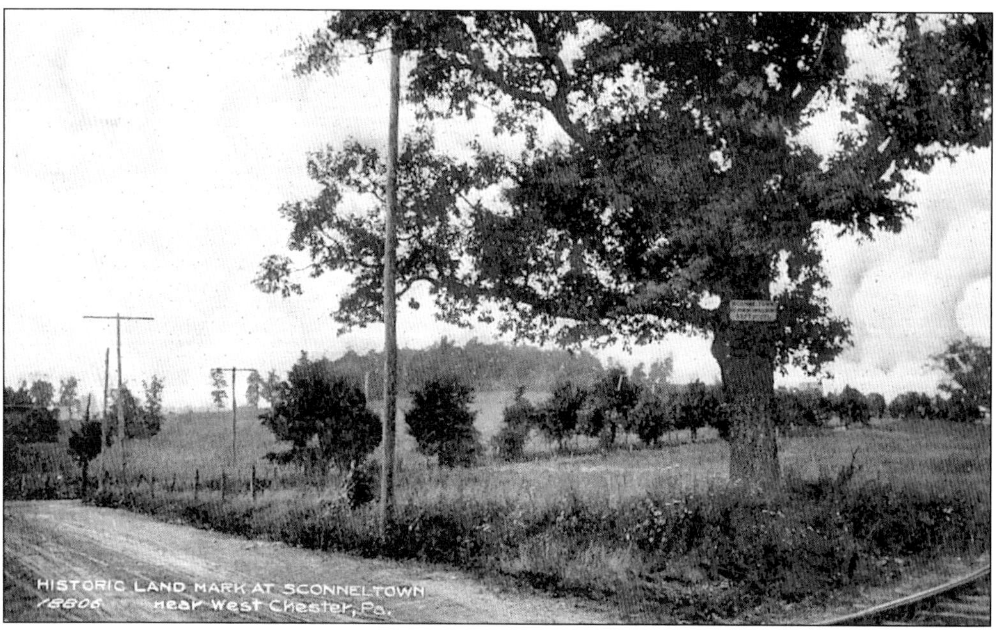

"Historic Land Mark at Sconneltown near West Chester, Pa." is the title of this card. Sconneltown was important during the Battle of Brandywine. It marked the area where the troops under British generals William Howe and Lord Charles Cornwallis turned to outflank Washington's troops. Washington—as at a previous battle at Long Island, New York, the year before—allowed Howe to surprise him with a flanking movement. The sign on the tree reads, "Sconneltown, Sept. 11, 1777," the date of the battle.

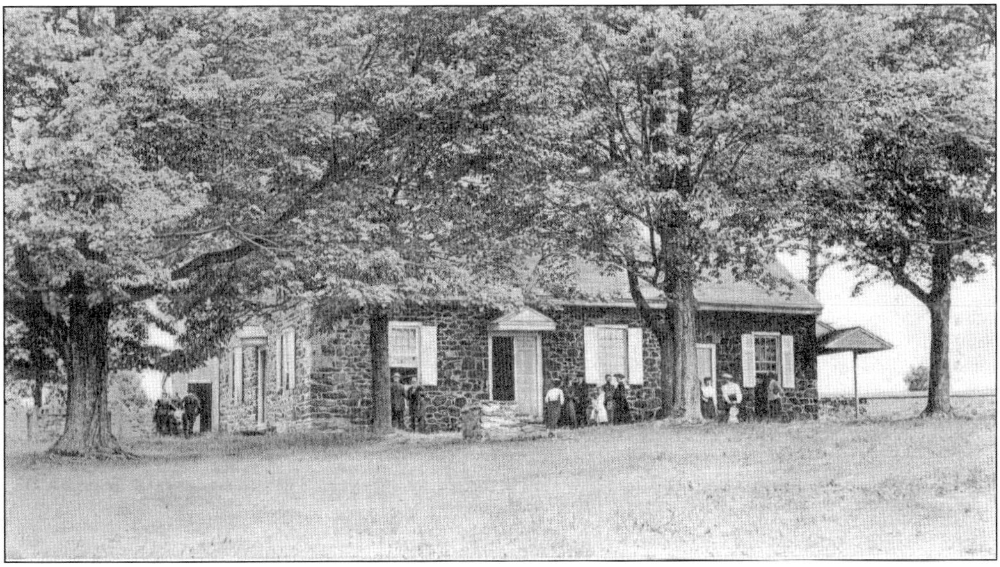

If you head due south from the historic marker at Sconneltown and follow the basic path taken by Howe's wing of the British army, you will find your way to the Birmingham meetinghouse. Several Quaker meetinghouses played roles during the day of the battle, September 11, 1777. The postcard above shows the Birmingham meetinghouse. The meetinghouse saw much warfare and was used as a hospital for the wounded. The card below, "Longwood Friends Meeting House, Hamorton, Chester Co., Pa.," is No. 282 in the S.J. Parker & Son series of the area. This meetinghouse was in the path of the second wing of the British army.

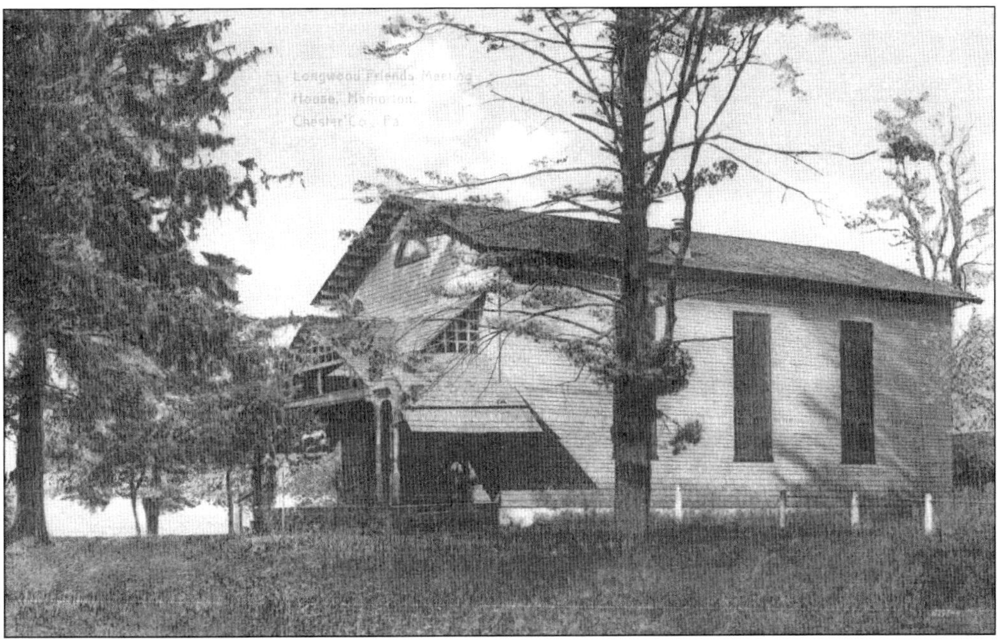

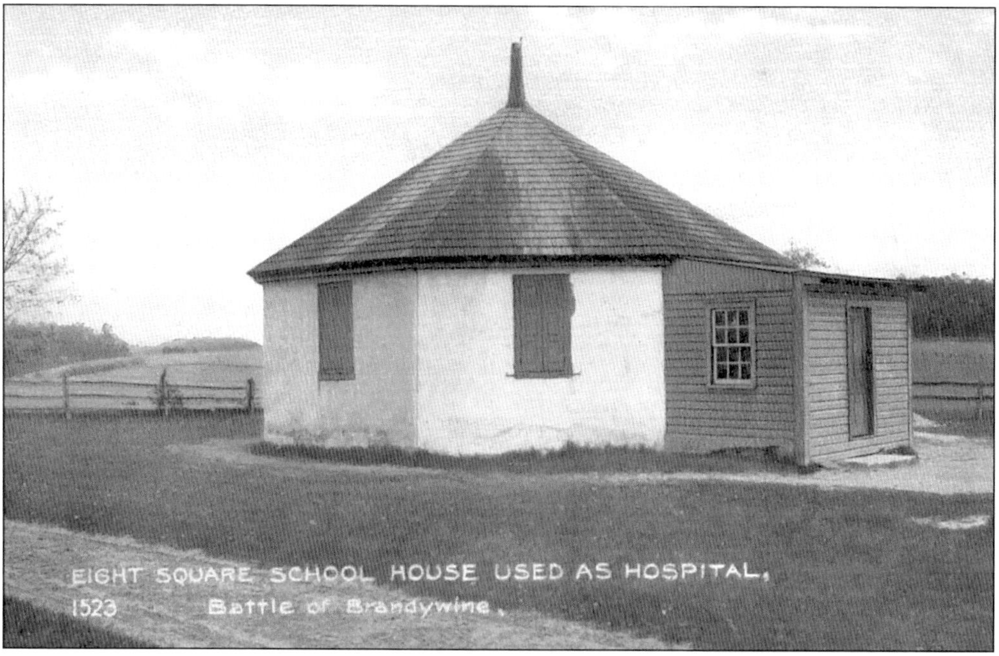

As with the Birmingham meetinghouse, many historic buildings survived for more than a century after the battle. The postcard above, "Eight Square School House Used as Hospital, Battle of Brandywine," shows one of a number of buildings used as a hospital after the bloody fighting that saw hundreds of casualties on each side. Below is the interior of the Birmingham meetinghouse.

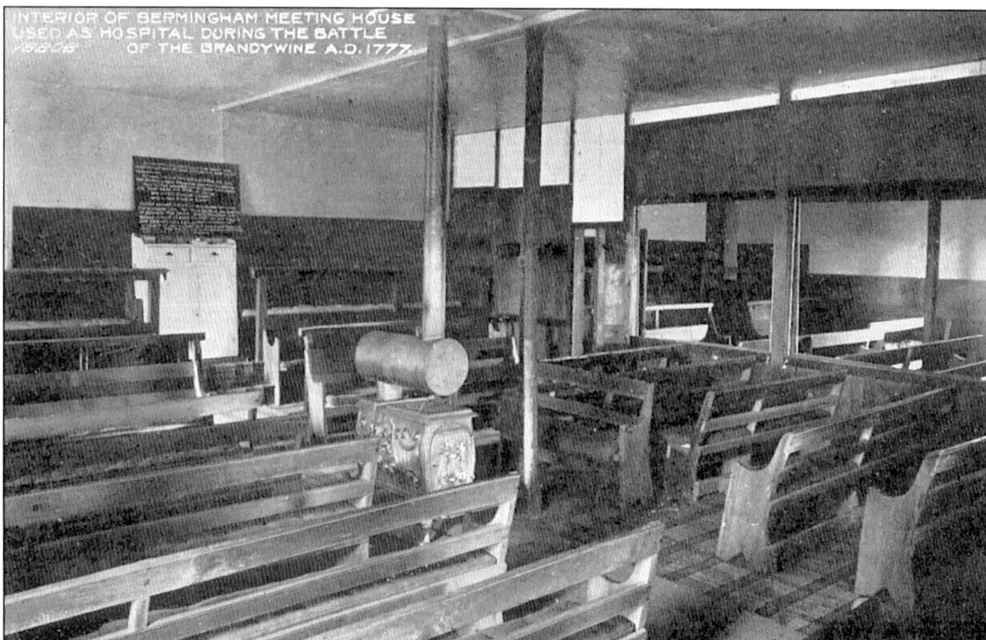

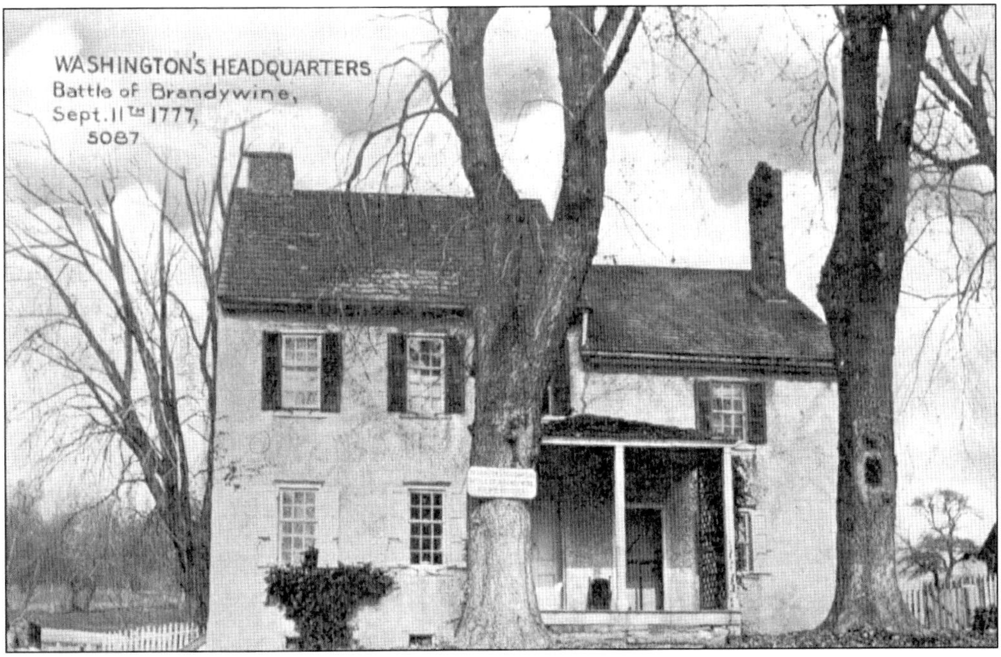

General Washington made his headquarters in a home owned by a Quaker, Benjamin Ring, near the Brandywine. Washington's new, young general from France, Marie Joseph Paul Yves Roch Gilbert du Motier Lafayette (better known as the Marquis de Lafayette), used the home of another Quaker family, the Gilpins. Washington gathered his army on the banks of the Brandywine and, on the day before the battle, held a meeting at his headquarters to give orders for what turned out to be the largest land battle of the war. Above is "Washington's Headquarters Battle of Brandywine, Sept. 11th 1777." The photograph to the right is "Lafayette's Headquarters, Battle of Brandywine, September 11, 1777, near Chadd's Ford, Pa." The credit for the photograph is given to George A. Wolf of Wilmington, Delaware. Many of the postcards to follow are Wolf's creations.

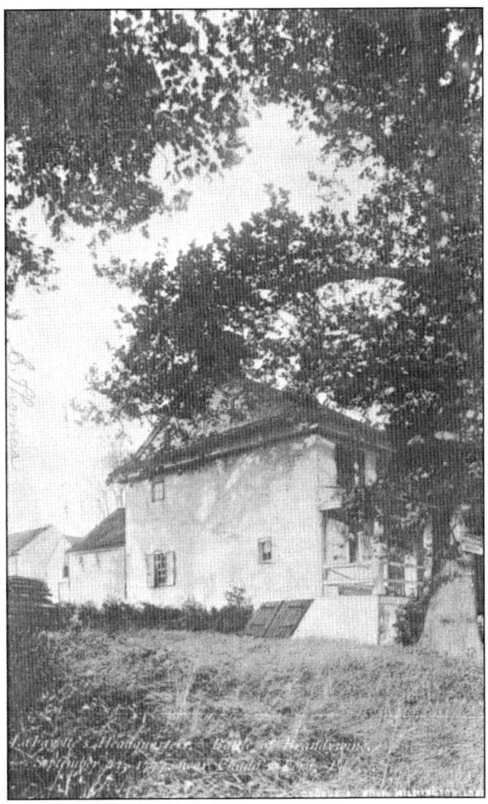

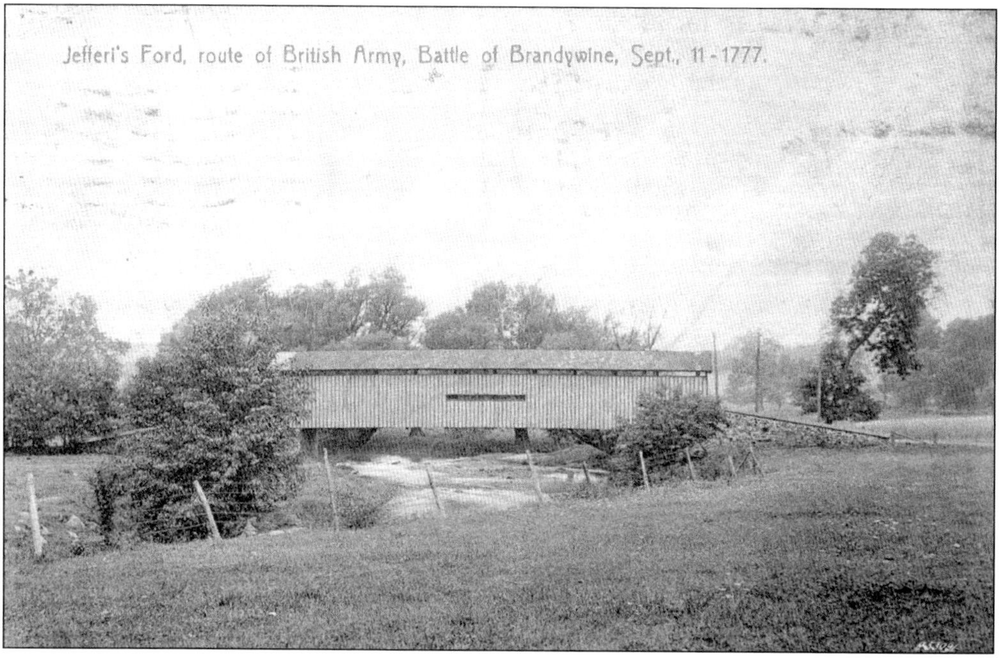

General Howe defeated General Washington by outflanking the Americans. A heavy fog on the morning of the battle and faulty intelligence allowed Howe's forces to slip out of Kennett Square unnoticed and march to the north. His forces needed to arrive in back of the Americans undetected. He almost succeeded but was discovered by several local patriots, who then reported to Washington. Howe had to ford the Brandywine at two places, including Jeffer's Ford. The card above, No. 177 of the S.J. Parker & Son series, shows Jeffer's Ford. The photograph below was taken to be used as a postcard and dates from the early 20th century. There is no photograph credit, but it appears to have been developed in Media, Delaware County, not far from the Battle of Brandywine.

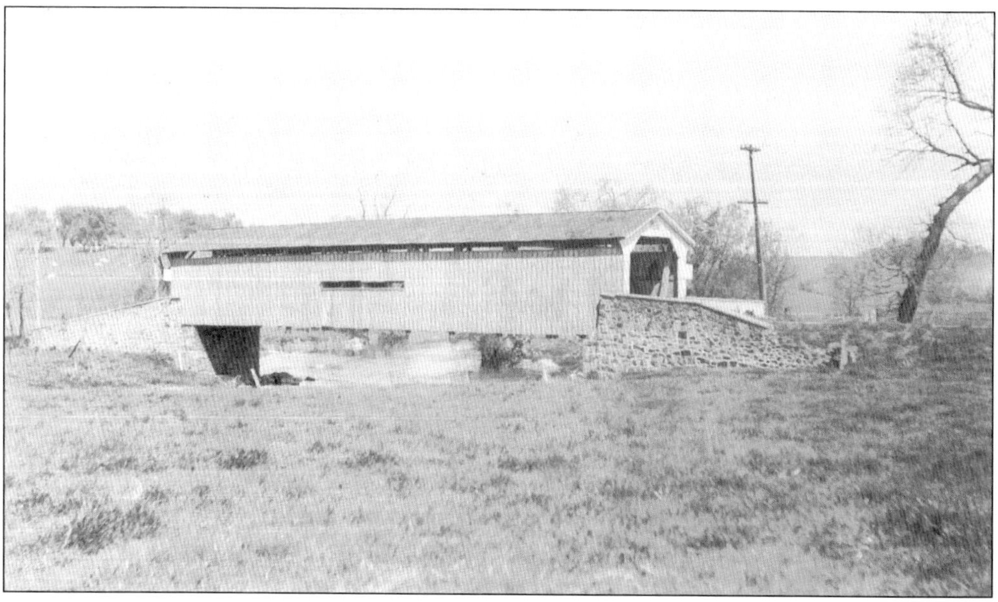

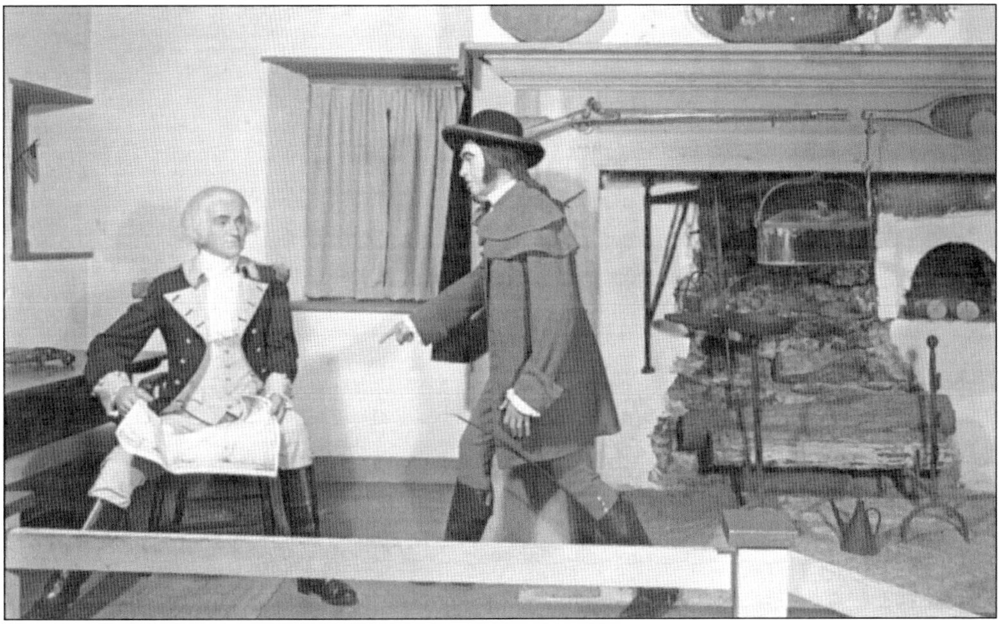

General Washington did not receive as much help as he expected from the residents of Chester County. The Quakers were sworn not to support either army, as they did not believe in war. Some Quakers did join the American army, and Gen. Nathanael Greene from New England served with distinction at Brandywine. The card above is a fanciful reenactment of the meeting of Squire Cheyney and General Washington. Cheney, after seeing Howe's forces fording the Brandywine, rode to General Sullivan to spread the alarm. Sullivan did not believe Cheyney, and Cheyney demanded to be taken to Washington. Washington also doubted Cheyney, but the report was soon verified by American scouts. The scene above was displayed for a time in Washington's Headquarters, shown below in a photograph taken by George R. King of Boston.

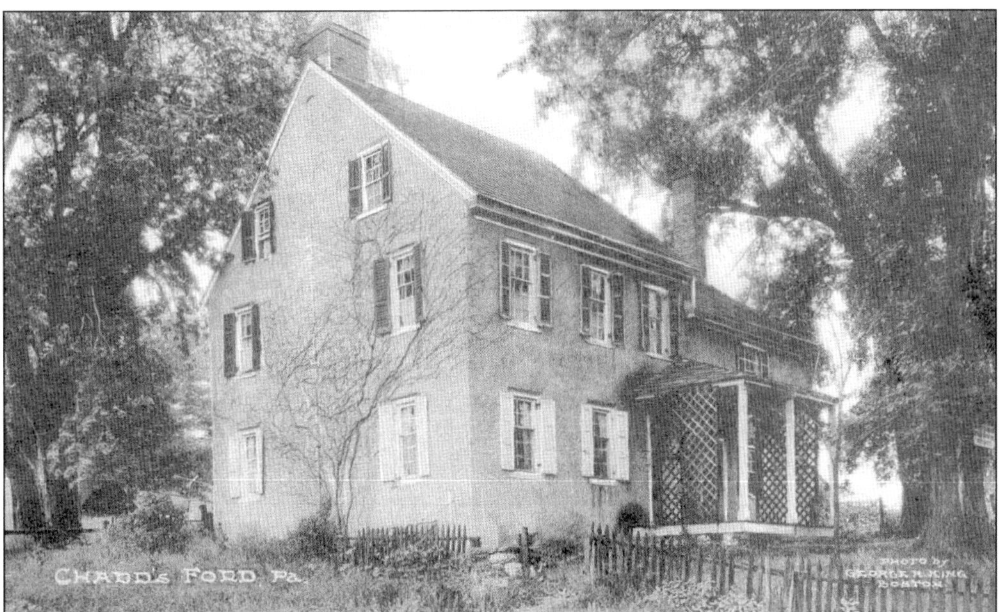

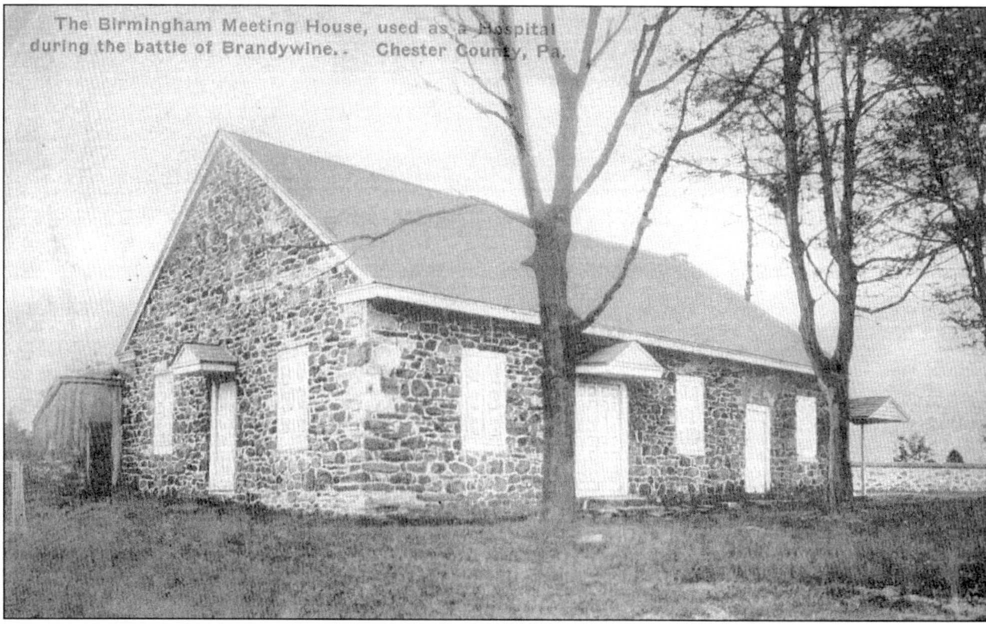

After receiving the warning from Squire Cheyney, General Washington rushed his troops to the vicinity of the Birmingham meetinghouse, shown above in a postcard published by a Coatesville company, C.N. Speakman and Sons. The Americans were driven south from the area of the meetinghouse to a section called Sandy Hollow. Several cannons still mark the areas of the battle. None of the cannons were actually used during the battle. The caption in the card below says, "Cannon marking the scene of the Battle of Brandywine, September 11, 1777." This card is another one by George A. Wolf and is postmarked 1906.

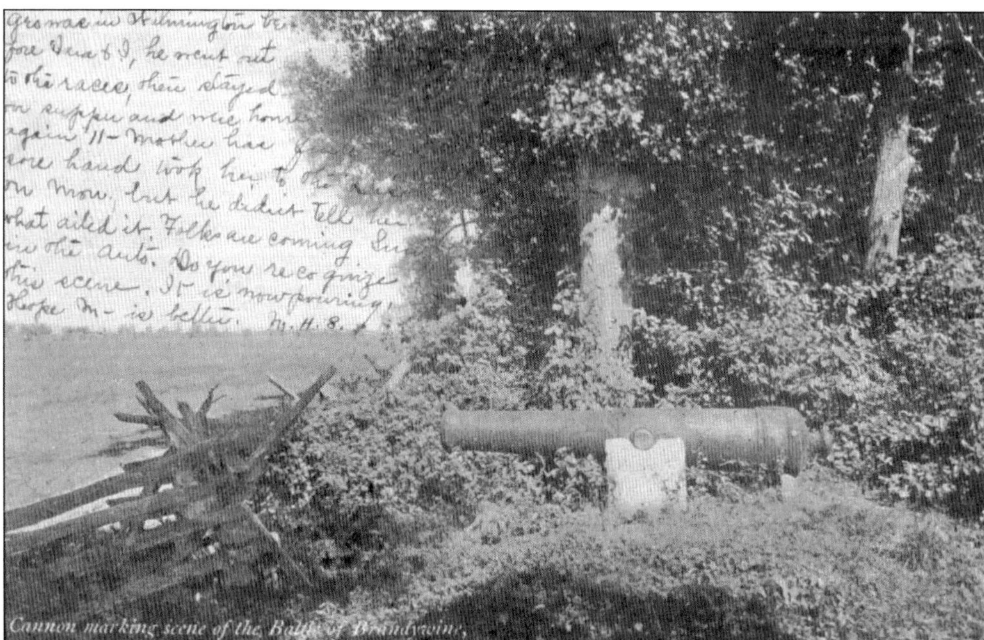

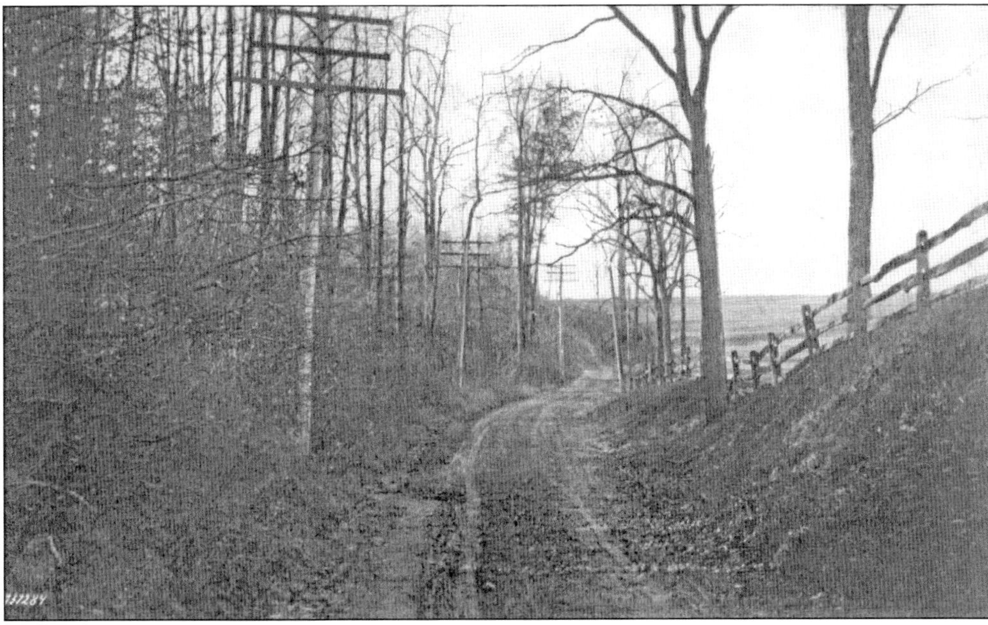

The fighting around Sandy Hollow was fierce. The above postcard says, "Sandy Hollow, scene of the last fighting Battle of Brandywine, and right of the American line." In the woods depicted in this scene, General Lafayette suffered a leg wound and won the respect of the American army. Also near this spot, brave Virginia troops fought and delayed the British long enough for Washington's army to escape to Chester city. At the Birmingham meetinghouse (below), while the fighting was taking place, a young Quaker talked to British officers and later recorded his observations. The card below notes that the Birmingham meetinghouse was built in 1763.

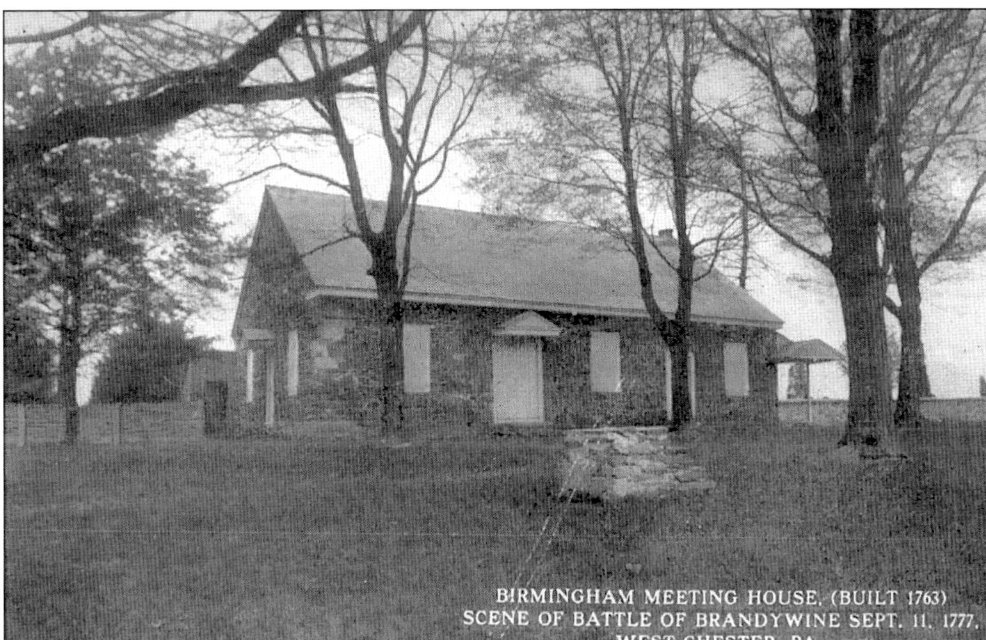

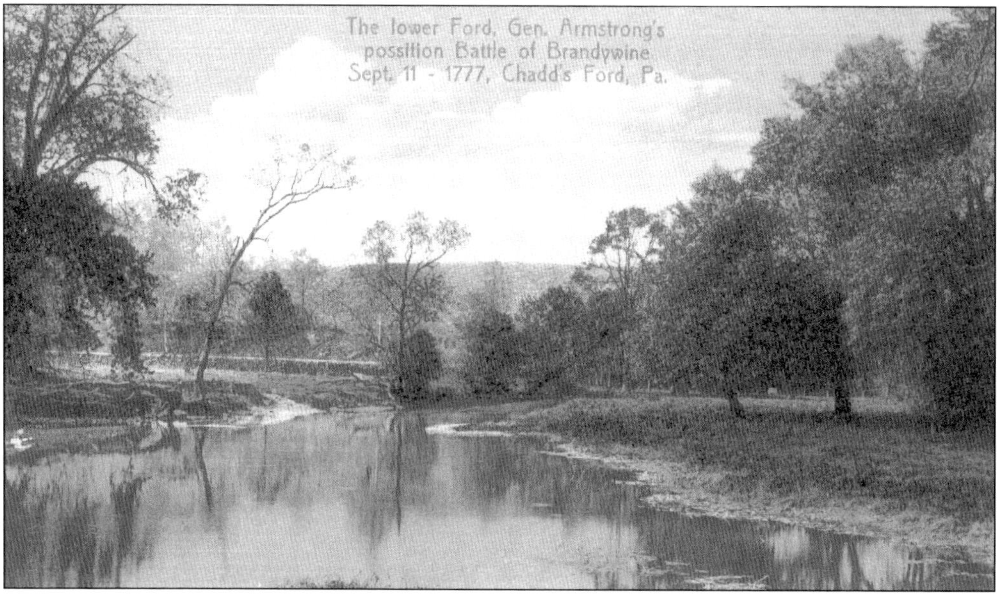

George Washington's army had many fords on the Brandywine to protect on September 11, 1777. The idea was to use the river as a defensive position and make the British attack his troops. Of course, if the British never crossed the Brandywine, they would be kept from Philadelphia. The postcard above shows "the lower Ford, Gen. Armstrong's possition [*sic*], Battle of Brandywine, Sept. 11, 1777, Chadd's Ford." Gen. John Armstrong commanded the Pennsylvania militia at Brandywine and held the southernmost position at Pyle's Ford. The British were not expected to attack this position, and no action took place at this location. The card below is an unusual card with both Washington's and Lafayette's Headquarters pictured. The postmark is September 11, 1907, the 130th anniversary of the battle. The postcard is one of the first to be allowed to have a divided back for both messages and addresses. The government allowed these cards beginning March 1, 1907.

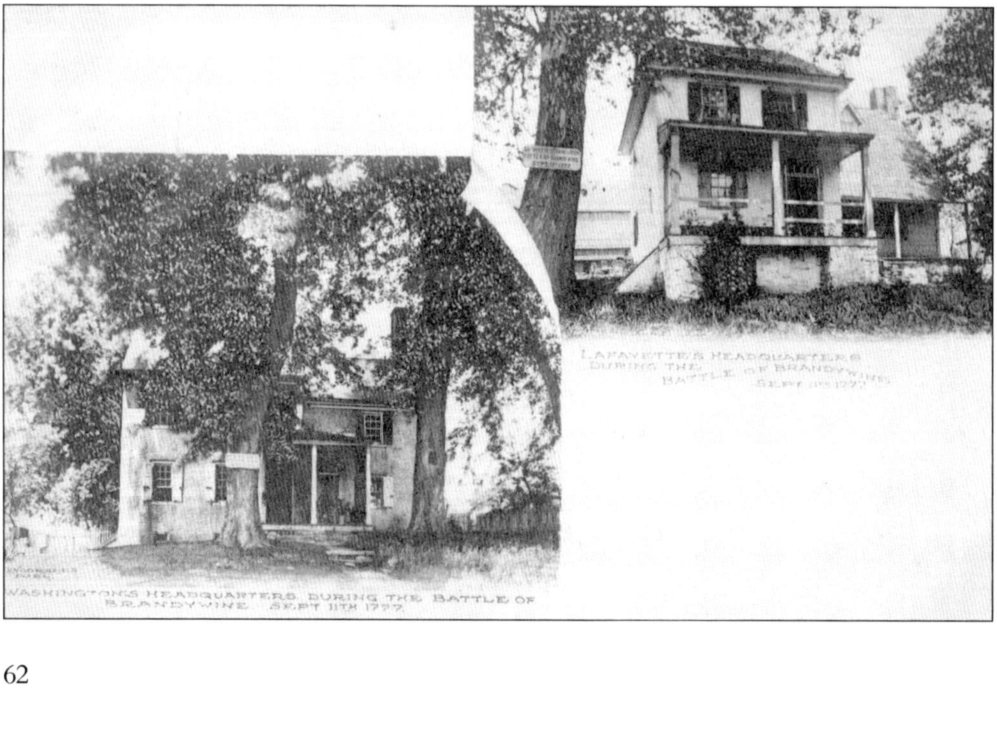

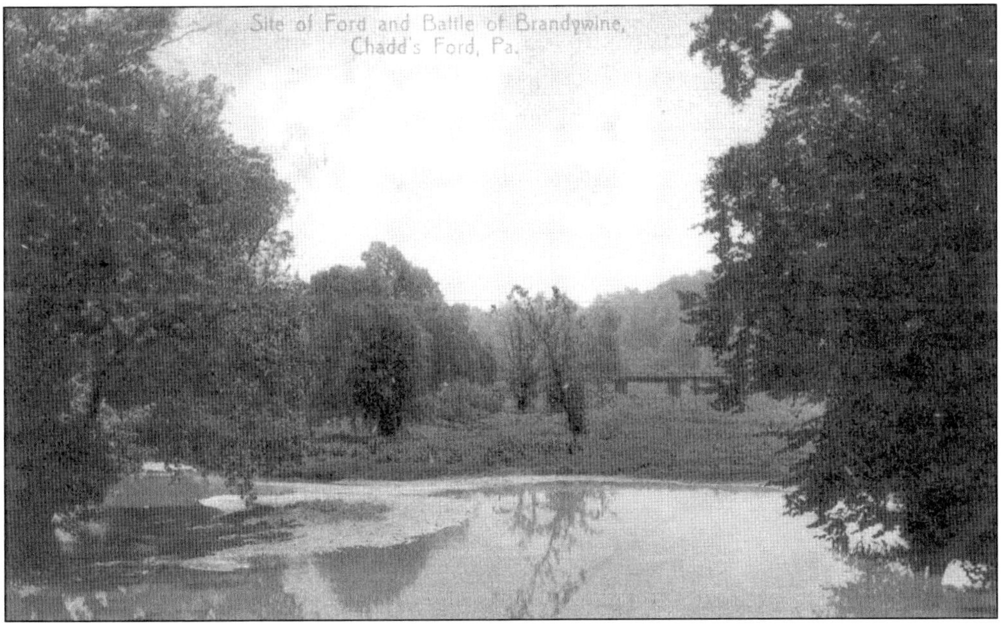

American general John Sullivan was in charge of guarding the northern fords during the Battle of Brandywine. At a conference the night before the battle, Sullivan was told the fords that the British were to use the next day did not exist. Misinformed, Sullivan did not have them covered, and Howe and Cornwallis outflanked the American army. The card above says, "Site of Ford and Battle of Brandywine, Chadd's Ford, Pa." The card is another one of S.J. Parker & Sons, No. 157 in the series. The card below says, "Anvil Tavern, route of British Army, Sept. 11 - 1777." The tavern was located close to what is now Longwood Gardens. Hessian general Wilhelm Knyphausen led half of the British army directly from Kennett Square to Chadds Ford. For a long time, Washington believed Knyphausen had the majority of the British army with him. When Howe attacked near the Birmingham meetinghouse, Knyphausen pushed across the Brandywine at Chadds Ford.

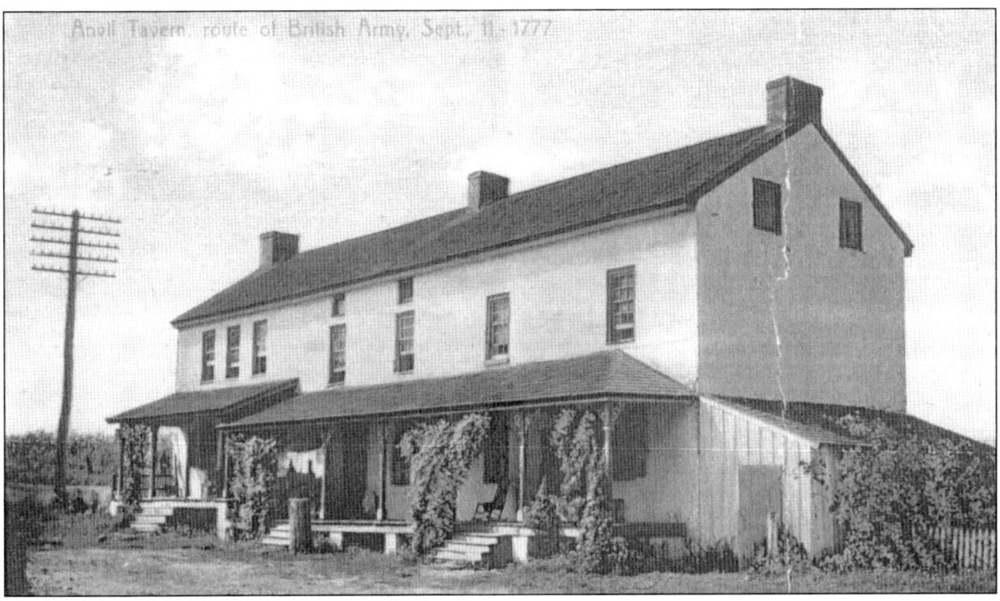

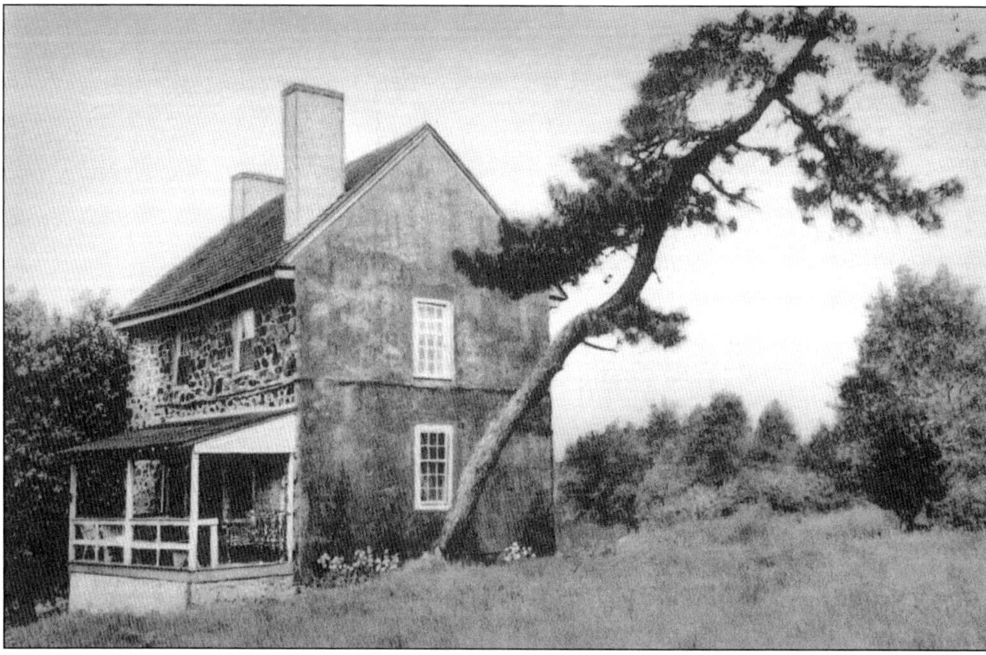

The card above shows "John Chad's House." John Chads, as he called himself, ran a ferry across the Brandywine just below Brinton's Run. He was the son of a shoemaker named Francis Chadsey. Many of the cards used in this book refer to the village as Chadd's Ford. Today, however, the area is most commonly known as Chadds Ford. The card below says, "Where the Battle of Brandywine was fought, 1777, on the Brandywine River, Pa." Part of the American artillery was located near Chads's home.

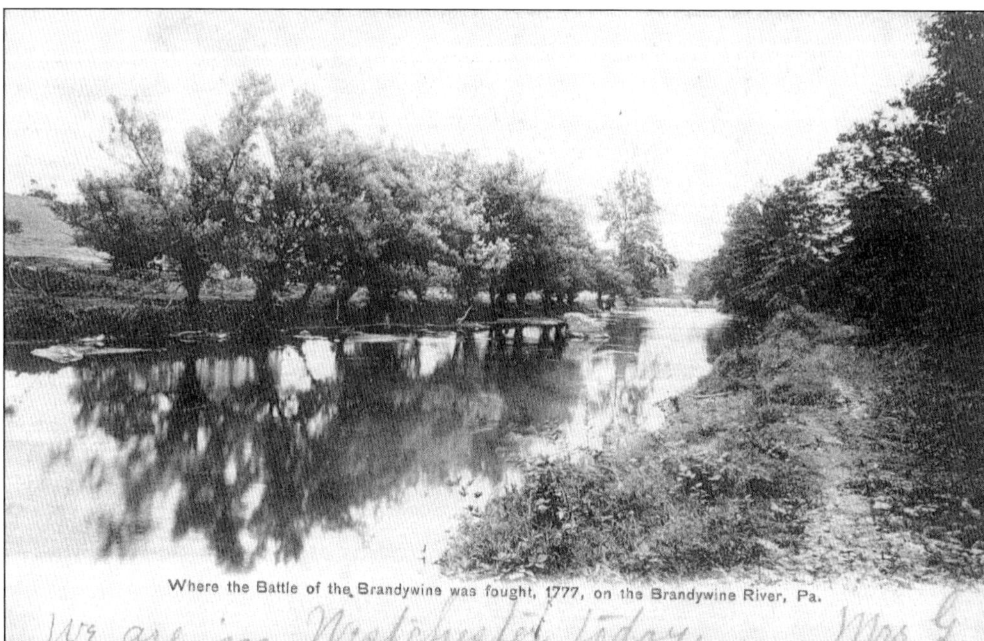

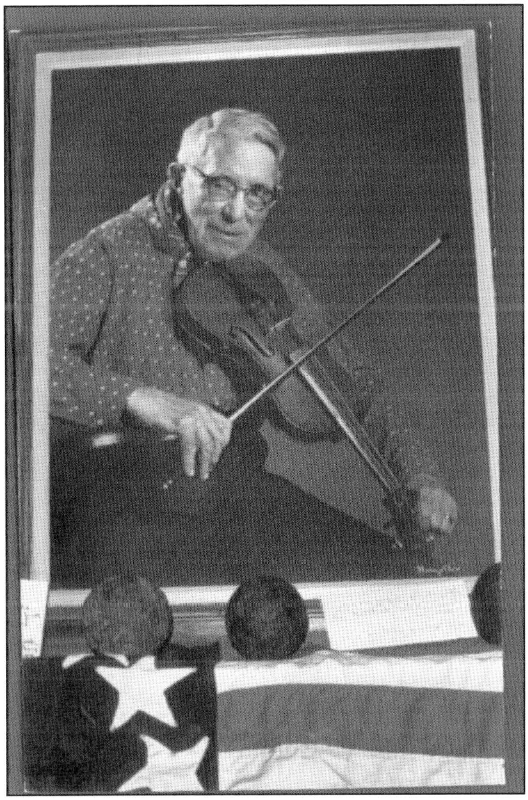

For many years, the Brandywine Battlefield, one of the most historic sites in the nation, was left to decay. The buildings that once housed Washington and Lafayette continued to be used as homes after the battle, and no effort concerning preservation was made until the 20th century. The person responsible for starting the preservation effort was Christian C. Sanderson (right), a teacher who at one time lived in Washington's Headquarters with his mother. He was a friend of the famous Wyeth family of painters. The card below notes that Lafayette's Headquarters was used on both September 10 and 11, 1777.

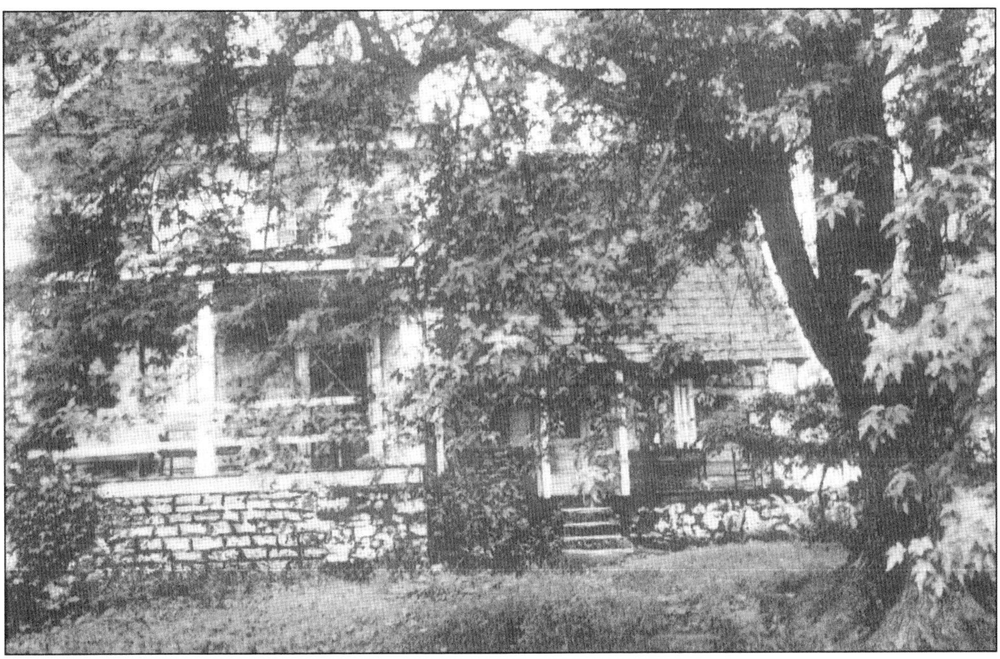

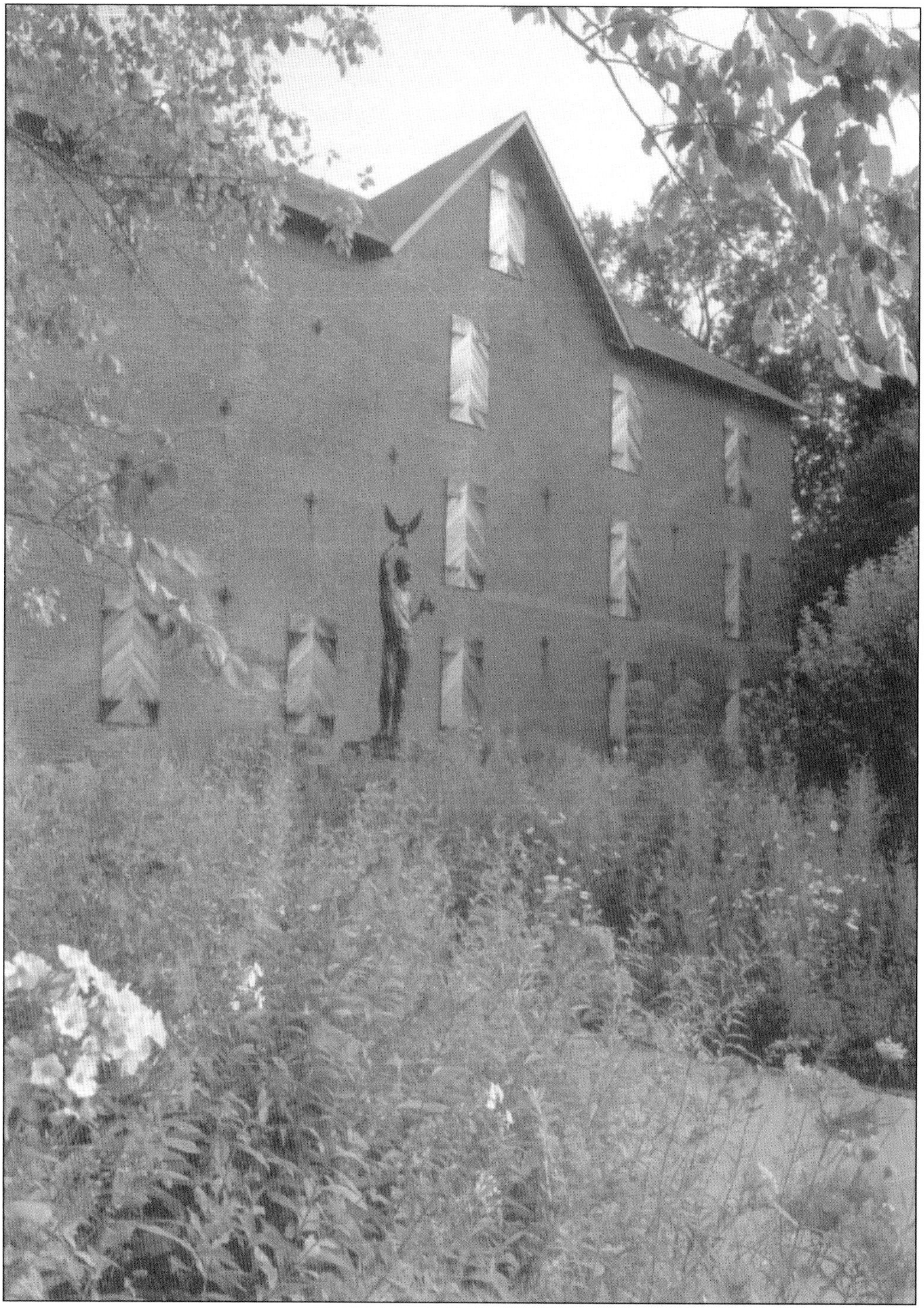

Besides the American Revolution battle, the Brandywine is also known for art made famous by Howard Pyle, N.C. Wyeth (Pyle's star pupil), and Andrew Wyeth (N.C. Wyeth's son), along with the rest of the Brandywine painters. The Brandywine River Museum at Chadds Ford, shown in the postcard, houses works by Wyeth and many famous painters. The museum began as the Hoffman's gristmill in 1864.

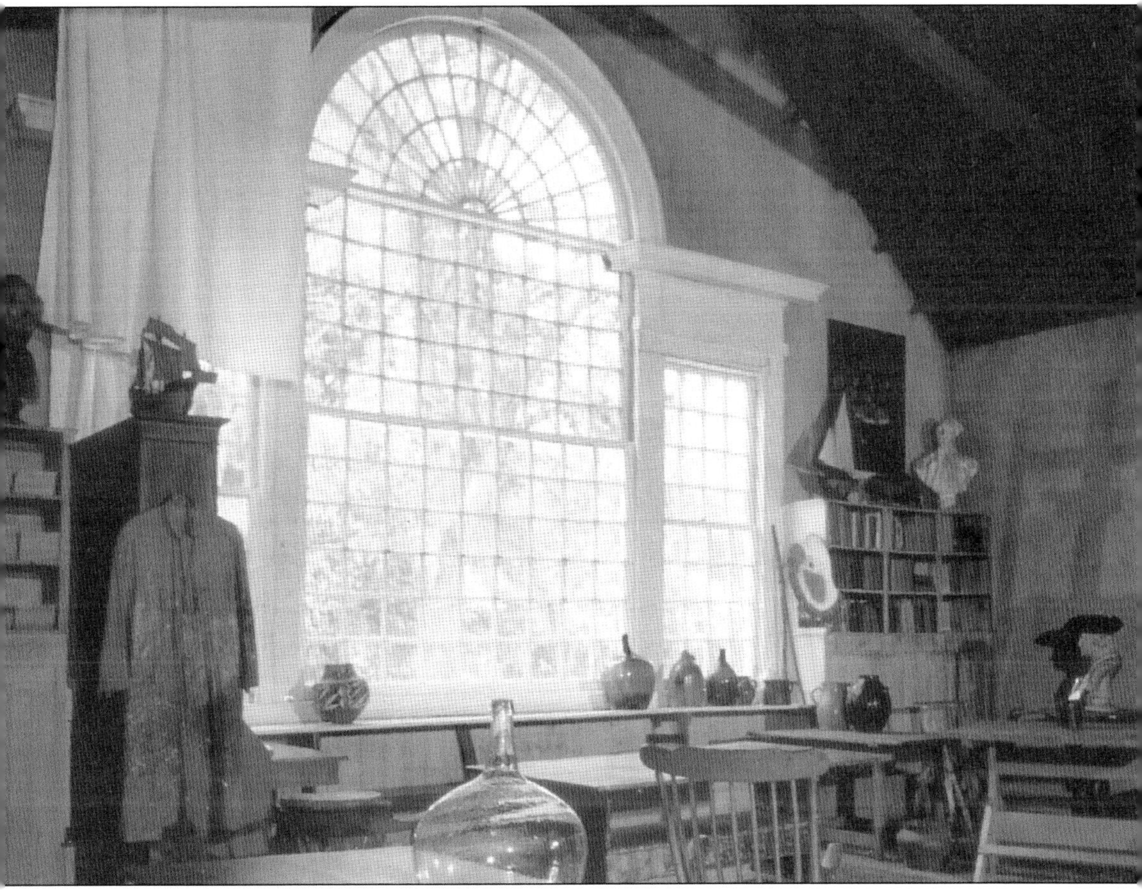

The N.C. Wyeth studio has been preserved and is part of the Brandywine Conservancy, as is the Brandywine River Museum. The interior of the museum is shown in this card issued by the museum, as are all of the cards concerning the Wyeths. N.C. Wyeth has been quoted as saying, "Never have I appreciated nature as I have in this place." Three generations of Wyeths have painted and lived along the Brandywine.

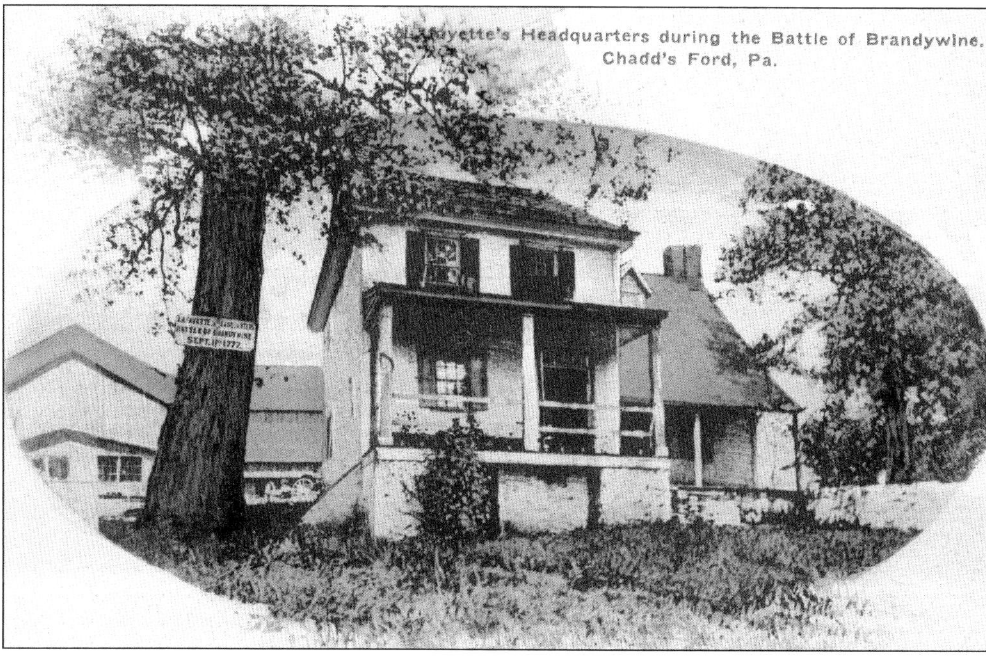

In 1941, Andrew Wyeth took his palette to the Brandywine and painted Lafayette's Headquarters. Much of the land surrounding the Battle of Brandywine has been preserved by the nonprofit Brandywine Conservancy. The efforts of the conservancy help to preserve the landscape as it looked during the battle.

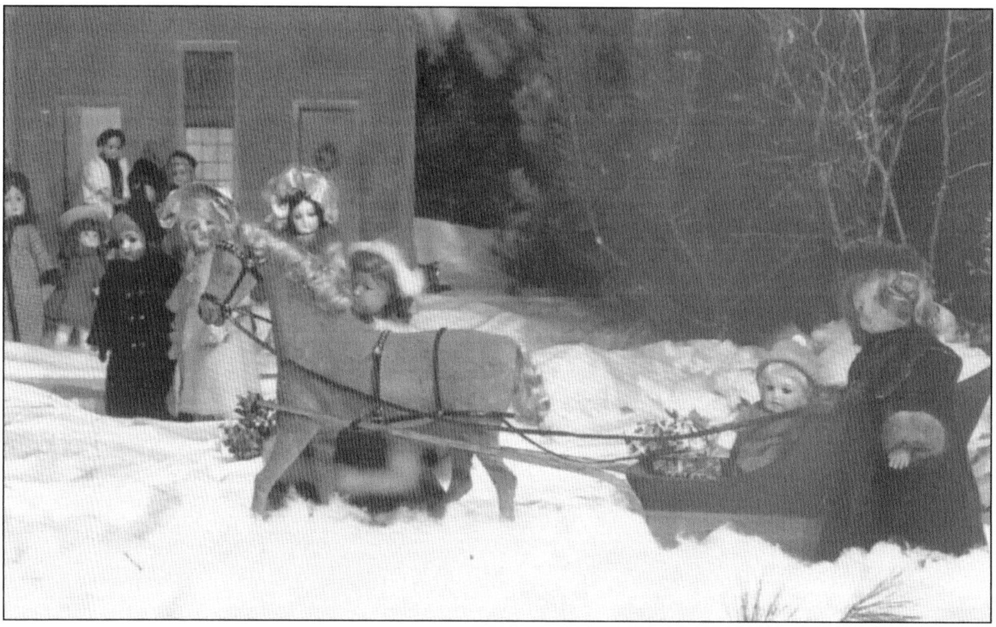

The Brandywine River Museum offers a number of special displays during the year, especially during the Christmas season. The museum is known for its annual electric train display that takes up a floor on one side of the three-story museum. Some seasons, the museum will have a doll collection set up in a winter scene to go with the trains. The antique dolls are from the collection of Ann Wyeth McCoy, daughter of N.C. Wyeth.

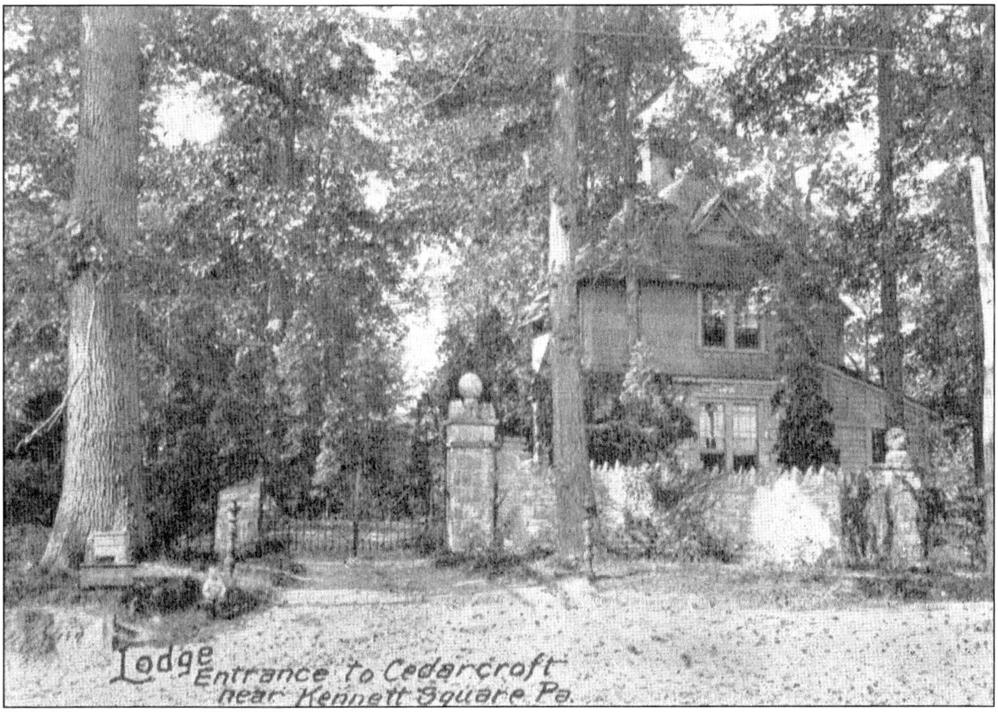

The southern section of the Brandywine was home to 19th-century writer Bayard Taylor. Born near the river, Taylor claimed his fame as an international poet, novelist, journalist, translator, and travel writer and then returned to the Brandywine. The postcard shows the entrance to Cedarcroft, Taylor's home near Kennett Square. Some of his works use this region of the Brandywine as the setting for his stories.

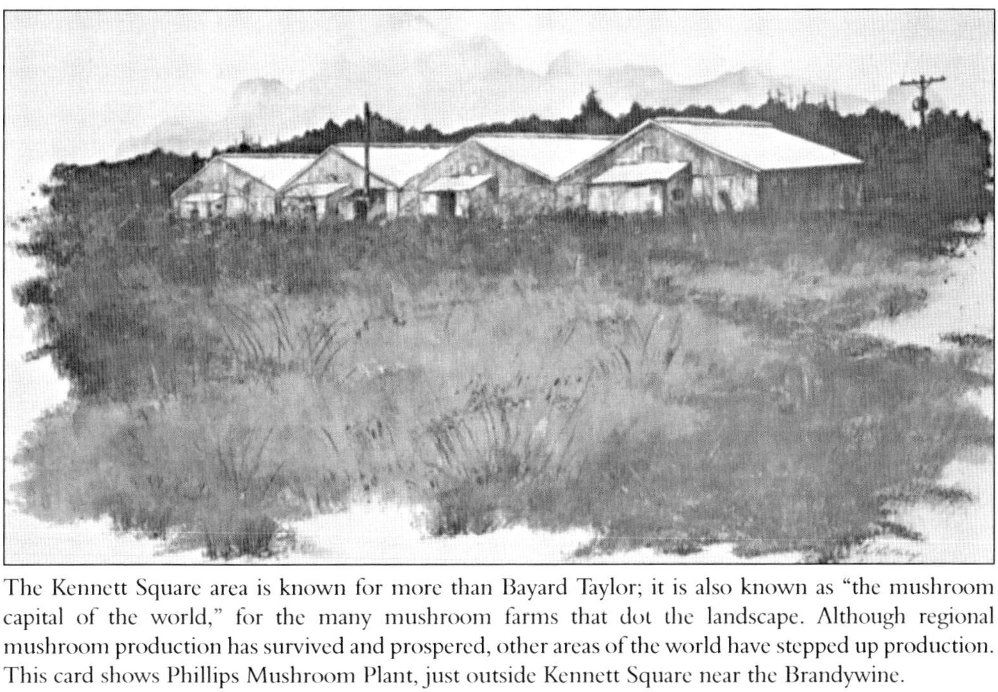

The Kennett Square area is known for more than Bayard Taylor; it is also known as "the mushroom capital of the world," for the many mushroom farms that dot the landscape. Although regional mushroom production has survived and prospered, other areas of the world have stepped up production. This card shows Phillips Mushroom Plant, just outside Kennett Square near the Brandywine.

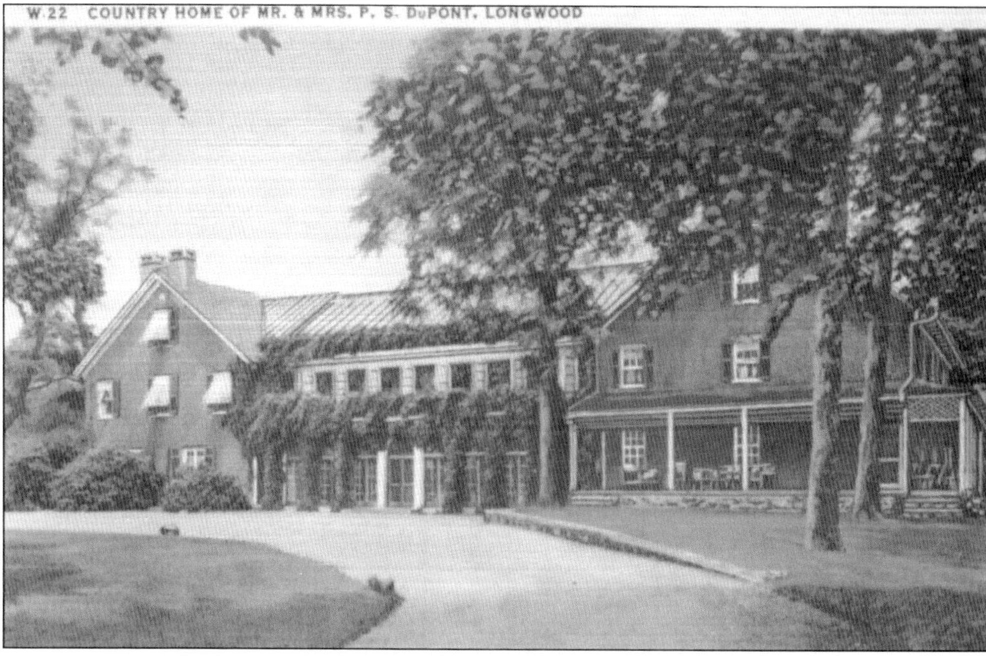

As the Brandywine flows past the final miles of Pennsylvania and into Delaware, one other cultural institution is linked to the river, the Delaware du Pont family, and Pennsylvania. It is Longwood Gardens, the world's premier horticultural display garden. Longwood Gardens, sometimes called the du Pont Gardens, was created by industrialist Pierre S. du Pont and offers 1,050 acres of gardens, woodlands, and meadows with 20 outdoor gardens and 20 indoor gardens. The postcard above shows the "country home of Mr. and Mrs. P.S. DuPont, Longwood between Kennett Square, Pa., and Wilmington, Del." The postcard below shows the "entrance to exhibition house, Longwood, near Kennett Square, Pa."

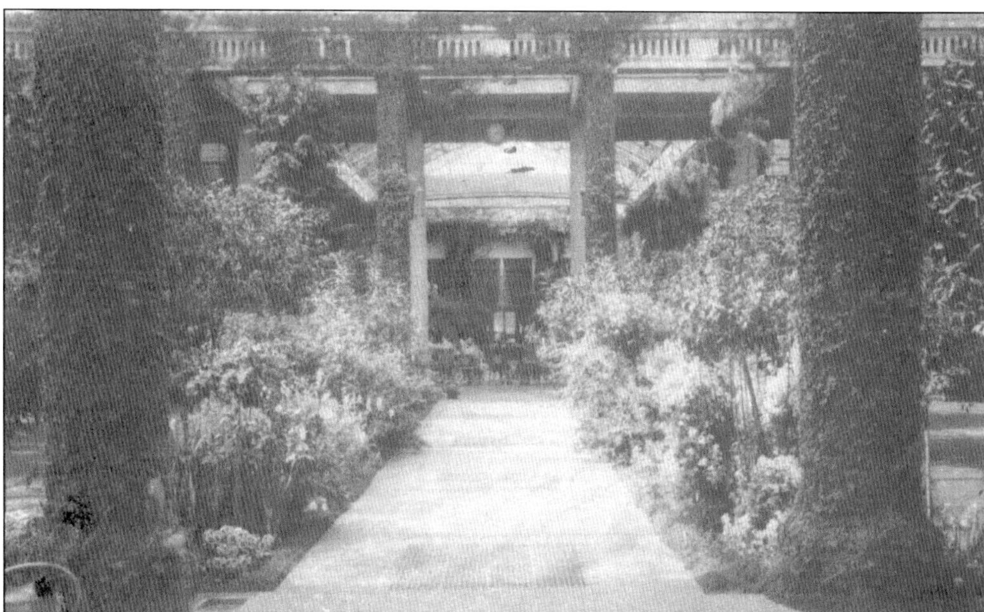

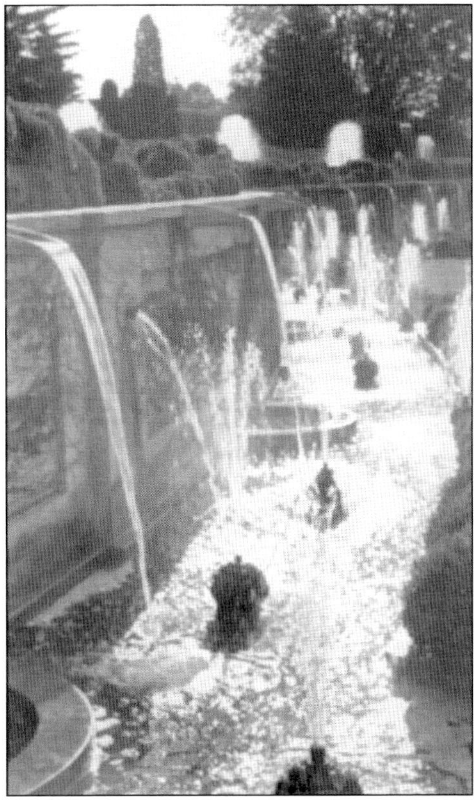

Longwood Gardens also contains four acres of heated greenhouses and more than 11,000 different types of plants. Longwood Gardens is one of the most visited attractions in Pennsylvania, ranking second to only the Liberty Bell in Philadelphia. Longwood Gardens also offers educational programs, including horticultural career training and internships. The postcard to the right shows the water as it cascades from the upper level to the basin of the fountains fronting the conservatory. The bottom card shows part of the gardens.

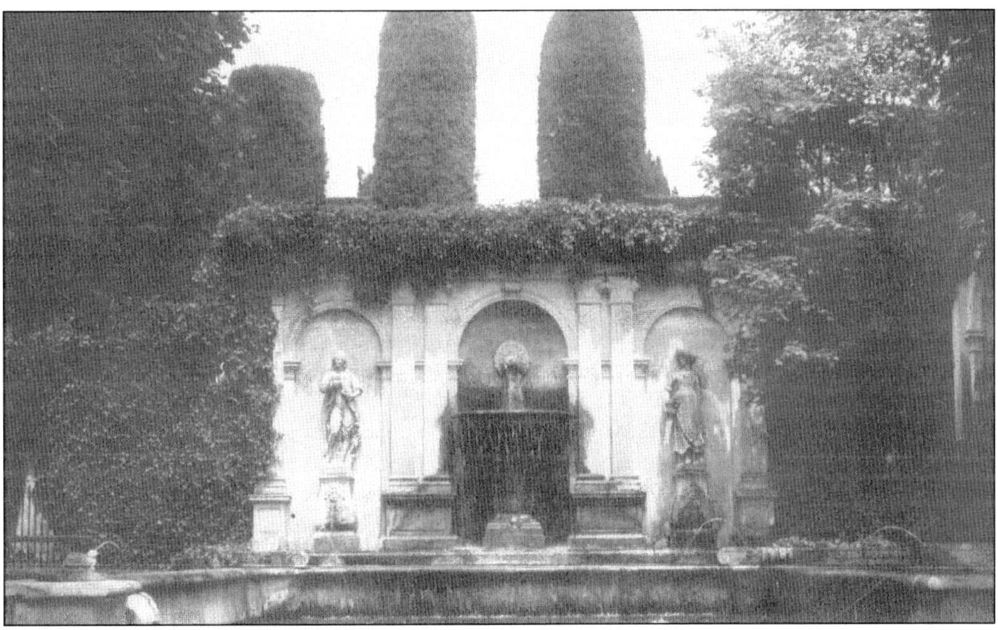

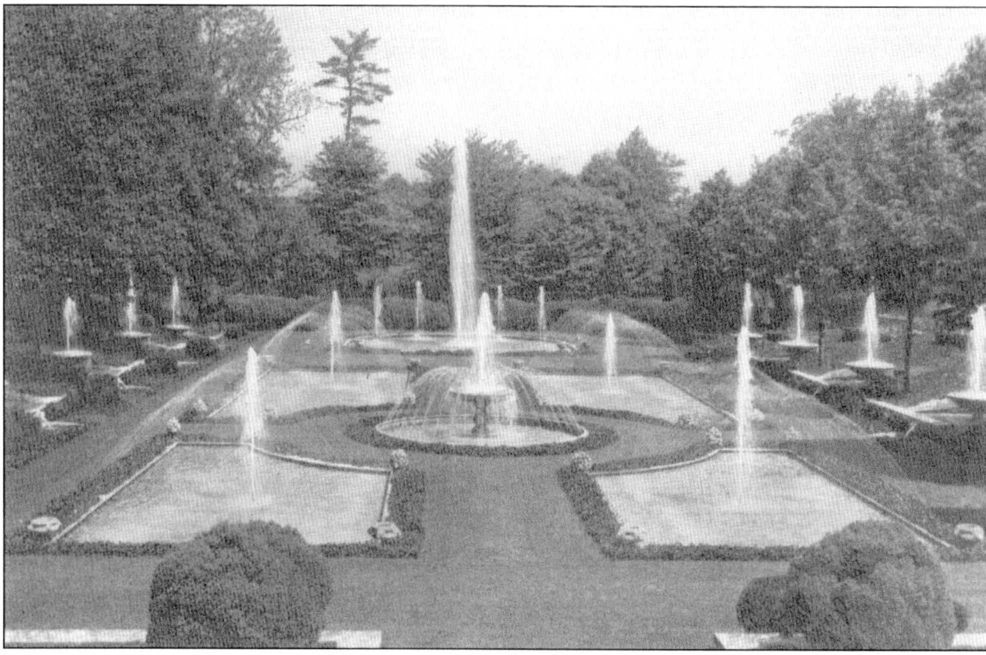

Water plays a big part of the outdoor displays at Longwood Gardens. The Italian Water Garden, pictured in the postcard above, is based on the Villa Gamberaia near Florence, Italy. The postcard below shows the Chimes Tower, waterfalls, and fountain reservoir. The chimes are played during various events. Pierre du Pont was the great-grandson of Eleuthere Irenee du Pont, who founded the DuPont chemical company. Pierre du Pont turned the family business into a corporate empire and used the fortune to develop Longwood Gardens. This land was part of the fields hunted and fished by the Lenni-Lenapi Indians.

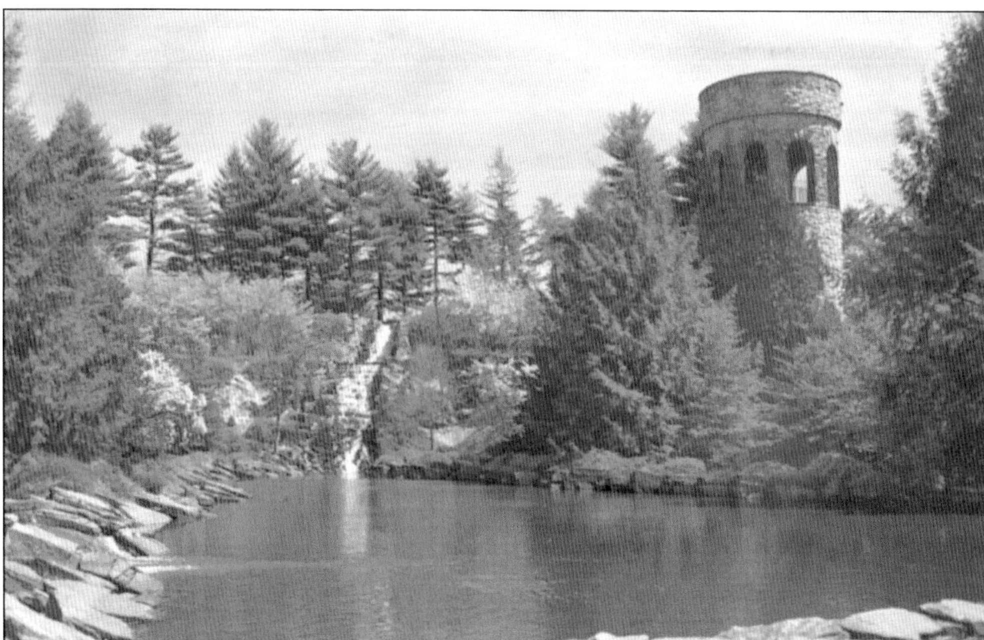

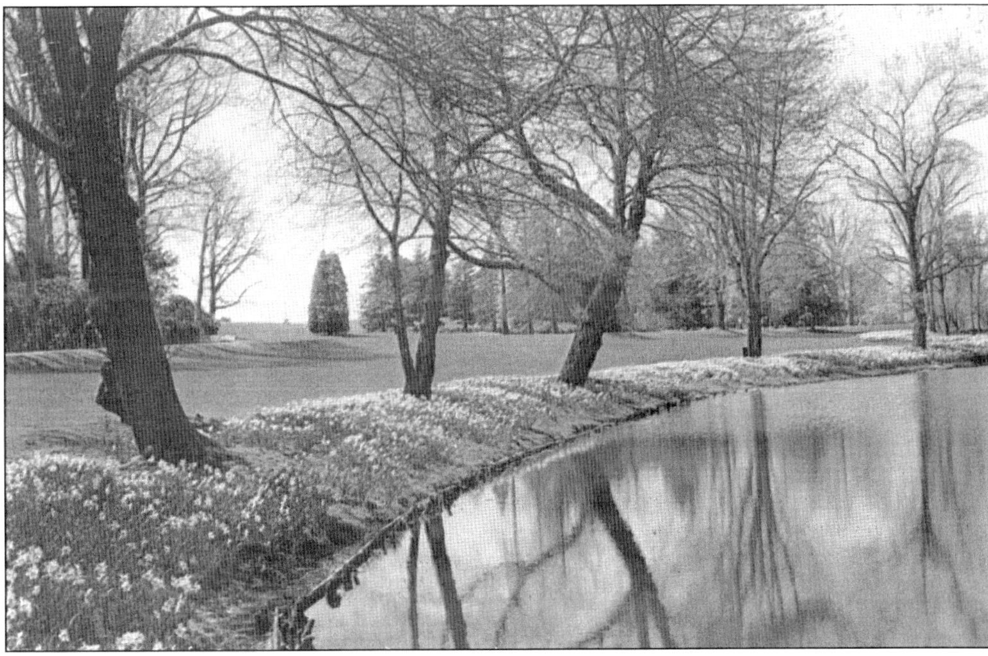

The land that comprises Longwood Gardens was part of the original William Penn grant. The land was sold to a Quaker family in the 1700s and became a working farm. An arboretum is reported to have been on the farm in 1798, just 21 years after the Battle of Brandywine. British and Hessian troops passed through this property on the way to confront Gen. "Mad Anthony" Wayne and other American units defending the Brandywine at the John Chad river crossing. The postcard above shows daffodils bordering a large lake at Longwood. The card below reads, "Sun Dial Garden, P.S. Du Pont Mansion Grounds, near Kennett Square, Pa."

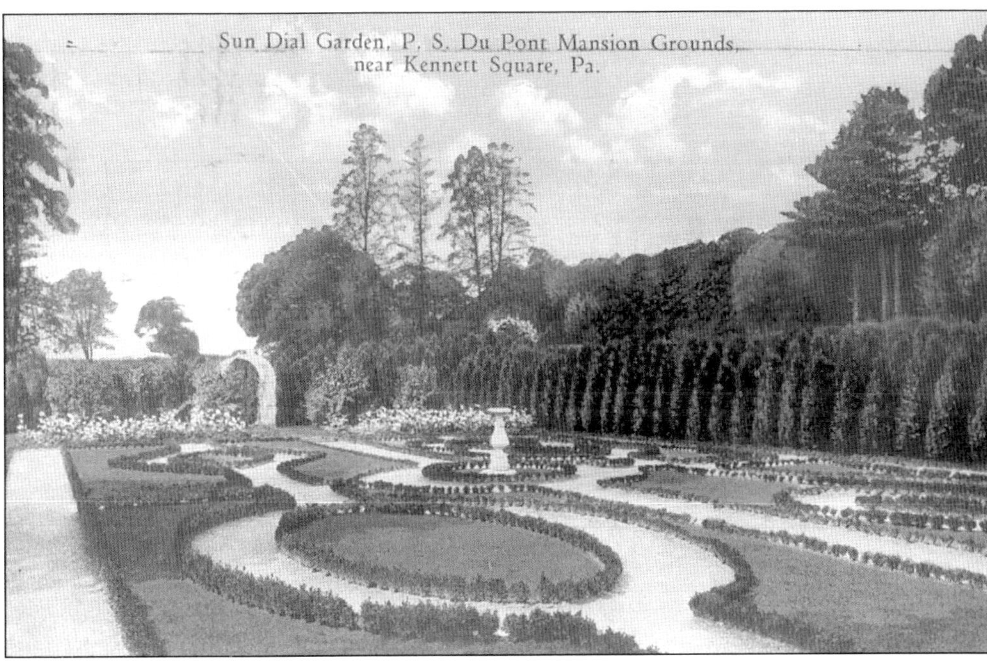

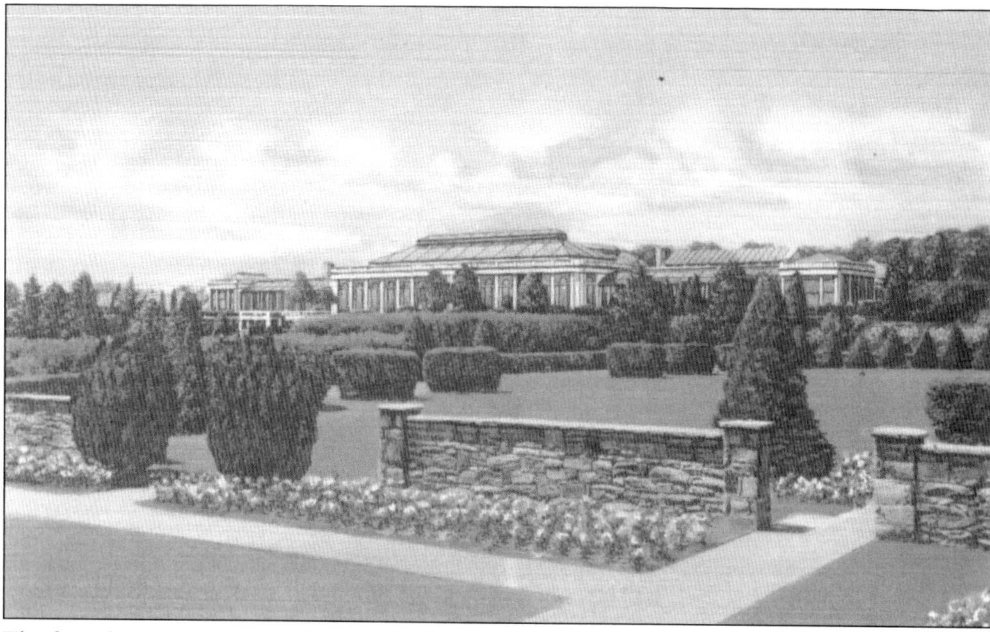

The farm that was turned into Longwood Gardens was purchased by Pierre du Pont in 1906. Du Pont worked to preserve the trees on the farm. From 1907 through most of the 1930s, du Pont created a large part of the gardens that are still seen by almost a million visitors each year. Throughout the year, the gardens are also used by numerous groups, many of which are nonprofit, to host various programs. The postcard above shows the main greenhouse of the conservatory. The greenhouse is 650 feet long, with more than 120,000 square feet under glass. The postcard below is titled "Open Theatre, P.S. du Pont Mansion Grounds, near Kennett Square, Pa."

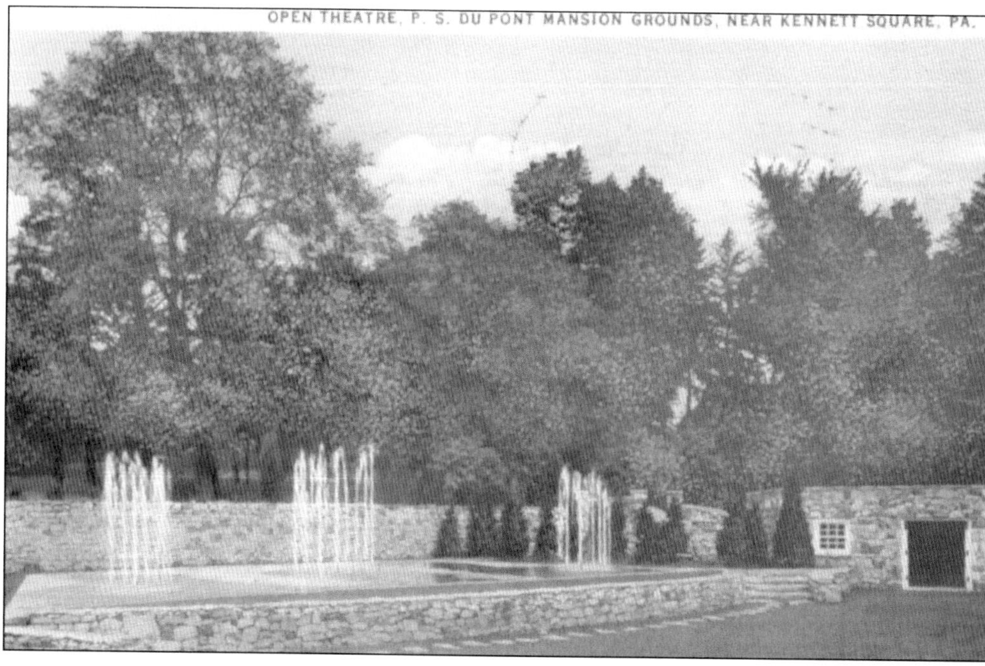

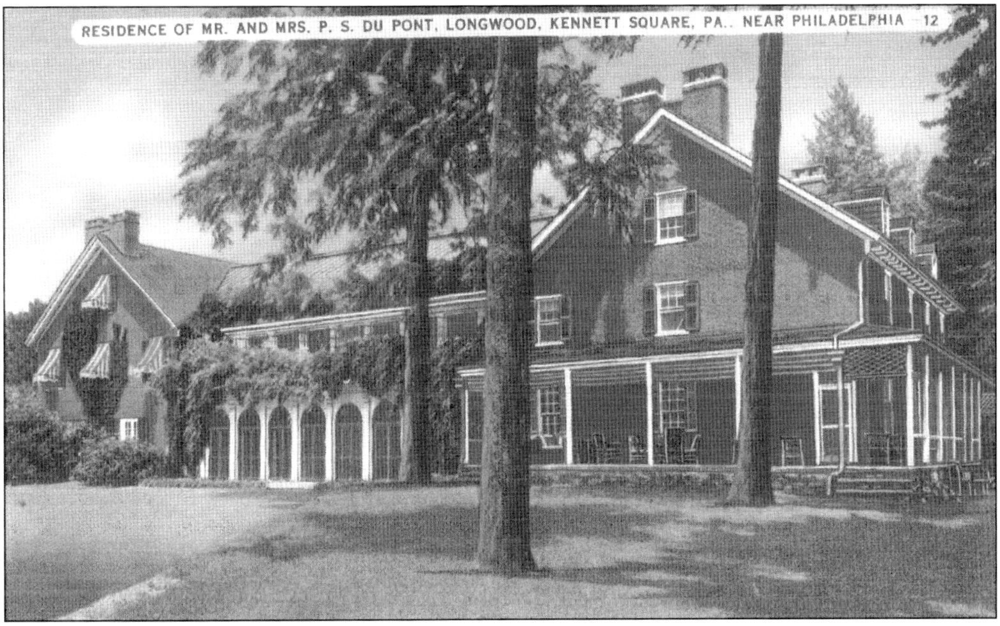

Those who collect postcards of Longwood Gardens should keep in mind that the cards can be filed under many different designations. The card above says, "Residence of Mr. and Mrs. P.S. Du Pont, Longwood, Kennett Square, Pa., near Philadelphia, Pa." This card could be filed under Longwood, Kennett Square, or Philadelphia. The only location commonly associated with Longwood Gardens is Wilmington, Delaware. Thus, the cards can be filed with cards from different Pennsylvania towns or with Wilmington in Delaware. The card below reads, "Chimes Tower, Longwood, between Kennett Square, Pa. and Wilmington, Del." This card omits the Philadelphia location of the card above.

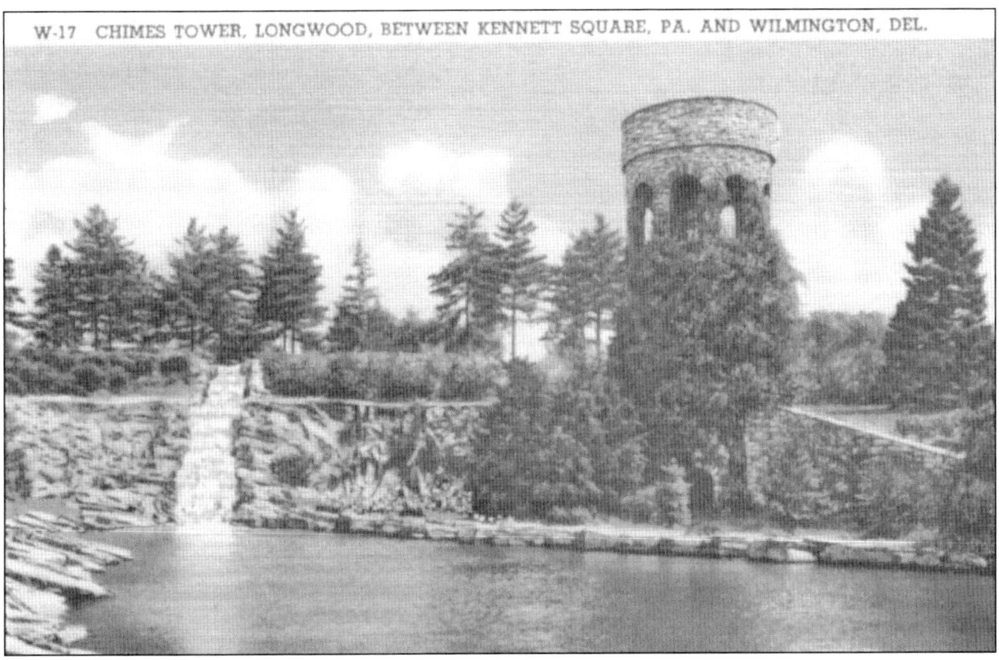

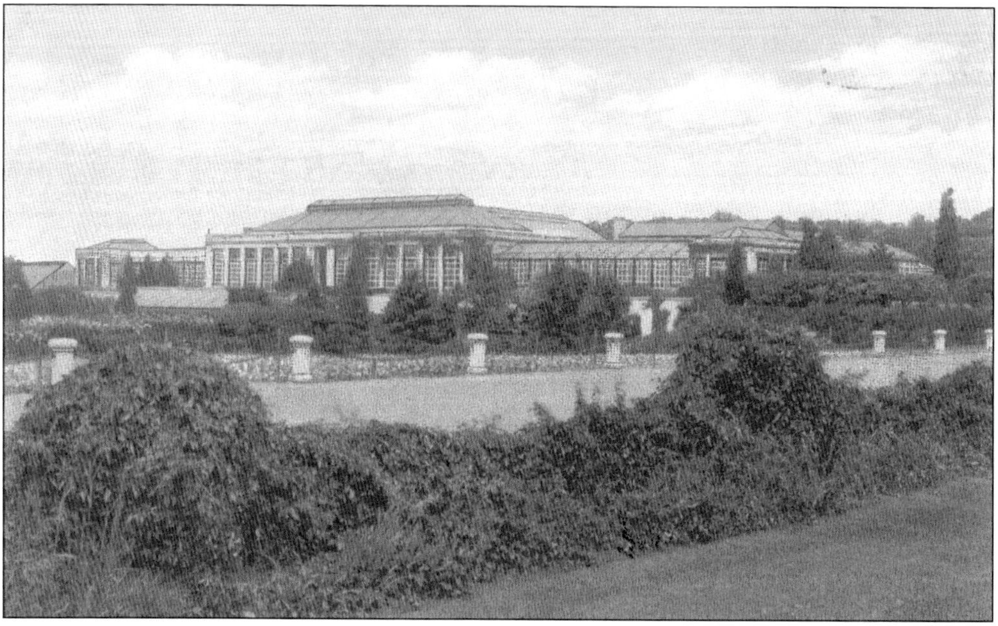

With the founding of Longwood Incorporated in 1914, preparations were made to prepare for the future of the property after the death of Mr. and Mrs. P.S. du Pont. In 1937, the Longwood Foundation was formed to handle charitable giving. The du Ponts did not have any children, but Pierre du Pont considered Longwood part of the family heritage. In 1946, he was given permission by the government for the Longwood Foundation to operate the gardens for "the sole use of the public for purposes of exhibition, instruction, education and enjoyment." Pierre du Pont was 86 years old when he died in 1954. His wife had died in 1944. He left behind a well-established horticultural tradition and a generous endowment. The two cards on this page depict different views of Horticultural Hall.

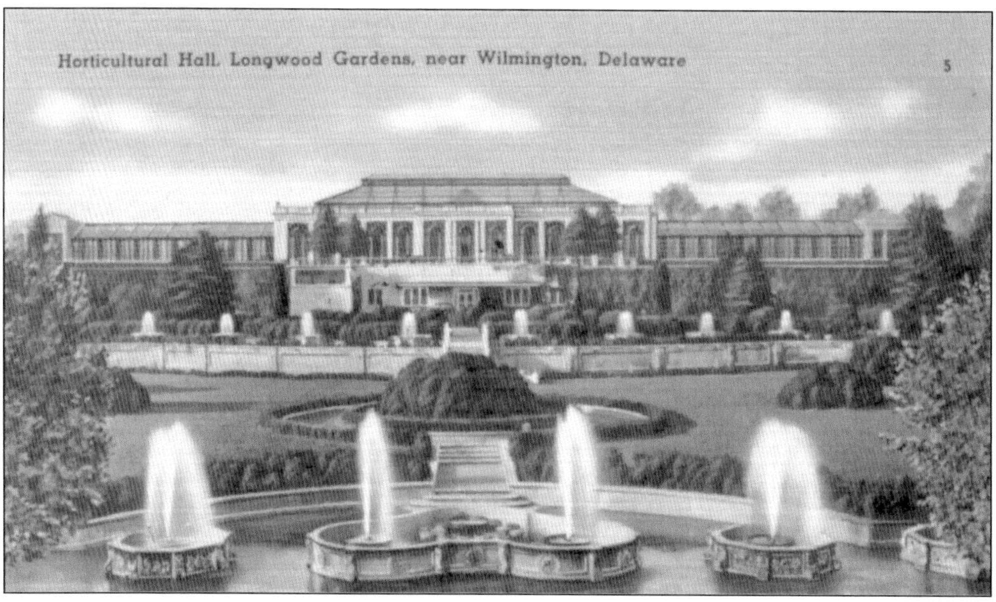

Three

BELOW THE MASON-DIXON LINE

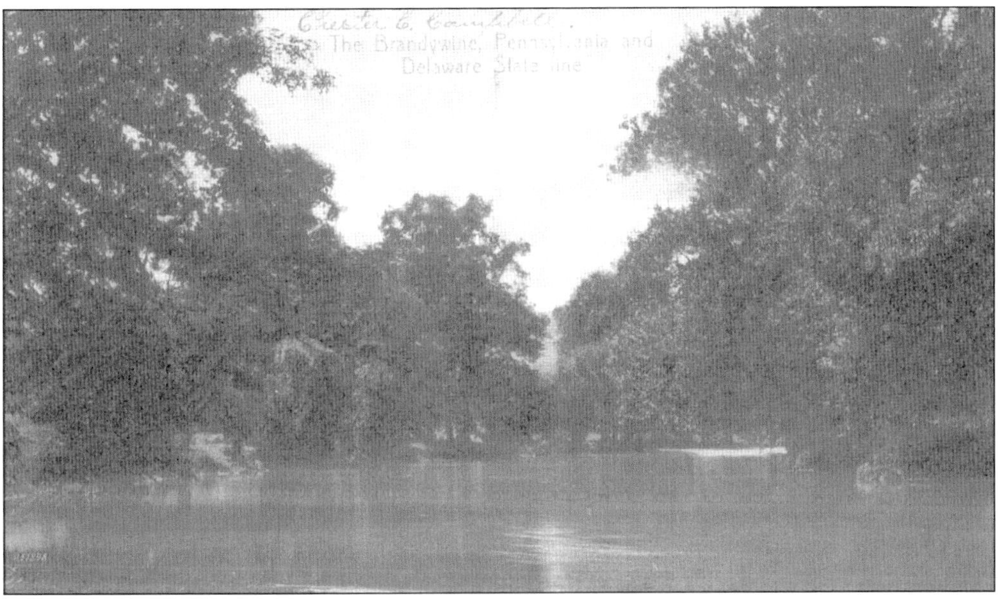

The Brandywine departs Chester County and Pennsylvania and makes its way through northern Delaware, into Wilmington, and eventually into the Christina River. More museums, including the Hagley and Winterthur, are on the Brandywine's banks where the du Pont family made its fortune.

As the Brandywine River departs the area of Chadds Ford where the Battle of Brandywine was fought, it continues through Mendenhall and several other small Pennsylvania villages before reaching the Delaware state line. This is the border marked by Mason and Dixon from the Stargazers' Stone in Newlin Township near Embreeville. This card, postmarked in 1908, shows the Brandywine at the Pennsylvania and Delaware state line.

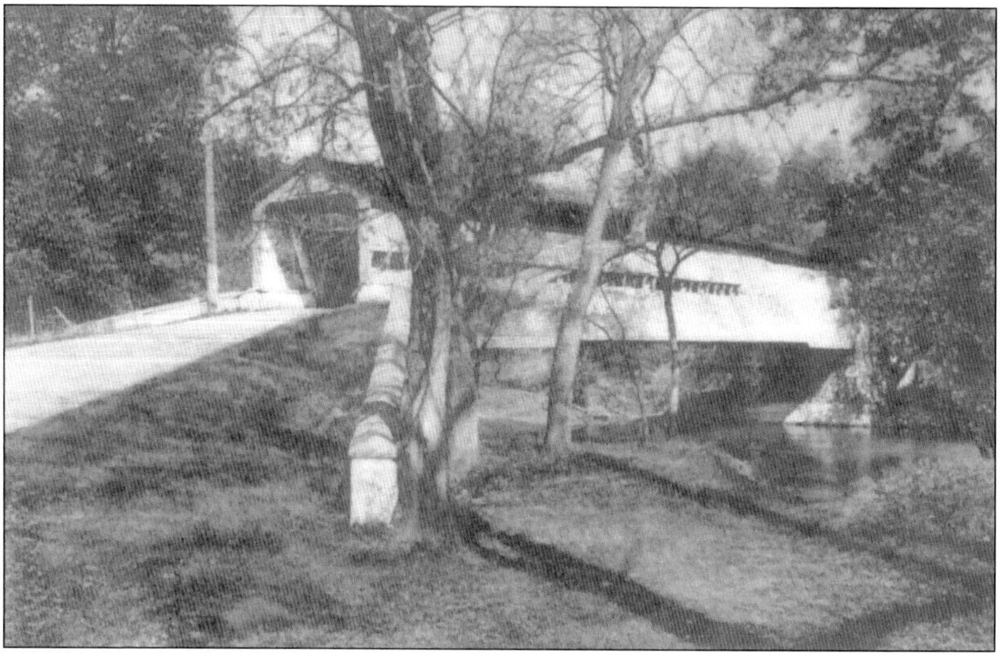

The Brandywine departs Pennsylvania and then returns to the commonwealth before leaving the state for good as it flows into Delaware. For many years, the Brandywine met a covered bridge called Smith's Bridge. The bridge was located about six miles northwest of Wilmington, Delaware. It was built in 1839 and was 154½ feet long. The card above, published by Mrs. J. Newcomer of Wilmington, Delaware, states that the bridge is still in use today. The more modern card with a photograph of Smith's Bridge over the "picturesque Brandywine Creek" has a hand-written note that says, "Shows what is left of Smith's covered bridge."

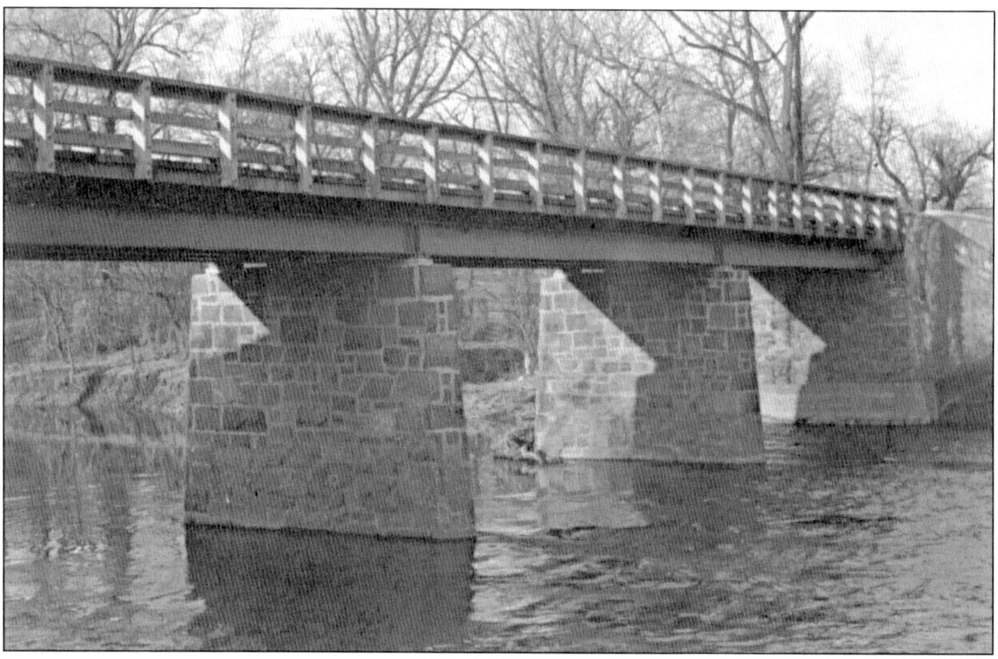

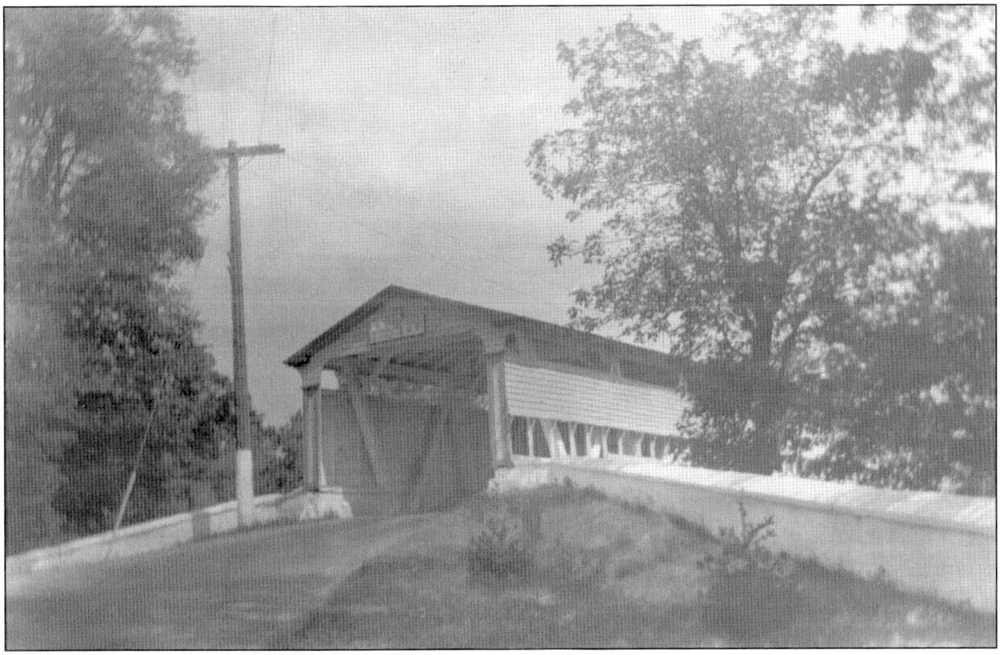

The following three photo postcards of Smith's Bridge were originally from the Chester H. Thomas covered bridge collection. Thomas was a noted photographer from the Kennett Square area. Ellanor M. Thomas published the photographs as postcards. The spelling of her first name came from the notation on the card. More of Thomas's photographs are reproduced in this book. One of the postcards notes that a catalog of the photographs was published in 1946. In the Delaware section, it notes, "41 Smith's Bridge, New Castle County, three views spanning Brandywine Creek." Since creeks and rivers are not specifically defined, some people call the Brandywine a river and others call it a creek.

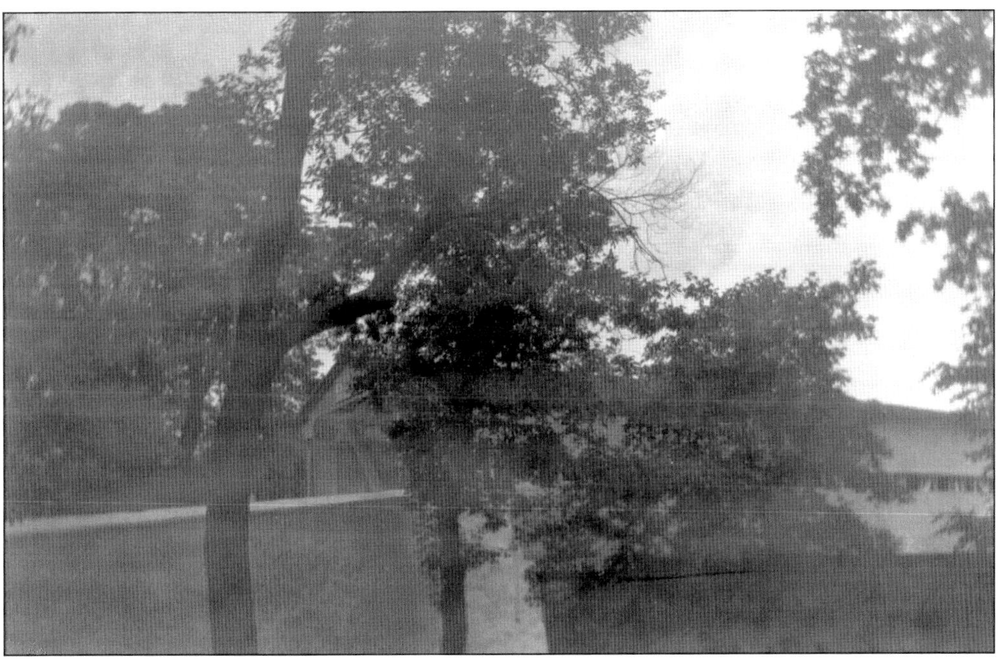

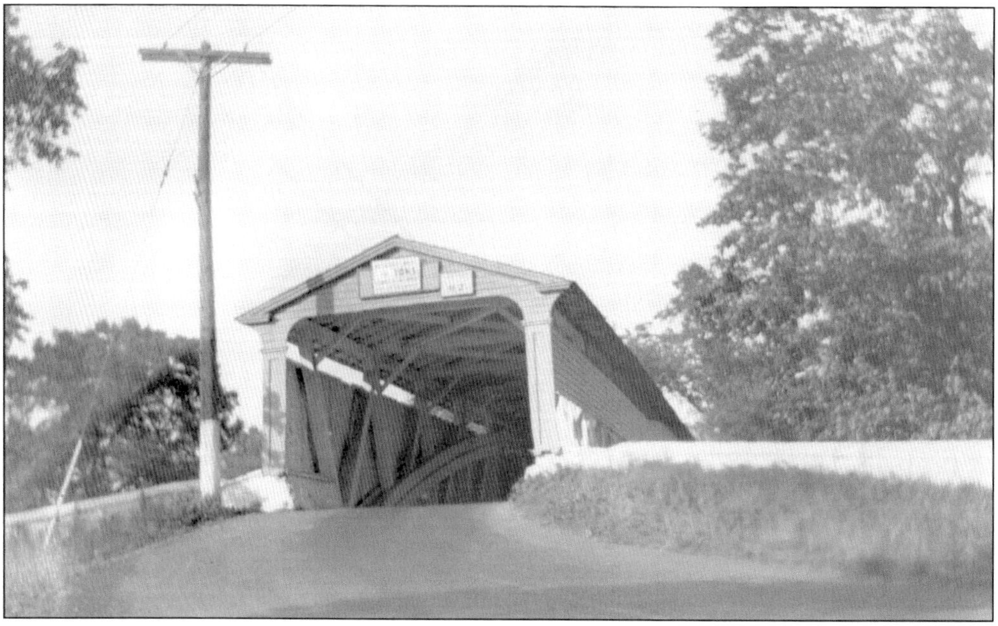

This is the third photograph of Smith's Bridge in the Thomas photo postcard collection. The bridge was named for Isaac Smith, who ran a succession of mills powered by the Brandywine. A number of large estates were built on the Brandywine at this point in the river, including the family home of Irenne du Pont, Granogue.

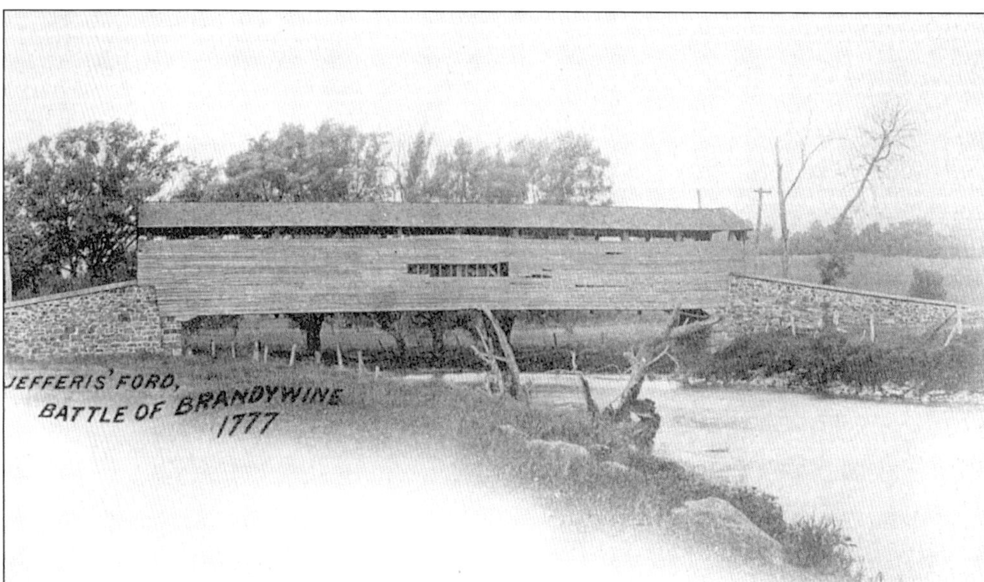

As with Smith's Bridge, many covered bridges along the Brandywine were demolished because of poor condition. In this card, missing boards are seen at the ford involved in the Battle of Brandywine. The Thompson Bridge, in Brandywine Creek State Park, was demolished in 1934.

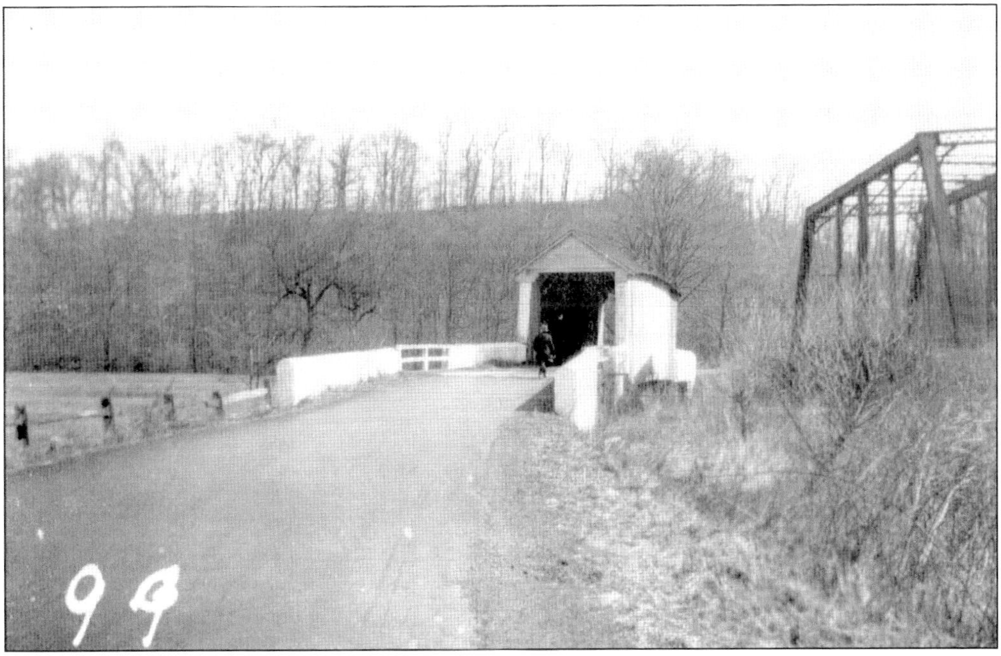

The postcard above is the fifth card in the Chester H. Thomas collection and notes that this covered bridge crosses the Brandywine at Ashland in New Castle County, near Mount Cuba. As noted earlier, there is no agreement on *river* versus *creek*. The Brandywine Conservancy calls it a river, while the Brandywine Valley Association believes it is a creek. The U.S. Geological Survey labels it a creek, while the Army Corps of Engineers designates it a river. The card below says, "Scenic Brandywine Creek with Washington St. Bridge in the background, Wilmington, Delaware."

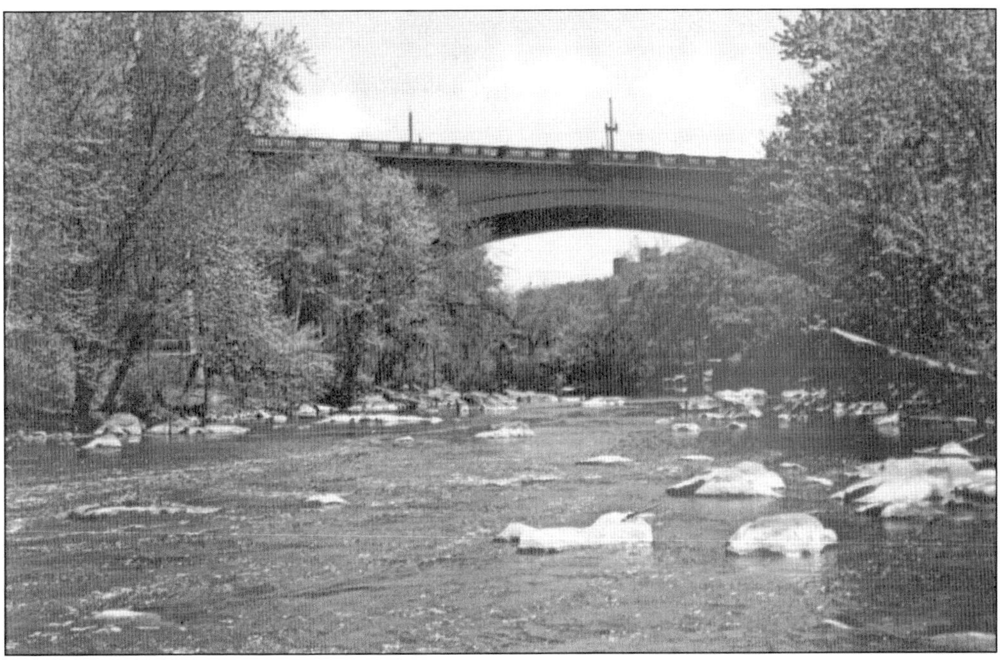

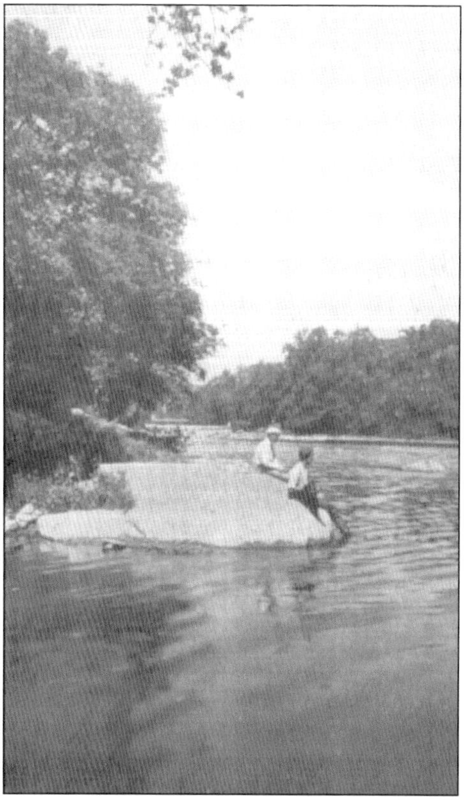

The postcards by George A. Wolf of Wilmington give a clear view of life on the Brandywine in Delaware during the early 20th century. Wolf's work can also be seen in the southern region of Pennsylvania. The card to the left is captioned "A Favorite Spot Along the Brandywine." The card below says, "The Historic Brandywine, Wilmington, Del." This card also has a hand-written note that says, "Canoe trip 22.ix.1906." Maybe the writer took a trip by canoe on this section of the Brandywine on September 22, 1906. All along the Brandywine, the river is used for canoeing, fishing, and other recreational pursuits.

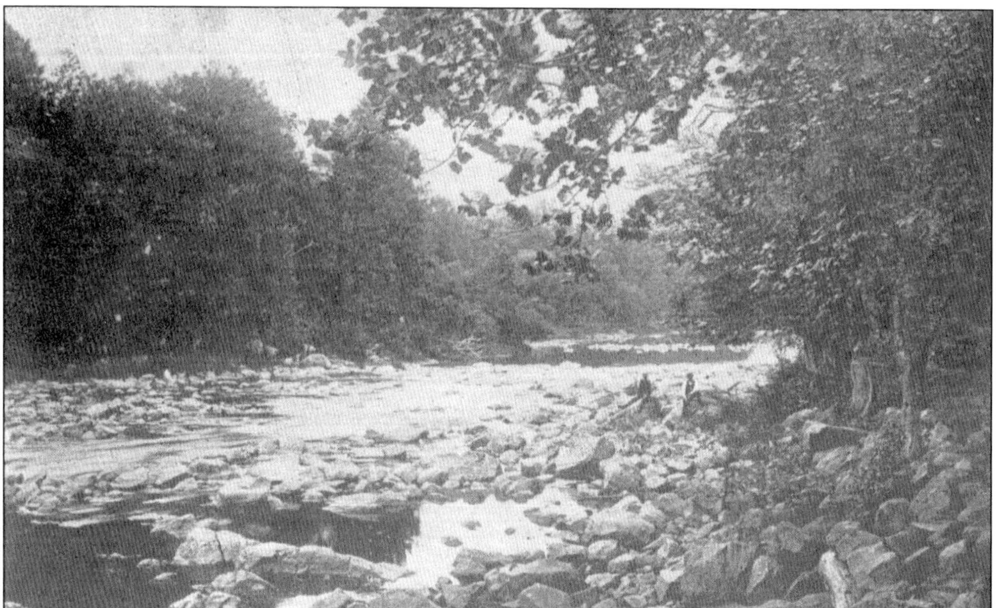

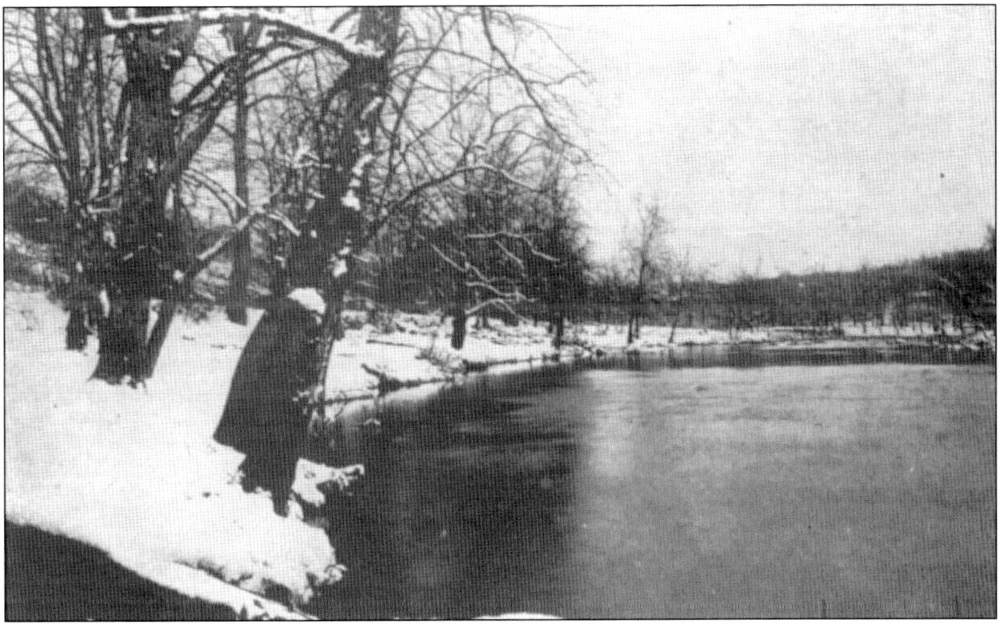

The beauty of the Brandywine is not confined to the spring and summer; the river is also picture-perfect during the winter. The two postcards on this page are devoted to winter scenes. The postcard above is captioned "Winter on the Historic Brandywine, Wilmington, Del." This is another postcard by George A. Wolf. The inscription by the sender says, "Love to all and a kiss for Elizabeth." The card below was published by Julian B. Robinson of Wilmington, Delaware, and the sender is thanking a friend in Wernersville, Pennsylvania, for sending seeds. It is postmarked October 1906. The Wolf card was sent in June 1906.

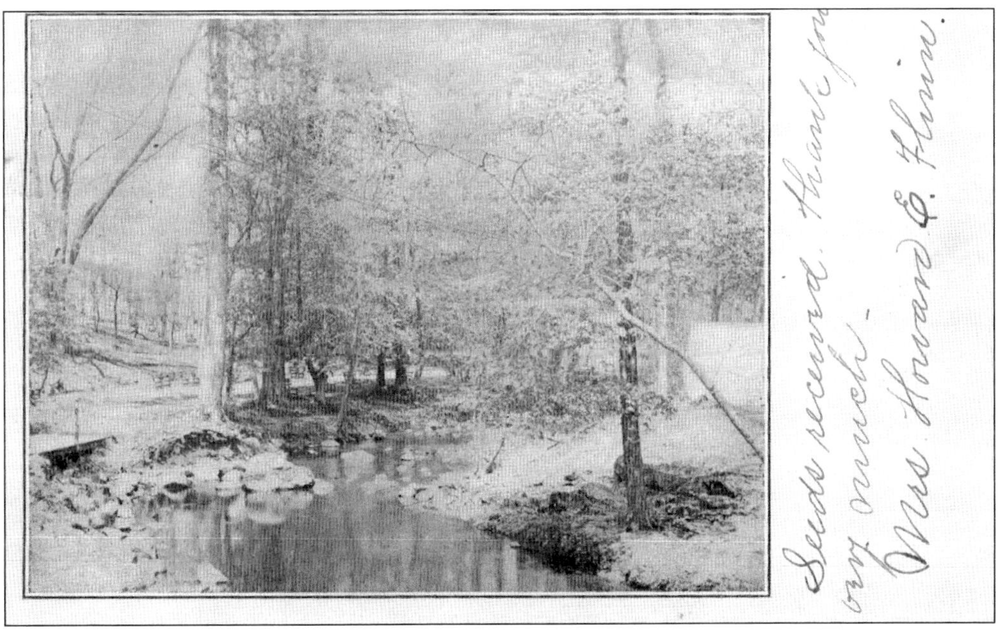

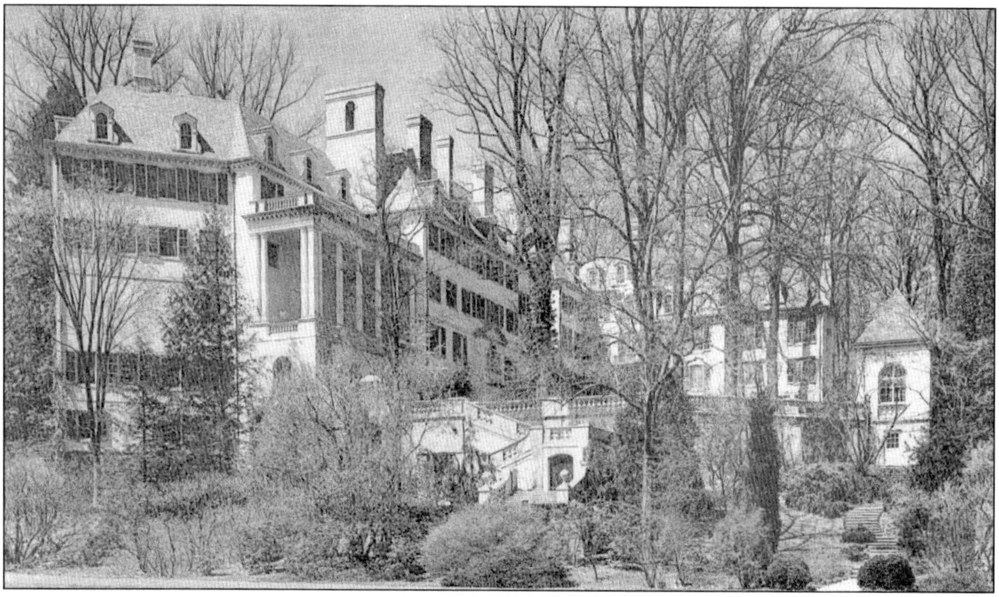

Henry Francis du Pont collected furniture and amassed about 83,000 decorative pieces. He constructed a nine-story French-style mansion to hold his collection. Today, it is a museum along Route 52 beside the Brandywine's path to Wilmington. In 1964, du Pont constructed a sign on his property that read, "Keep this view open forever." A portion of Winterthur, his estate, was a working farm at one point, and the land is now park of Brandywine Creek State Park. The postcard above shows the south side of the Winterthur Museum, while the card below shows the north side.

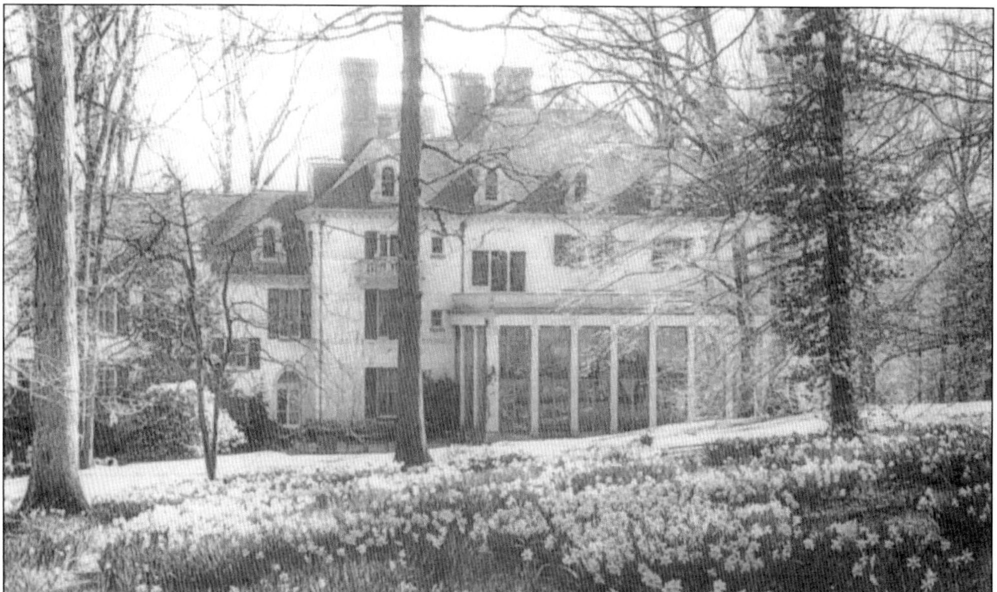

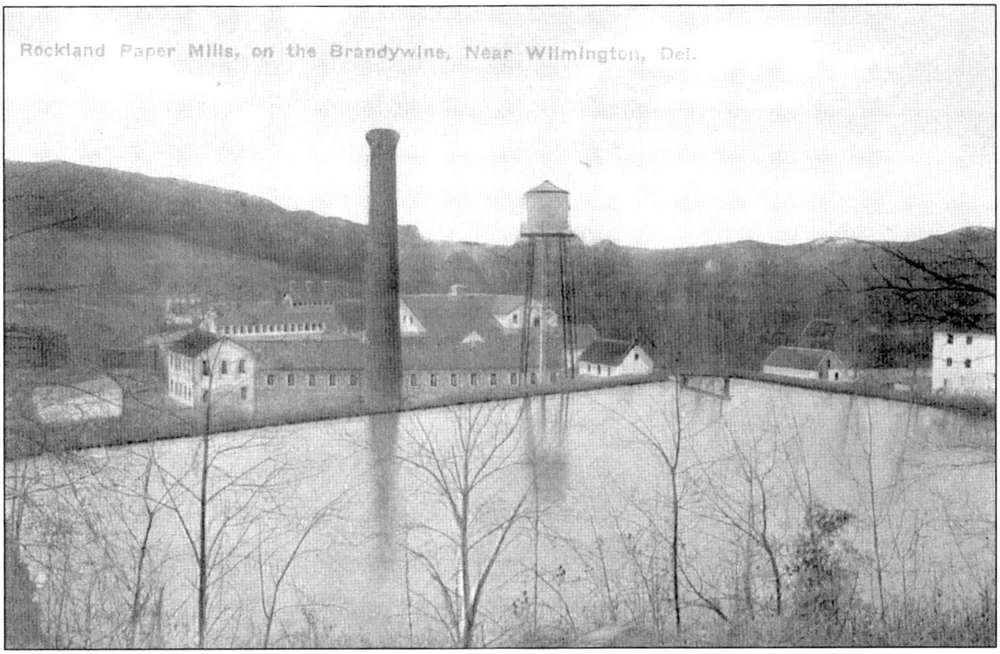

Seen in the photograph below, the Washington Street Bridge was located before the Brandywine reaches Wilmington. Rockland Paper Mill, on the Brandywine, was located on land that is now part of Brandywine Creek State Park. A dam was built in Rockland to aid the generation of power. William Young started his paper mill at Rockland in the late 1700s. The next property belonged to the du Pont family. The Wilmington sender of the postcard below, postmarked 1925, asks the recipient to begin an exchange of postcards. He requests views of post offices and monuments.

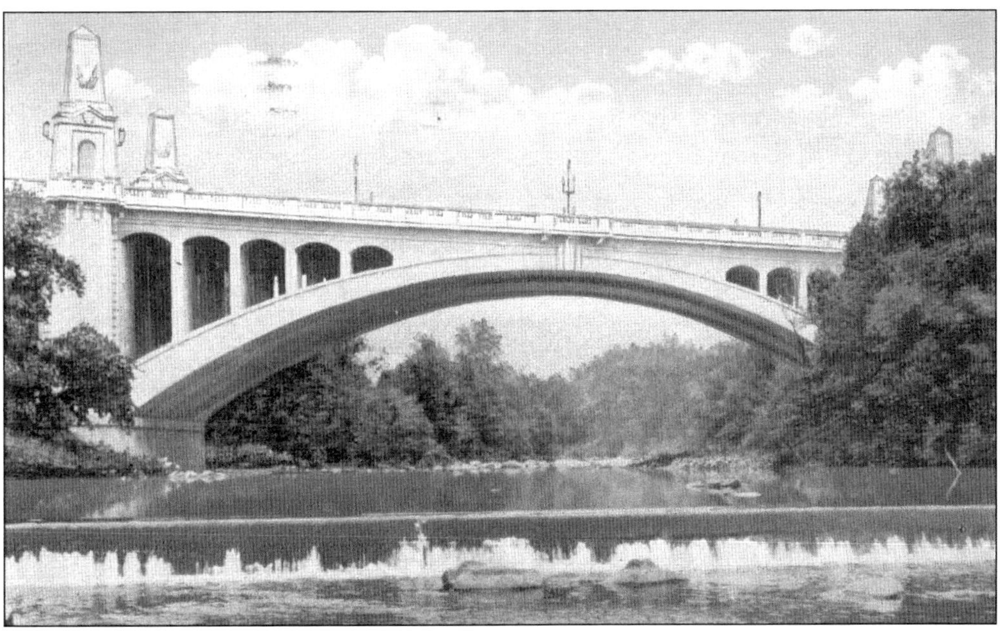

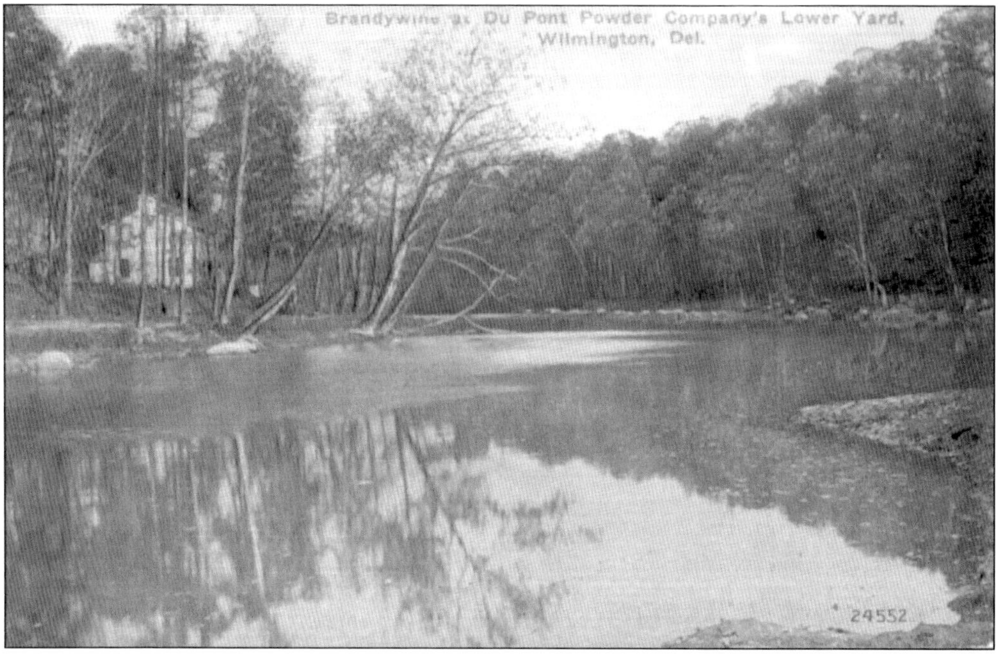

The du Pont fortune was made on the banks of the Brandywine with gunpowder mills. Eleuthere Irenne du Pont came to the United States when political unrest was taking place in his native France. Du Pont settled on the Brandywine River and put to use the lessons he learned from a famous French chemist. His father, a diplomat who corresponded with Benjamin Franklin and Thomas Jefferson, joined his son in Delaware but eventually returned to France. Eleuthere stayed. The Brandywine at the DuPont Powder Company's lower yard is shown above. Below is a view of Eleutherian Mills, the black powder mills, painted by Bass Otis, our country's first lithographer, as it appeared *c.* 1840.

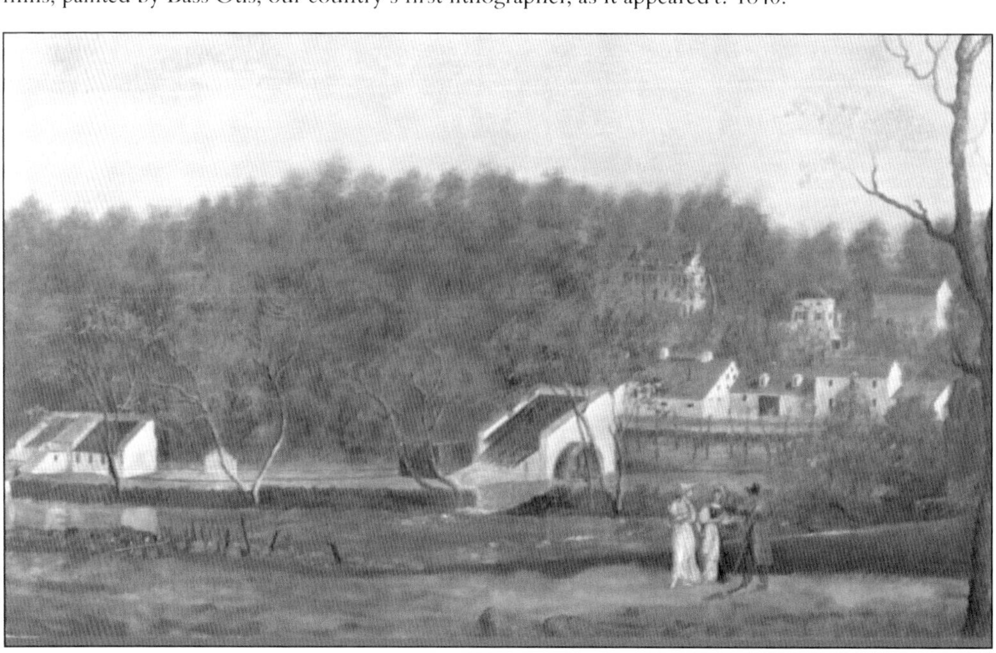

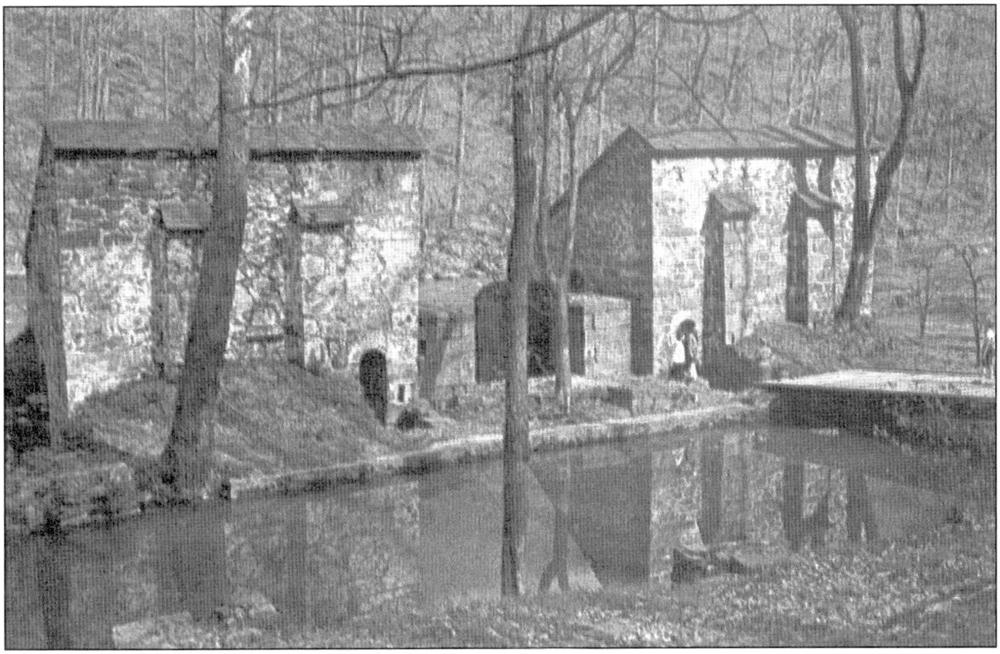

The pair of black powder du Pont mills shown in these postcards were constructed from 1822 to 1824 and are called "the Birkenhead." These mills produced powder for 117 years, and their products were used during the 19th century to further canal building and the mining industry across the United States. Of course, the powder also was used by American troops in a number of conflicts, including the Civil War. The mills ceased operation in 1921, and the mills are now part of the Hagley Museum along the Brandywine River just north of Wilmington.

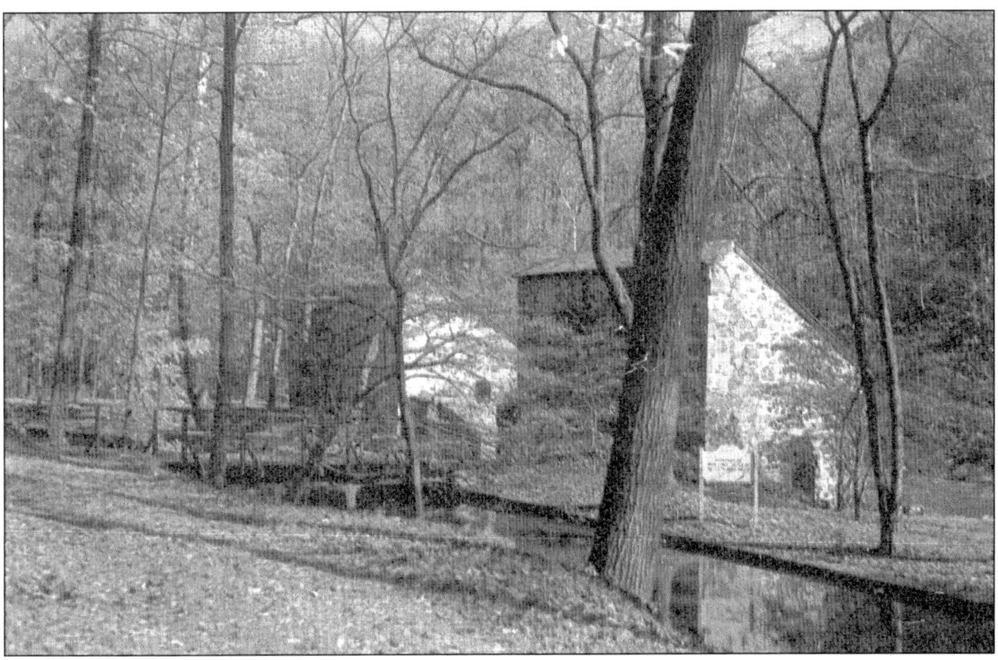

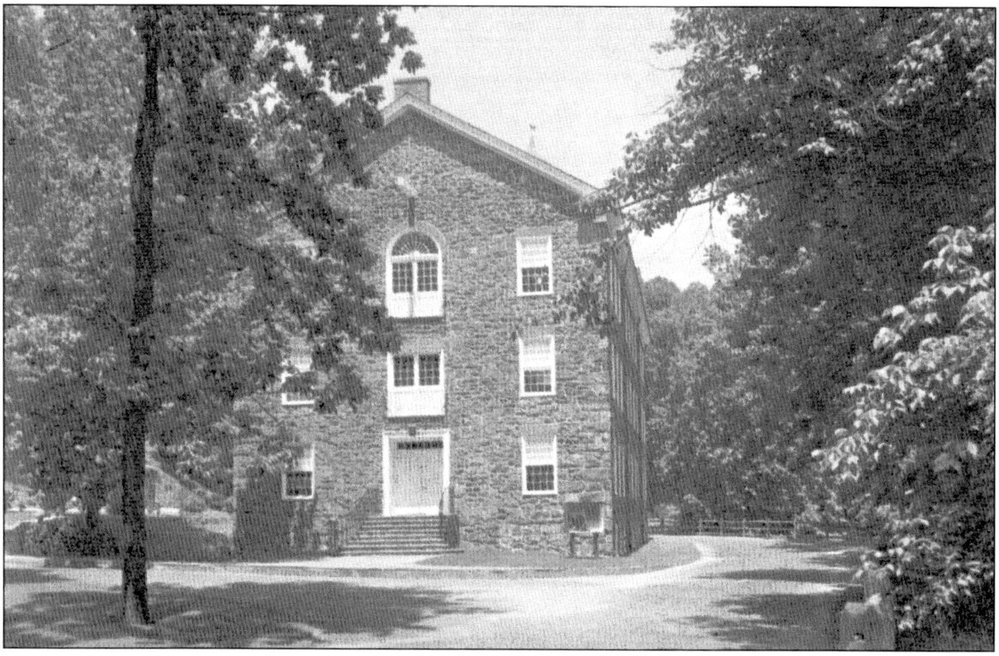

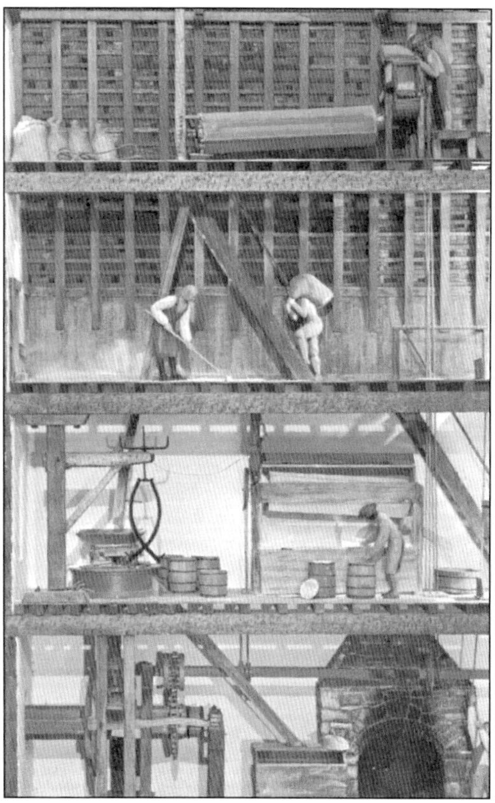

The mills connected with the Hagley Museum were not limited to the production of black powder. The postcard above shows an 1814 textile mill. The mill opened as a museum of early American industry in 1957. It has exhibited a number of working models and diagrams of water-powered mills. The postcard to the left shows an 18th-century flour mill exhibit from the Hagley Museum. E.I. du Pont used 65 acres along the west bank of the Brandywine to build his mills. They were built south of gristmills, paper mills, and textile mills. To meet increased demand for black powder during the War of 1812, he purchased land known as Hagley.

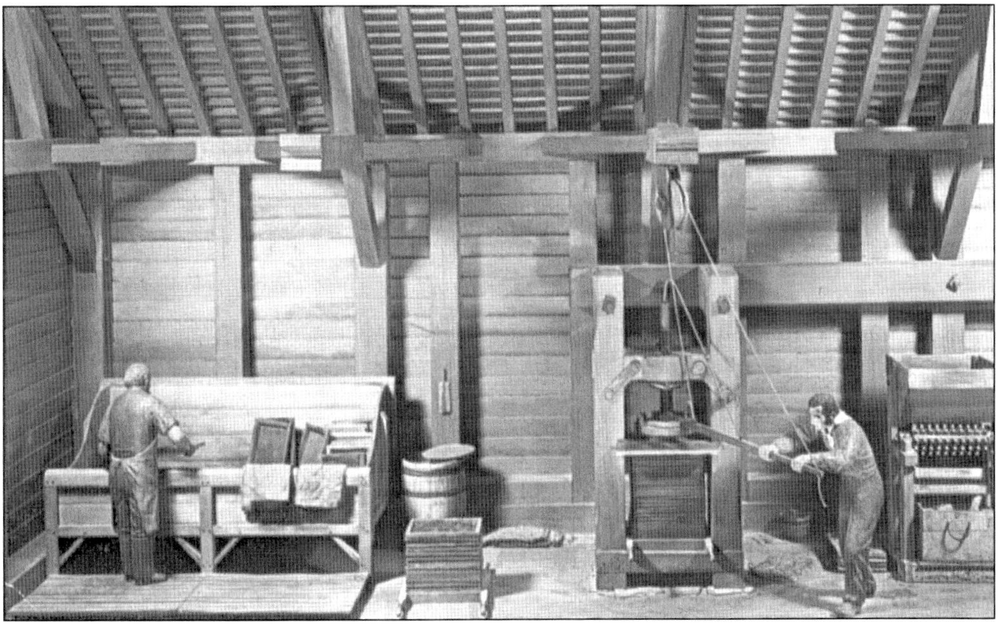

The Hagley Museum has used dioramas to show modern-day Americans how the nation's army was supplied with black powder during the early days of this country. The postcard above shows the press house, an important step in the manufacture of black powder in the du Pont mills. The card below says, "After being pressed and broken into chips, black powder was taken to a graining mill and sieved through oscillating screens." When the mills closed after World War I, the company diversified into the production of other industrial products and consumer goods.

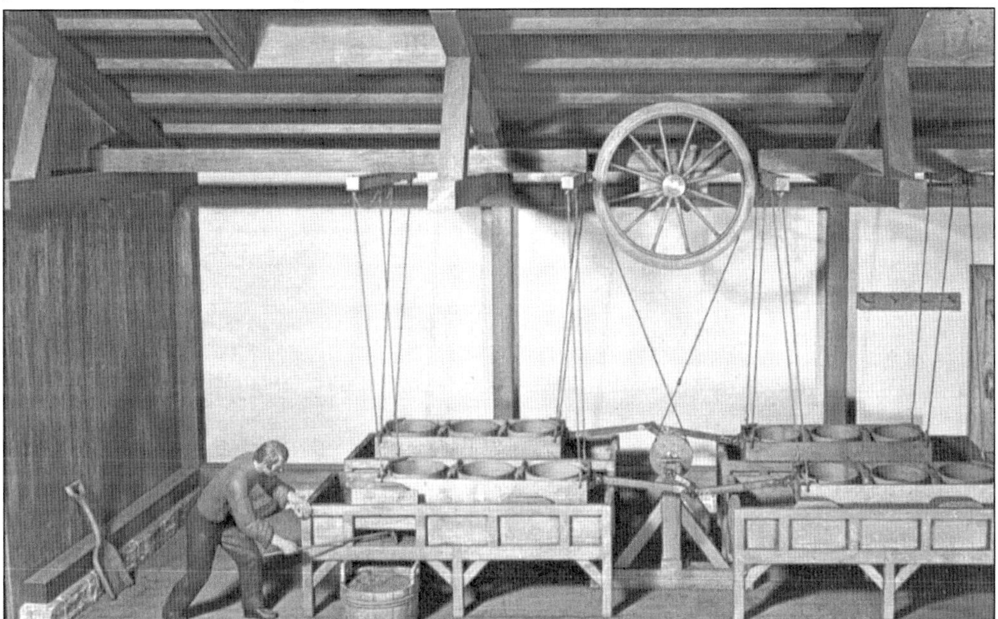

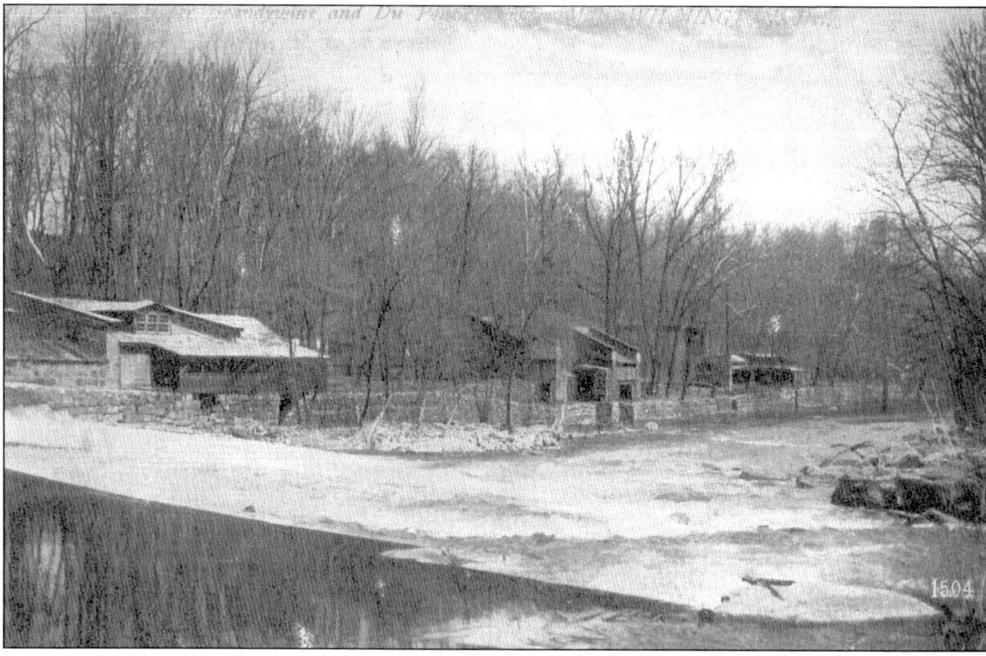

The card above, postmarked 1907, is titled "Upper Brandywine and Du Pont Powder Mills, Wilmington, Del." and offers an overall view of the mill. The mill employed a number of Irish workers who came to the United States seeking their fortunes. The plant also had workers who emigrated from England, Italy, and France. The Brandywine, at this point, is a short distance from Wilmington itself, as depicted in the postcard below. The card, which shows the Brandywine as it flows by Park Drive, calls the Brandywine a "Historic Creek."

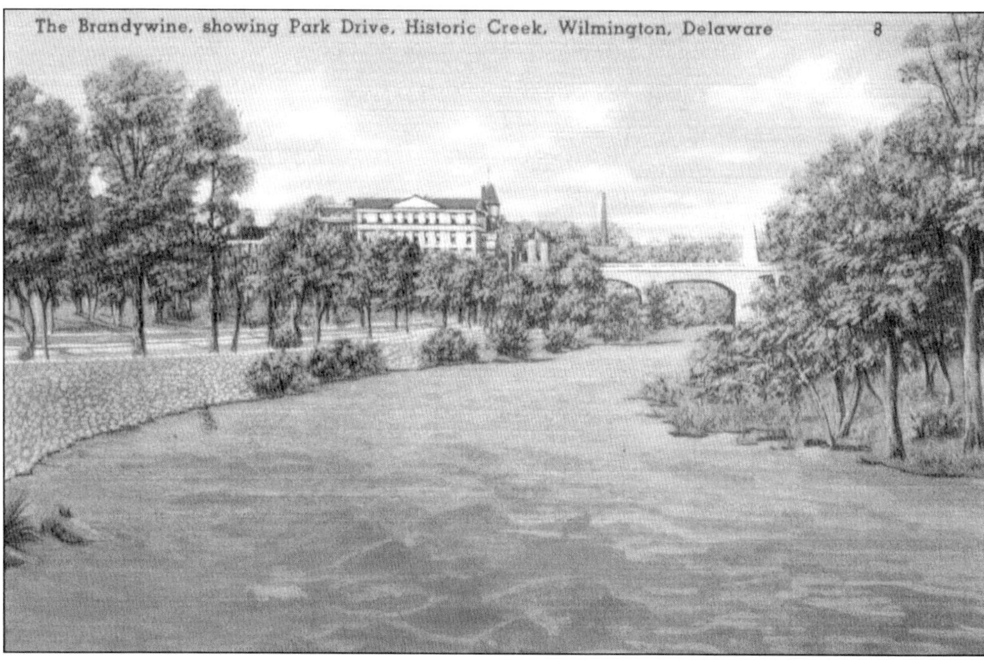

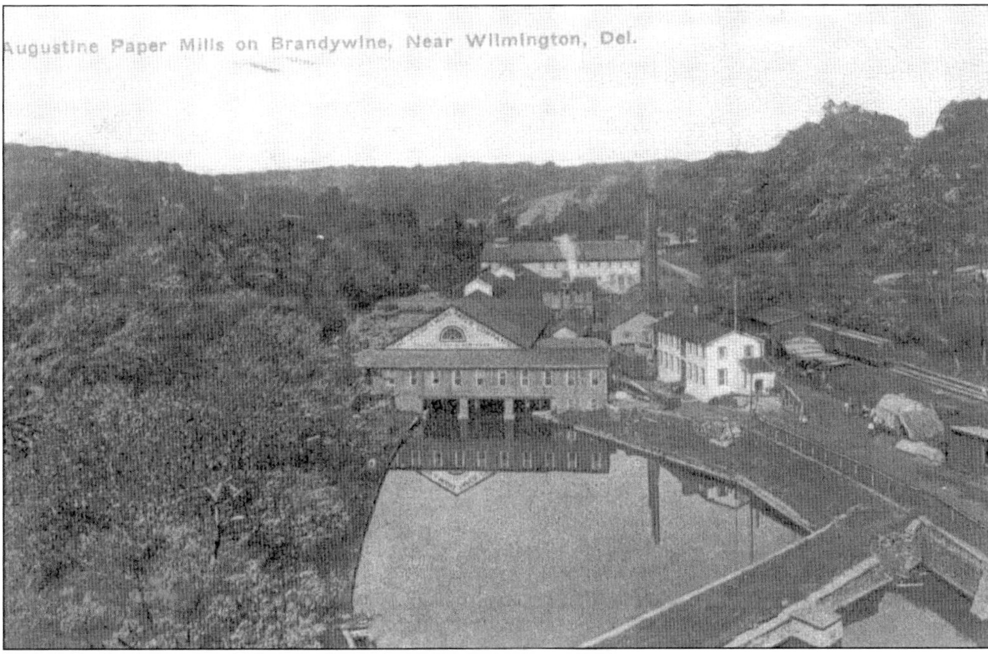

Downingtown did not have the only paper mills on the river. Delaware had the Augustine Paper Mills, near the city of Wilmington. The card above gives a clear view of the Brandywine and the paper mill, while the card below depicts the dam that aids the work at the mill. The dam is located above Riddle's and Augustine Mills. Norma, the sender of the card above (postmarked 1911), says she is ashamed of herself because, two weeks before, she wrote a letter to her friend Hester Fulk of Martinsburg, West Virginia, and forgot to mail it. Norma promises to author another letter to Hester.

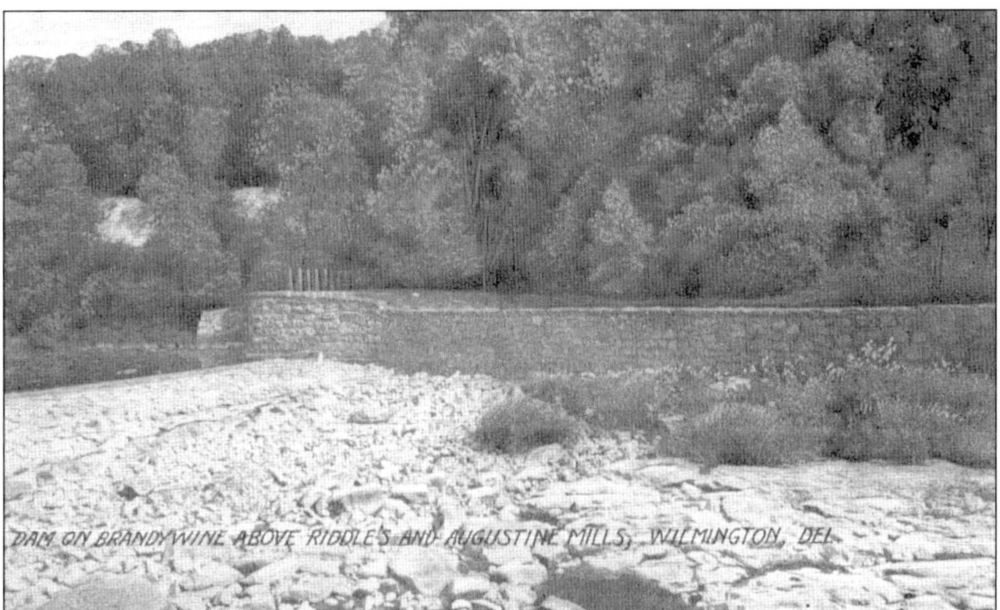

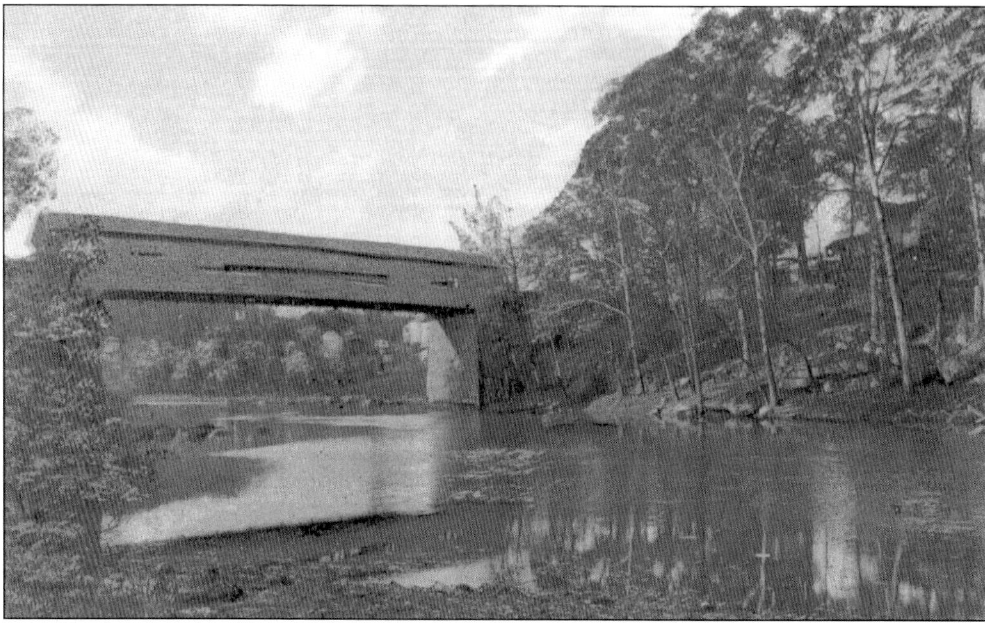

This card shows an old covered bridge over the Brandywine at Rising Sun, near Wilmington. The village of Rising Sun is at the end of what used to be Wilmington's streetcar line. It was a village of mills and workers' houses and has been called by various names besides Rising Sun, including Henry Clay, du Ponts Banks, Rokeby, and New Bridge.

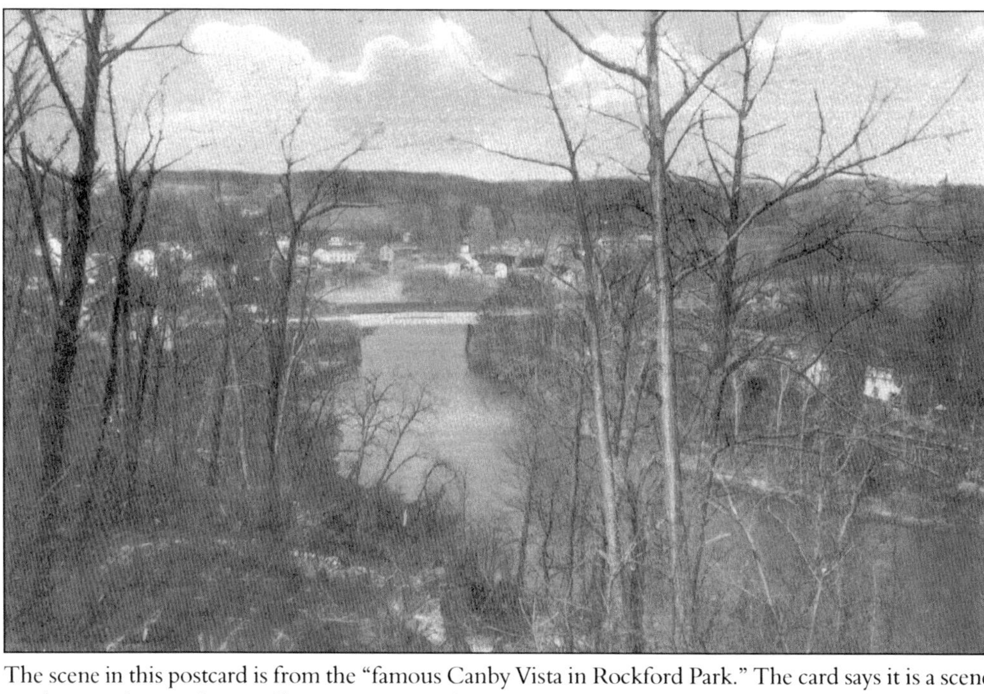

The scene in this postcard is from the "famous Canby Vista in Rockford Park." The card says it is a scene up the Brandywine from William Marriot Canby's Memorial. Oliver Canby built the first gristmill on the lower Brandywine in 1742. The mill was near King's Road that led from Philadelphia to Baltimore and was a good place to buy grain, meal, and flour.

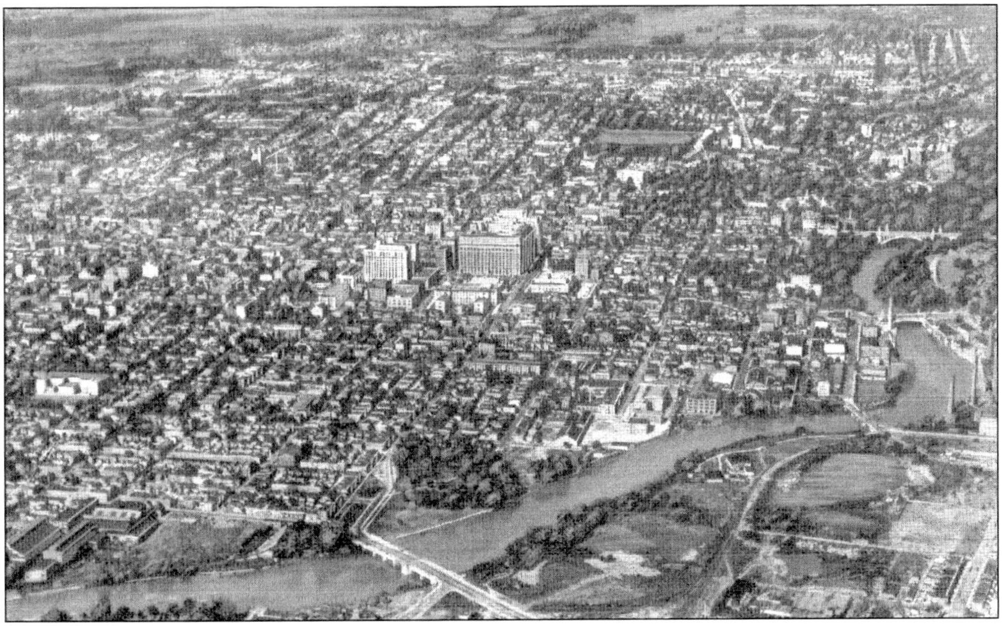

Wilmington is the largest city in Delaware and certainly one of the most important centers of business in the United States. The rivers that make up its borders define the city. As the postcard above states, "Wilmington is located at the junction of the Christina and Brandywine Rivers. The town was laid out in 1731." The city did benefit from the du Pont family and the fortune it made from black powder. The postcard below is from the Hagley Museum's black powder exhibit building.

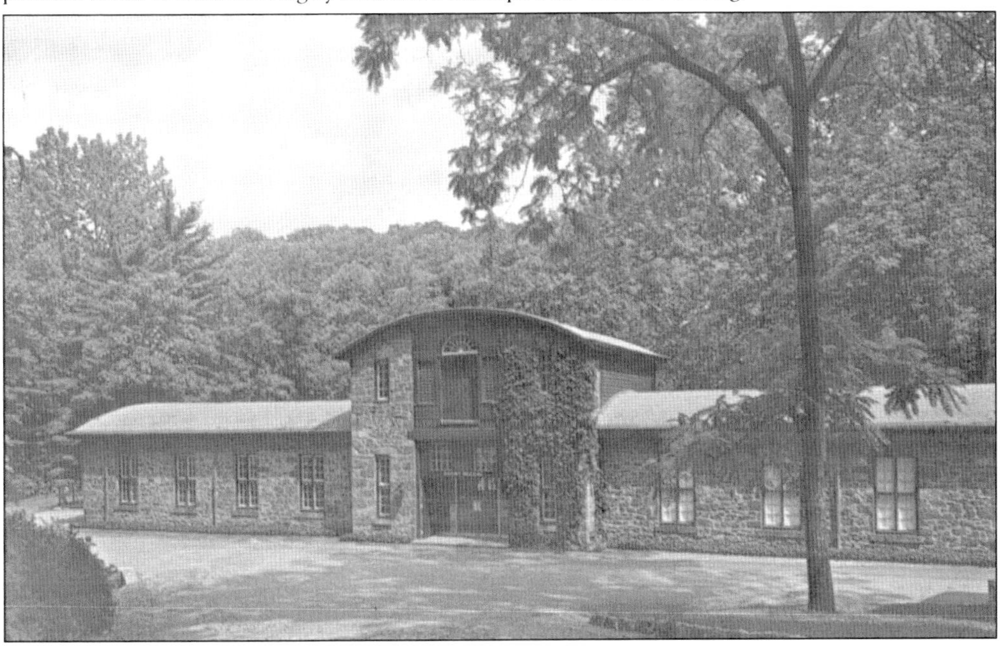

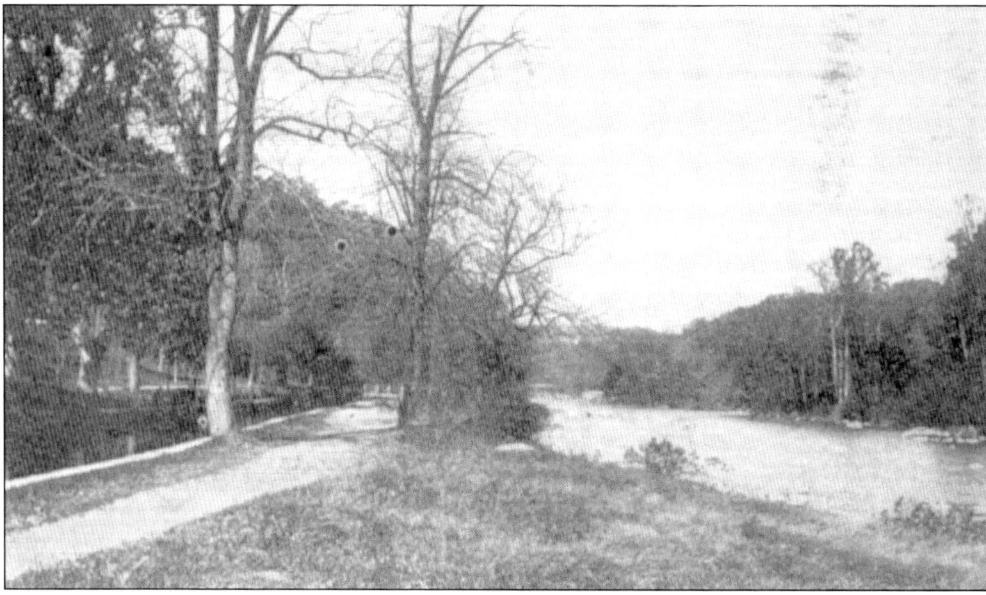

The Brandywine has meant a lot to the citizens of Wilmington for a number of different reasons, not the least of which is its survival. The river was responsible for much of the city's drinking water over the years. The Brandywine has also been a scene of gentle tranquility, as depicted in the two postcards on this page. The postcard above, sent by "Bertie" in May 1906, shows an uncluttered view of the Brandywine. The postcard with a 1910 postmark depicts a more forceful river. Both postcards are published by McIntyre and Company of Wilmington, Delaware.

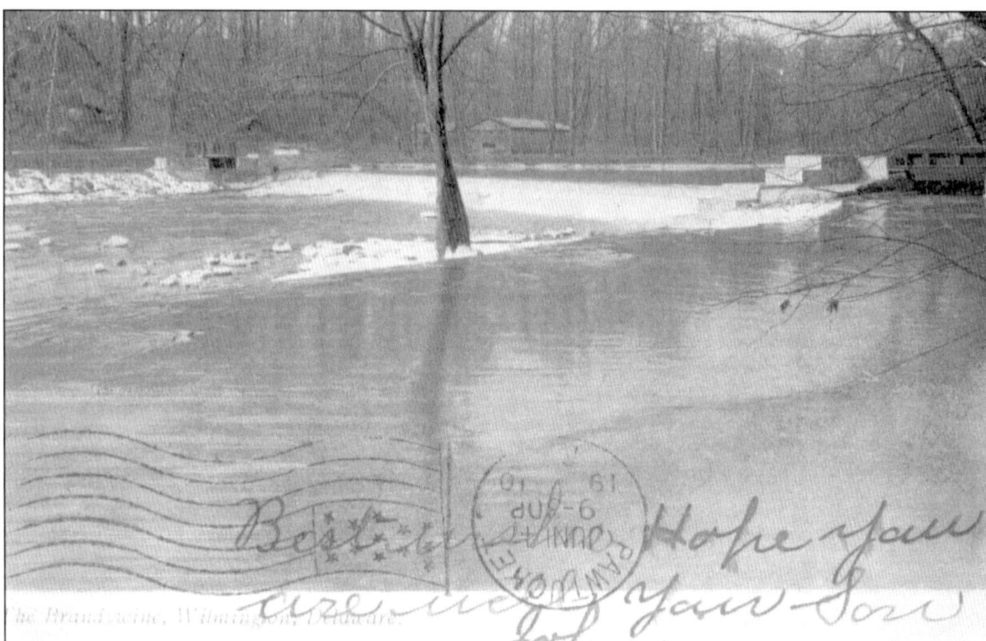

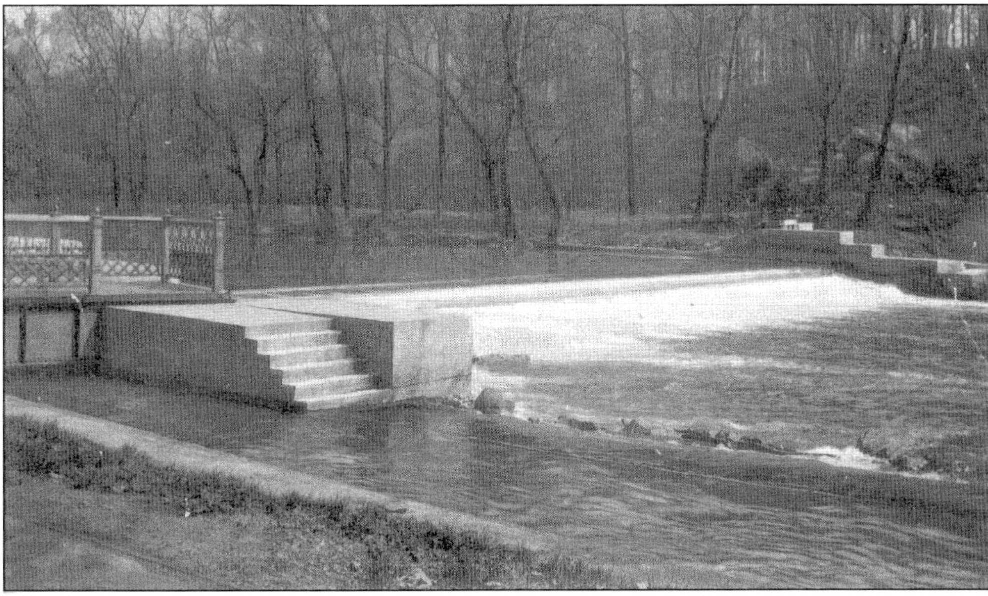

The flow of water from the Brandywine has always been important to Wilmington. At times, the river did not cooperate, and a series of dams and raceways was constructed to supply water for the inhabitants of the city. The First Dam, as it is called, played an integral part in the early development of the area. The dam was used to supply water to the many mills operating near the Brandywine. The postcard above shows the First Dam, located in Brandywine Park, Wilmington, Delaware. Below is a photograph of the dam published by Julian B. Robinson of Wilmington.

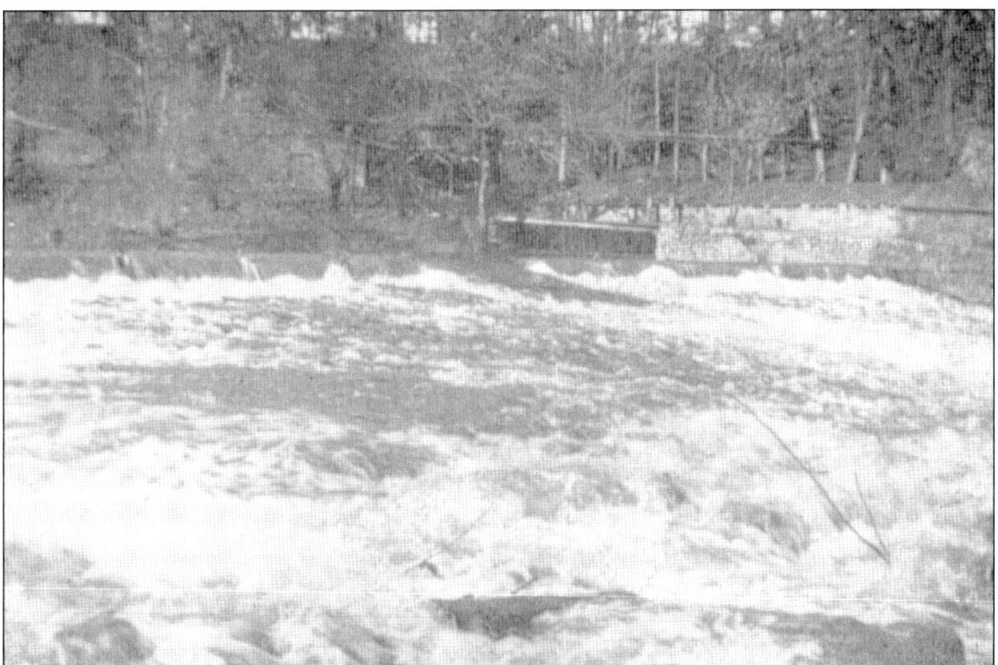

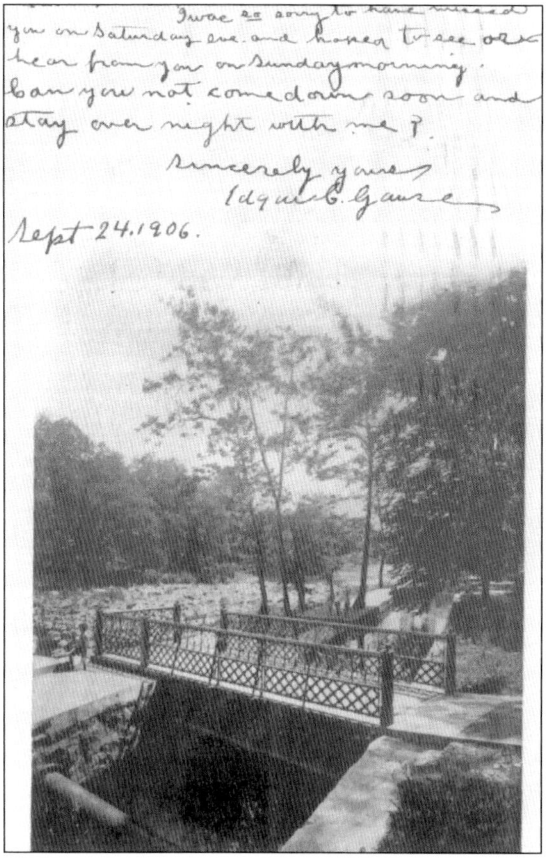

Sometimes, postcards were sent along the Brandywine in the opposite direction of the flow of the river. The postcard to the left was taken in Wilmington at the "Headgates of the Raceway," and traveled upriver to West Chester, on the banks of the east branch of the Brandywine. The recipient of the card is asked to come to the sender's home to stay overnight, since the two of them missed seeing each other on a recent visit. The postcard below is titled "Bridge over South Race at Jefferson Street." Both cards are by George A. Wolf of Wilmington.

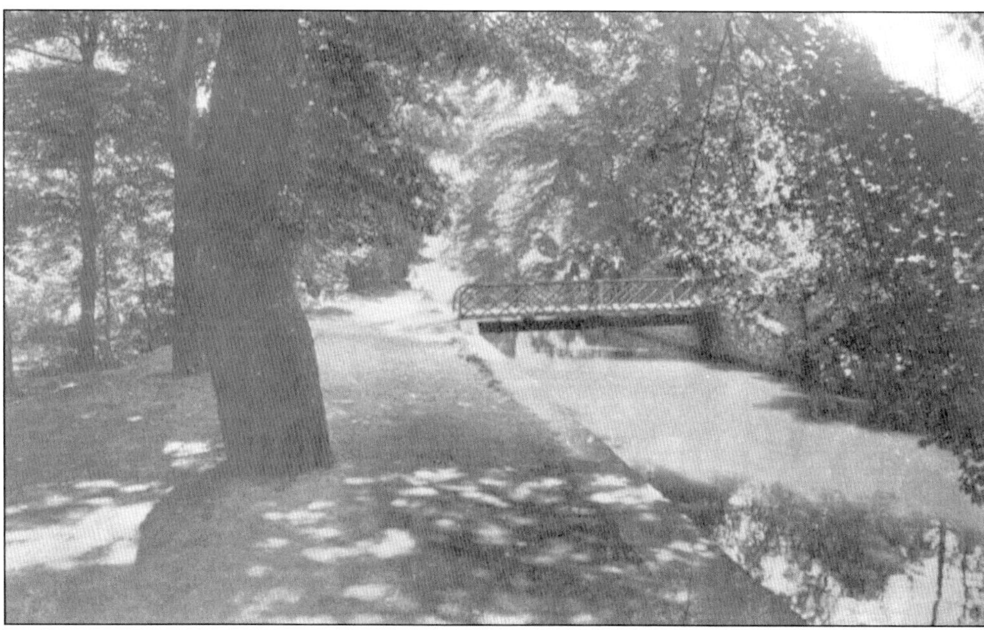

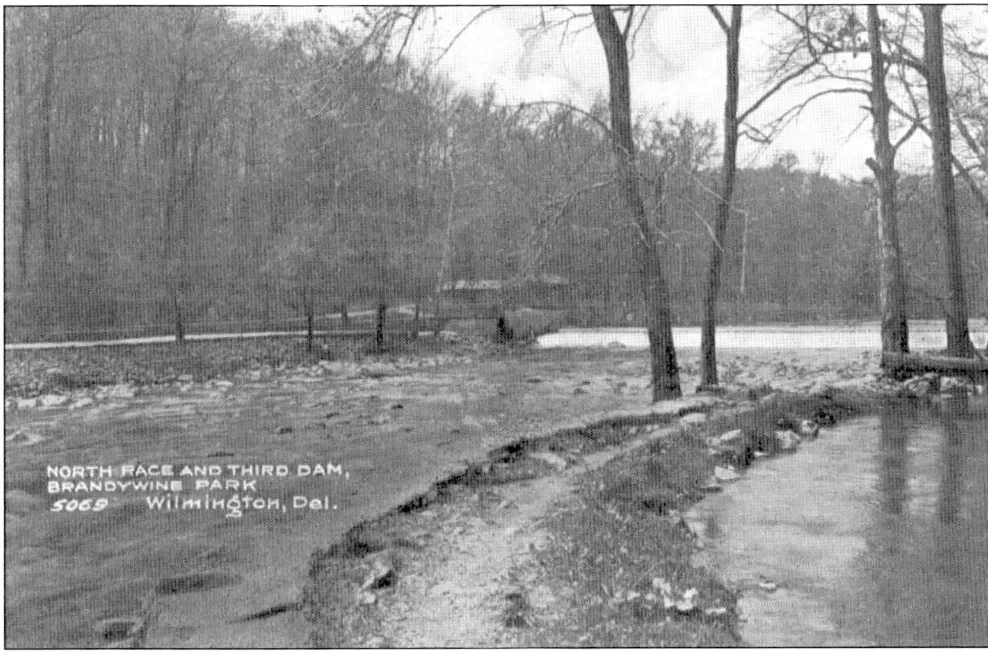

One of the mills that received power from the Brandywine was an early-19th-century woolen blankets manufacturer located in a brick mill downriver from the Tyler McConnell Bridge, which crossed Route 202 and Kennett Pike. The mill, once owned by a member of the du Pont family, burned in the 1840s but was rebuilt. The mill was later used as a performing hall for the Tankapanicum Orchestra, named for what some believe was the Native American name of the Brandywine. The two postcards on this page are of the Third Dam at Brandywine Park. The one below was produced in 1908, and both appear to be from the same series of cards. One is numbered 5066, and the other 5069.

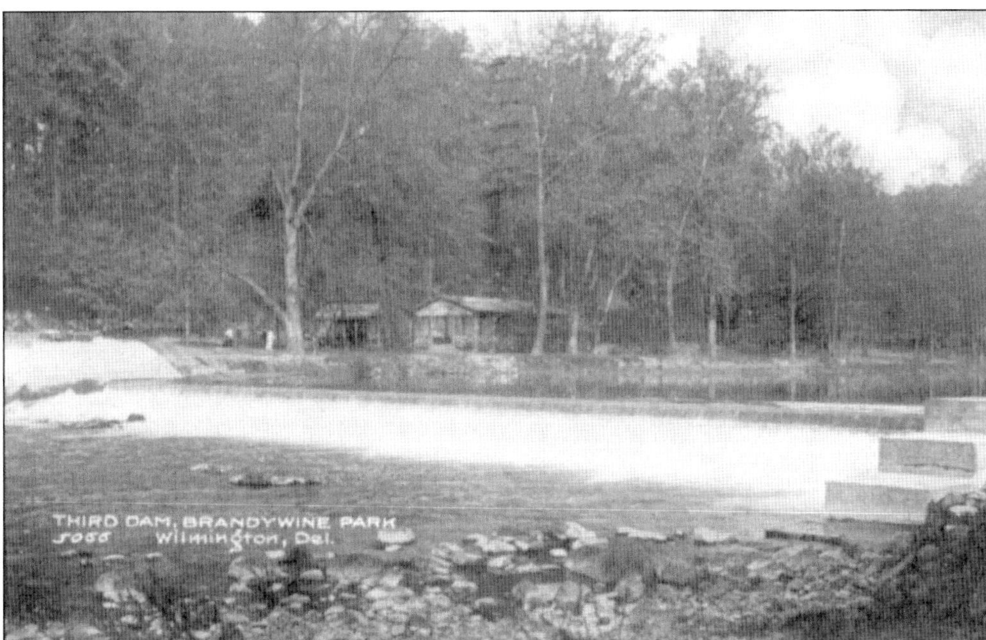

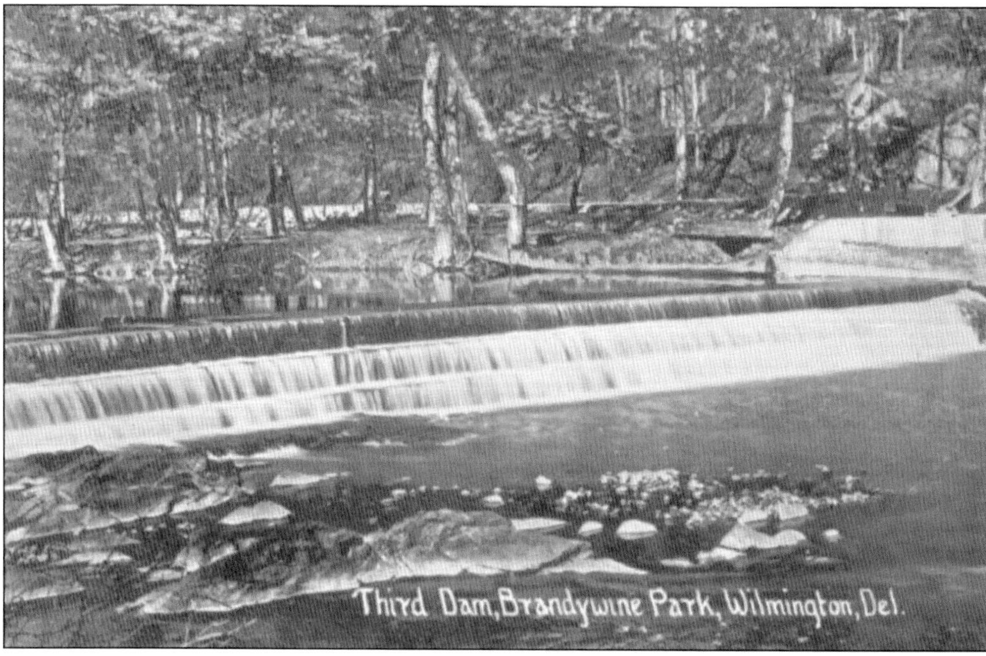

To keep its strength, the Brandywine is fed by creeks and runs, such as Pancake Run and Thundergust Run. This is the section where Rising Sun received its name. The constant supply of water necessitated the dams and raceways. In the postcard above is a view of the Third Dam at Brandywine Park, while the postcard below has three views of the raceways on the north side of the Brandywine. The bottom card is dated 1906 and was sent to a child by her father. It is another of the George A. Wolf cards.

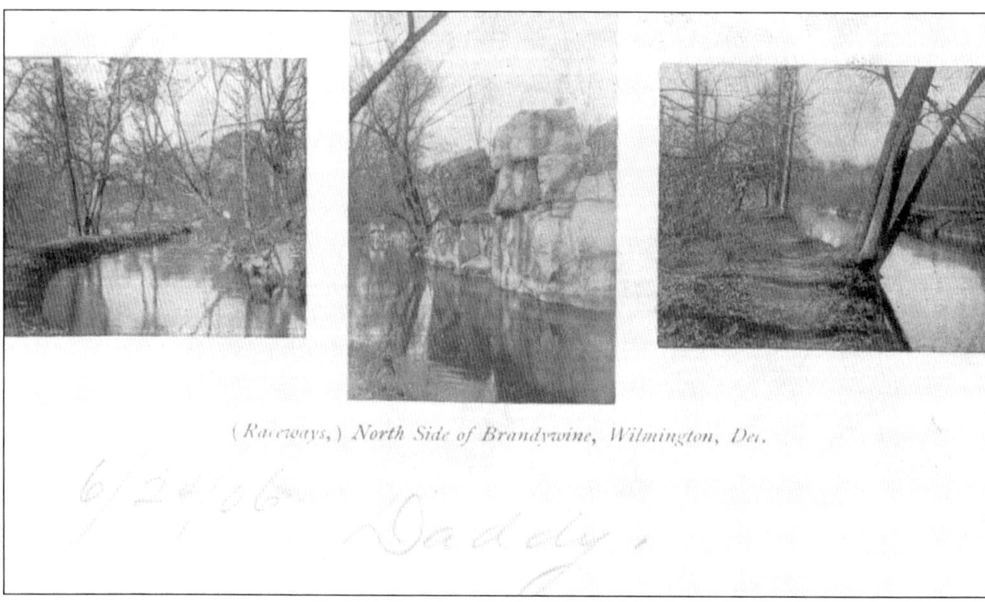

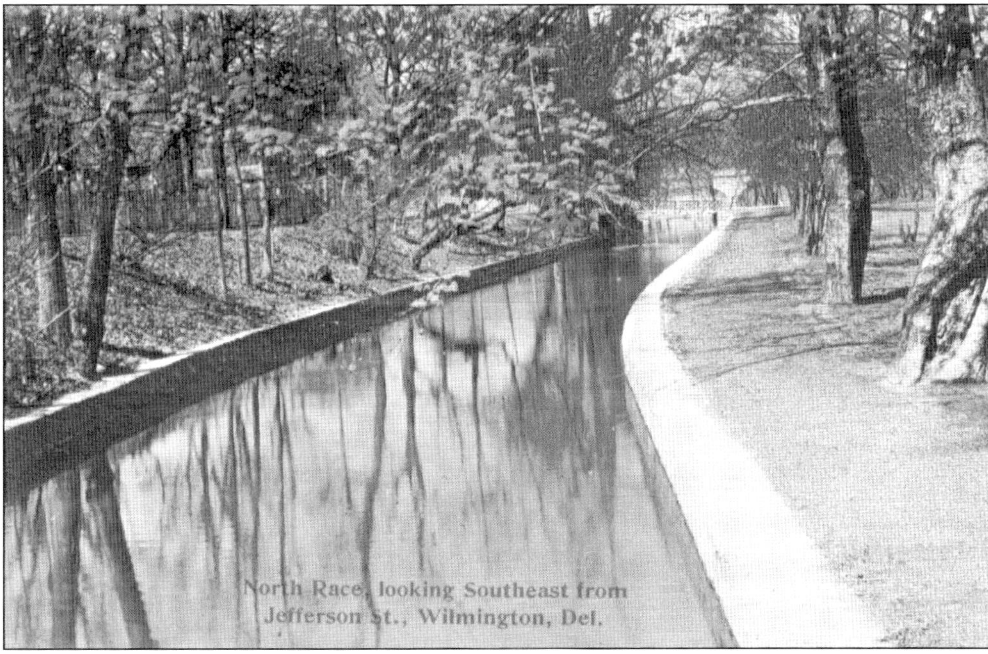

Not all of the mills along the Brandywine in Delaware were originally connected with the black powder mills of the du Ponts. In the early 1800s, one of the buildings was used as a cotton-spinning mill. It was located on the east bank of the Brandywine. The mill was named after Henry Clay, a leading politician who supported American businesses. The mill was eventually used to fabricate powder containers in connection with the du Pont operations. The two postcards on this page show views of the North Race. The card above looks southeast from Jefferson Street, and the card below looks southeast from Franklin Street.

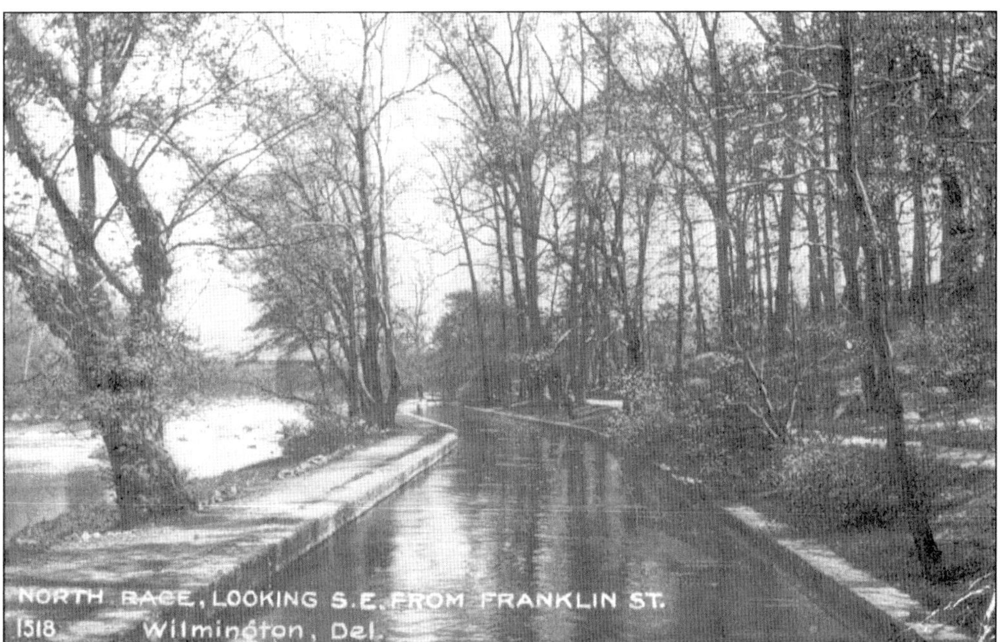

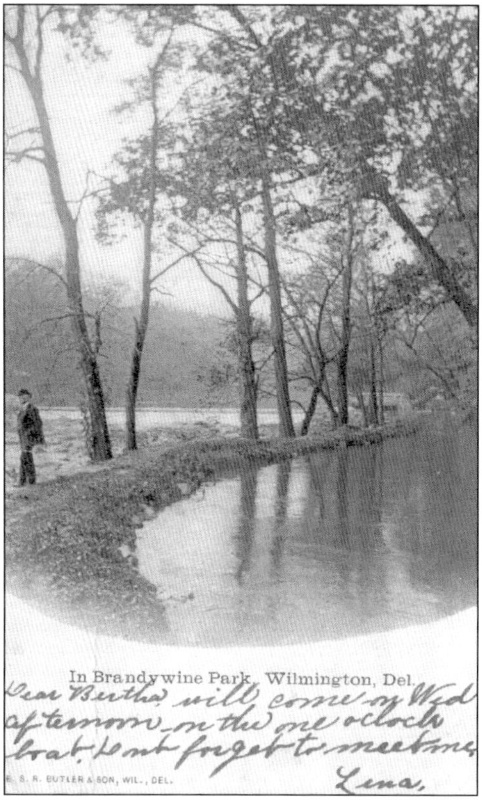

The Brandywine River now is associated with many recreational areas of Wilmington. The remains of an old Native American camp are part of a city park, and on the opposite hill is Rockford Park, named for an old ford in the ravine. In the card to the left, postmarked 1905, a man is shown strolling in Brandywine Park and looking out into the river. The card is by E.S.R. Butler & Son Company of Wilmington. The card below shows Park Drive at the entrance on the Brandywine. The note on the card expresses a hope that a relative is recovering from an illness. The postmark is 1913.

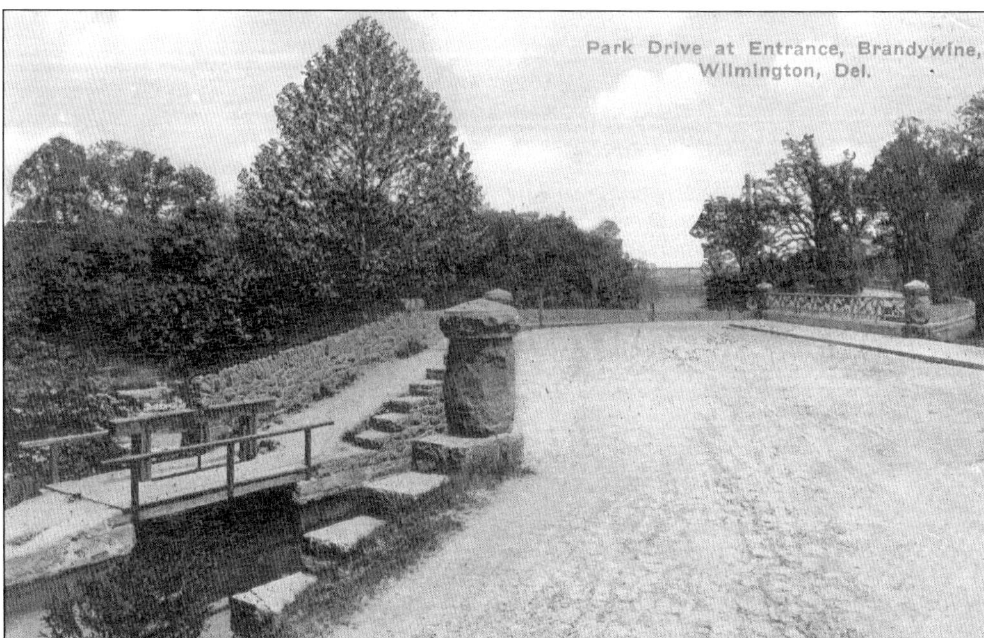

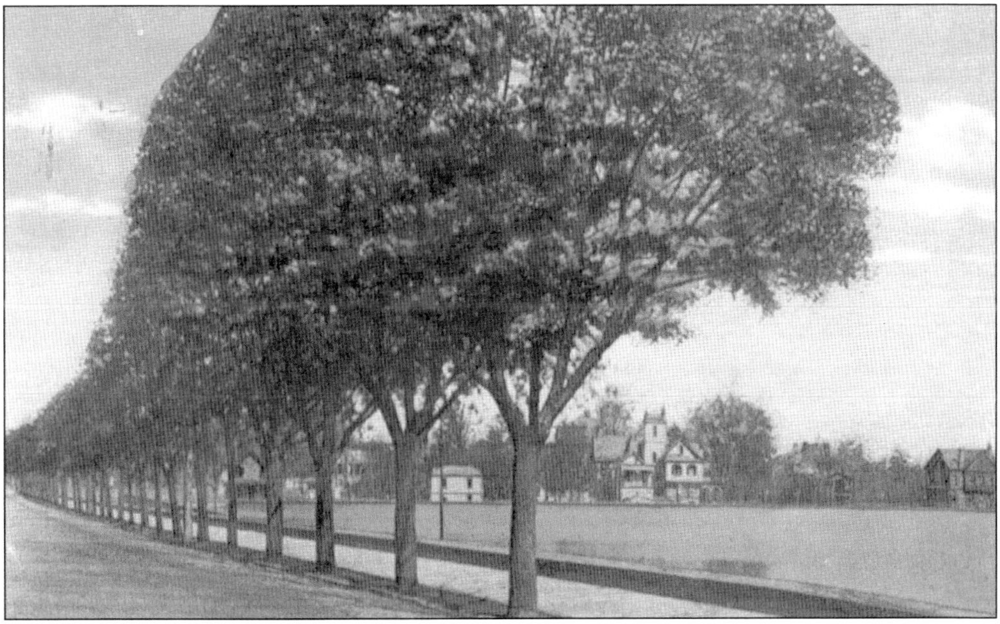

Water is always an important commodity and is becoming scarce as the population increases in the Brandywine River Valley. Rockford Tower, located in Rockford Park, can store half a million gallons of water brought up from the Brandywine for treatment downstream to supply the western section of the city. The Rockford Tower is the centerpiece of the park and is well known by residents of the city. In the postcard above, dated 1918, the city's reservoir is shown. The postcard below shows Park Drive along the Brandywine.

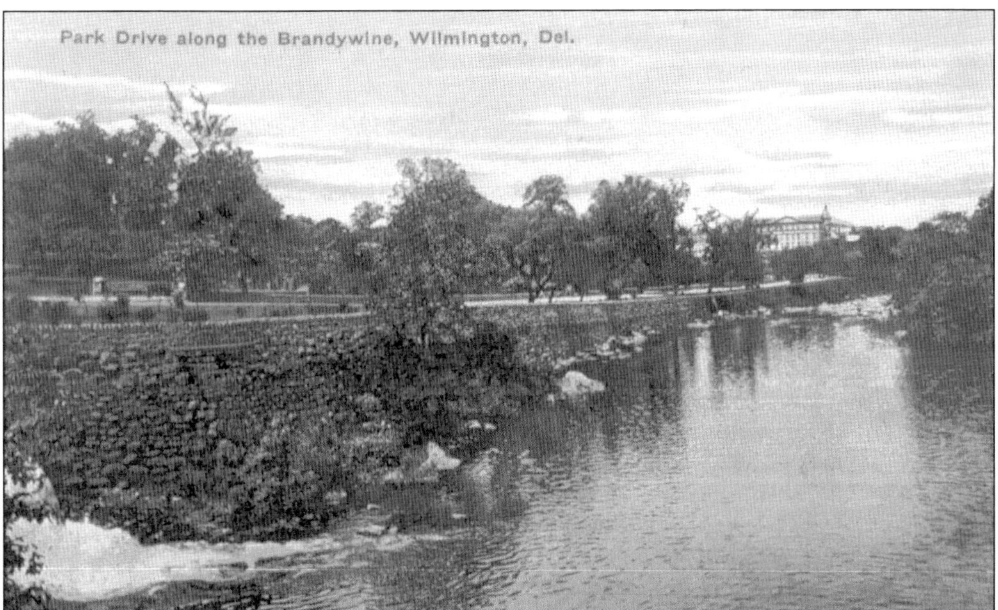

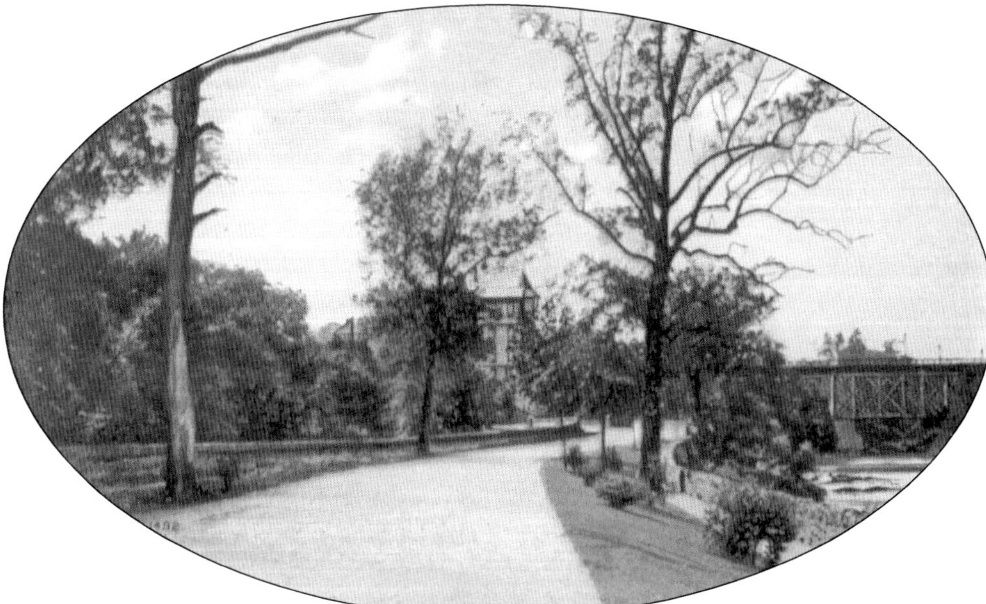

One of the mills along the Brandywine was the Bancroft Mills. The family business began almost as soon as the Quaker family reached Wilmington in the early 1800s. It was a book cloth dyeing business, and one order went for Bayard Taylor's Prince Dekalion. Taylor was one of the most noted writers of his time and grew up along the Brandywine near Kennett Square. Samuel Bancroft left a collection of pre-Raphaelite paintings to the Delaware Art Museum, which is near the Brandywine. The museum is shown below. The postcard above is a view of the Brandywine and Park Drive at Brandywine Park.

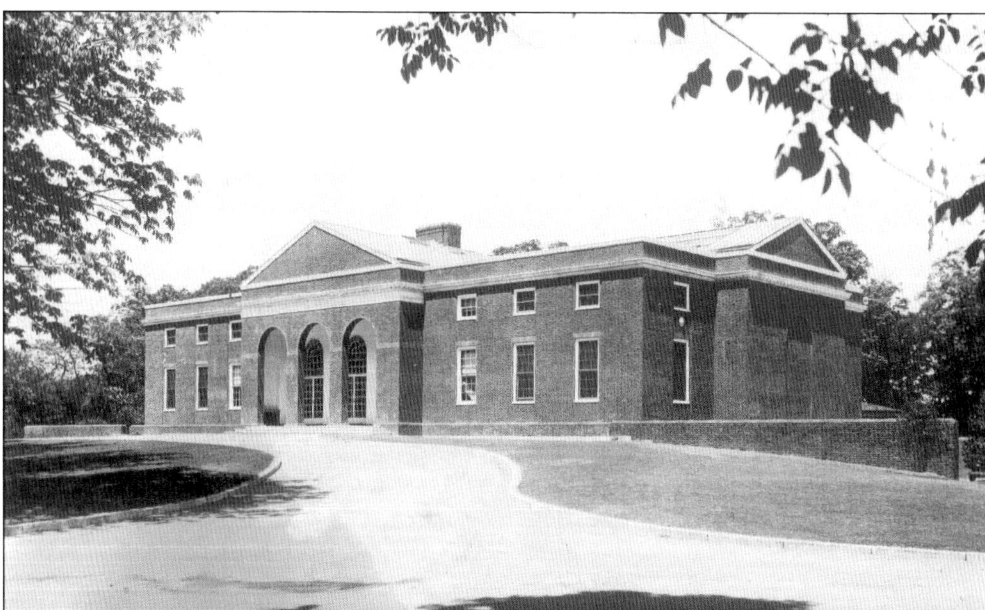

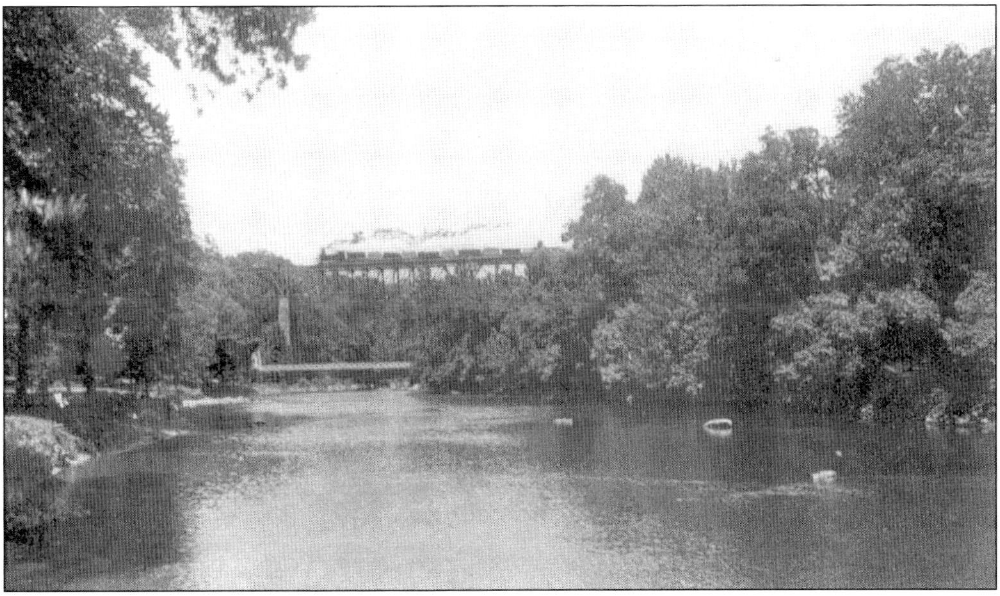

Another mill below Rockford was opened in the late 1700s by Joshua and Thomas Gilpin. The Gilpin family owned the home used by General Lafayette during the Battle of Brandywine. The Wilmington mill was first used to hand-press sheet paper. Later, a member of the family invented a machine to make continuous roll paper. Also, the family was the first paper maker in America to use chemicals to bleach rags. The postcard above is by George A. Wolf and shows the suspension bridge and Baltimore & Ohio bridge across the Brandywine. The bottom card is a view of the same site from Brandywine Park.

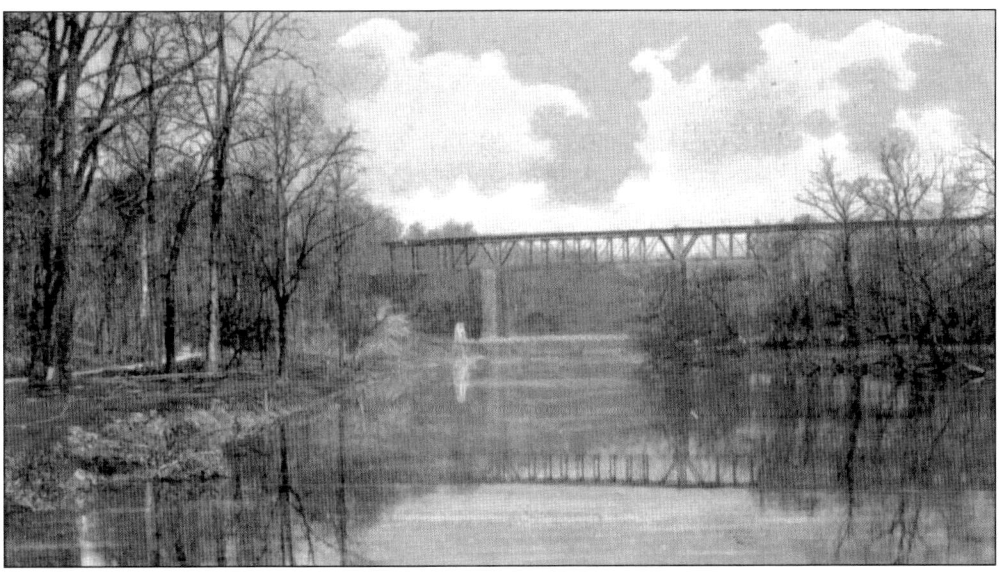

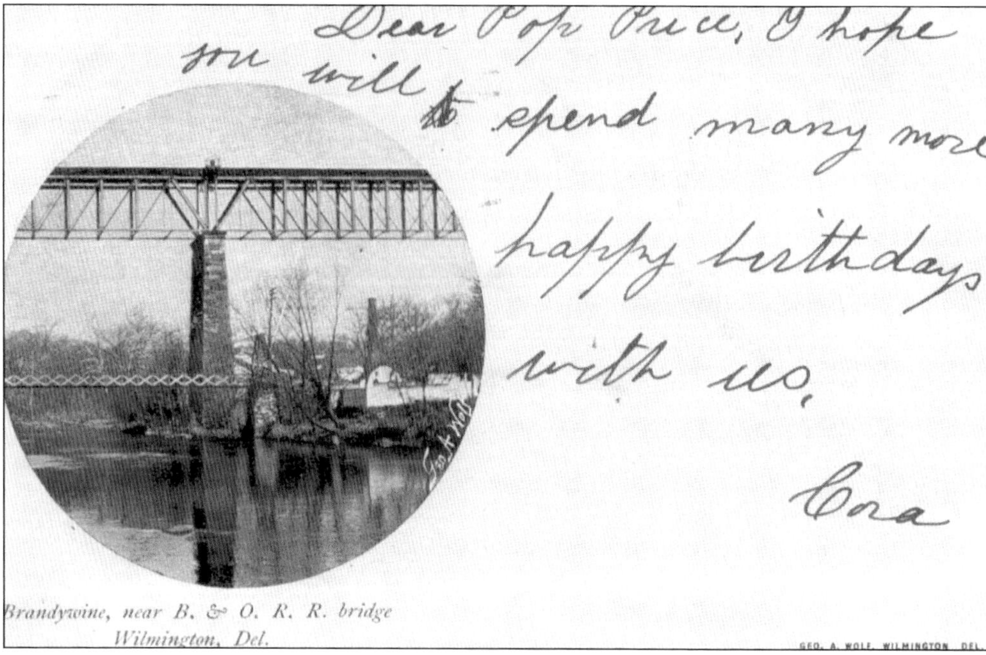

The Baltimore & Ohio bridge crossing the Brandywine River is a picturesque spot and has been the subject of many different postcards. The suspension bridge can be seen just above the Brandywine in both of the postcards. The card above is one of the George A. Wolf series. It is a birthday greeting from a grandson to his grandfather. The address just says 1302 King Street, City. The city is understood to be Wilmington. It also depicts one of the many mills along the banks of the river. The card below is No. 1519 of a series published by the Souvenir Postcard Company of New York and was printed in Germany. It does not have a postmark, but it predates World War I.

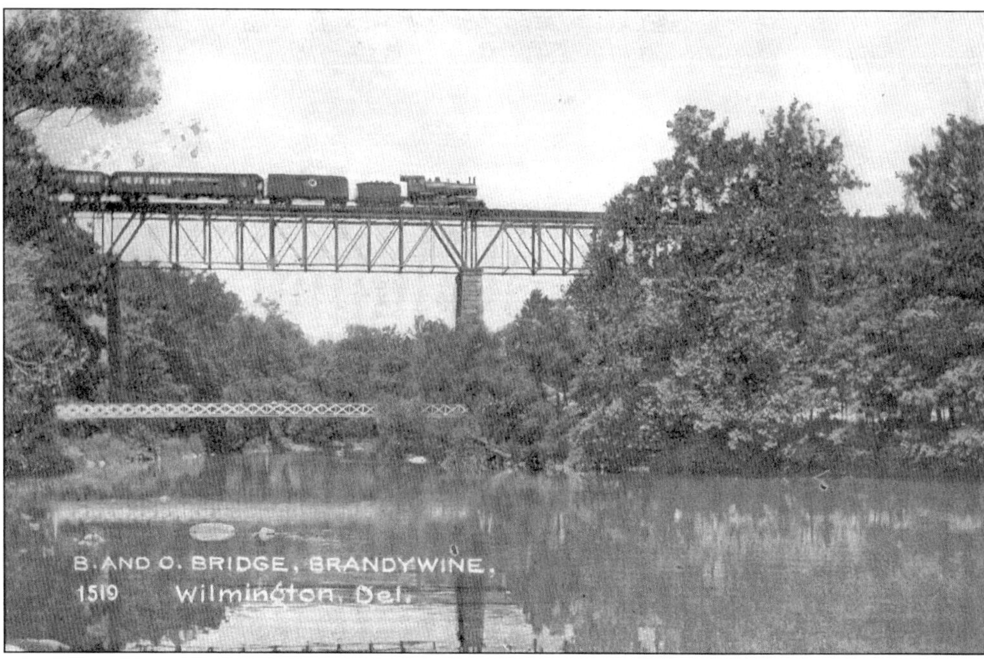

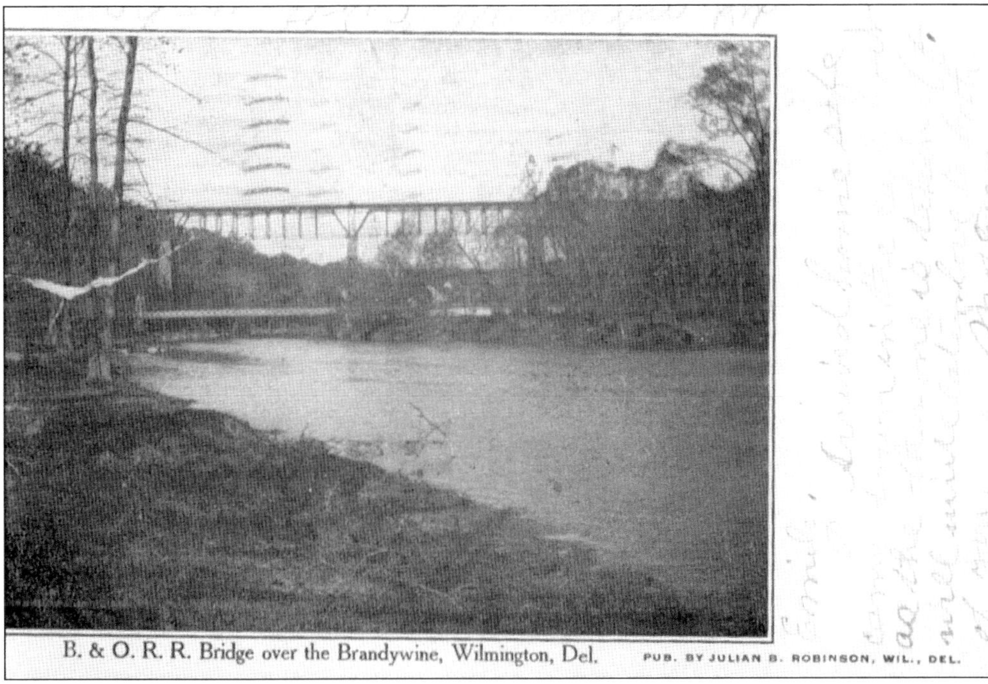

The view of the Brandywine with the Baltimore & Ohio bridge in the top postcard was published by Julian B. Robinson of Wilmington. Robinson and Wolf used many of the same scenes in their postcards and give the most realistic looks at Wilmington and the Brandywine at the turn of the century. The caption in the postcard below says, "View of Brandywine, B. O. Bridge in the Distance, Wilmington, Del." The card was printed in Germany and published by the American News Company of New York and Germany. It is No. A2707 of a series.

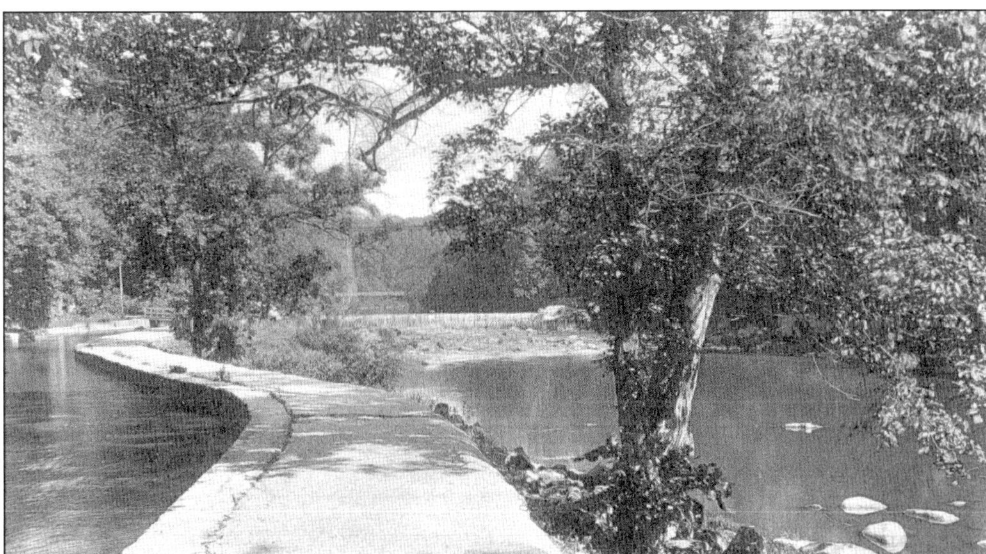

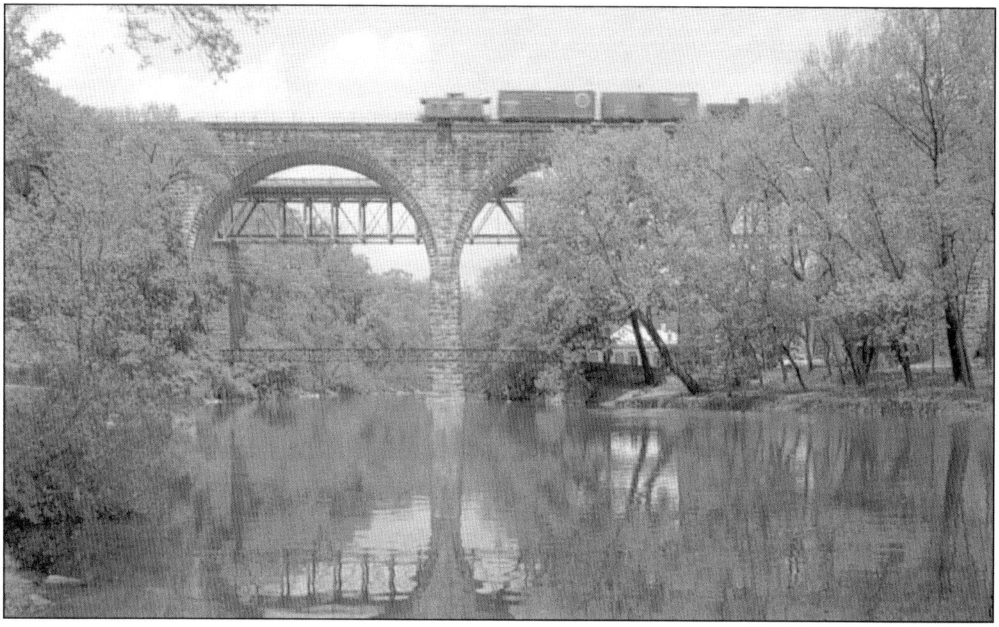

The old Baltimore & Ohio bridge can be seen from Brandywine Park. The bridge was constructed in 1910. Ten years later, the old railroad bridge, which can be seen through the arches in the postcard below, was converted into a crossing highway for use by the public. Once converted, the bridge became known as the Augustine Cut-off Bridge. The original swing span was replaced by a suspension bridge. Close to the Brandywine, the old swinging footbridge can be seen in both of these postcards.

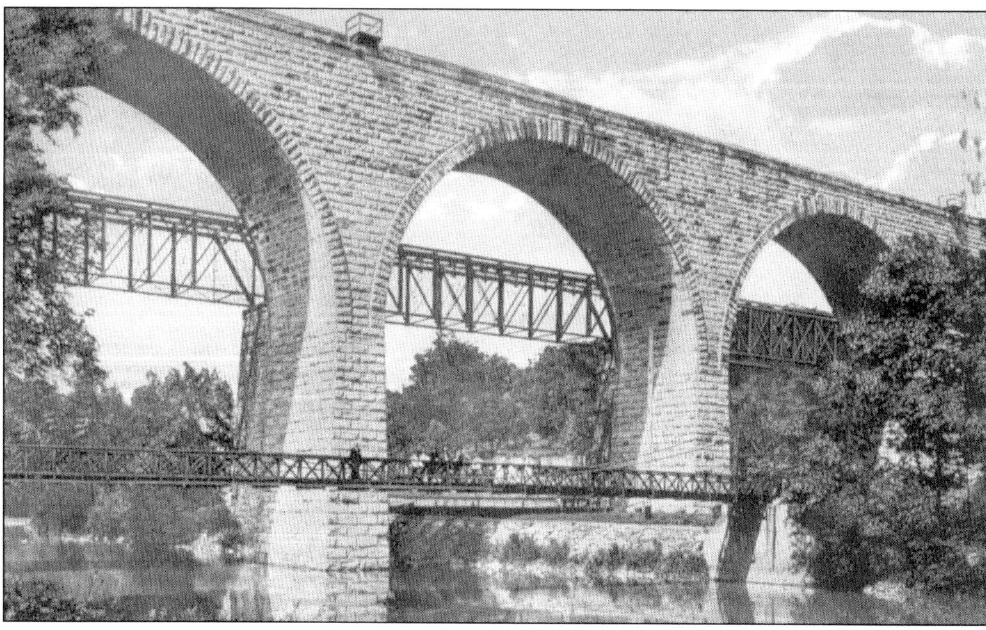

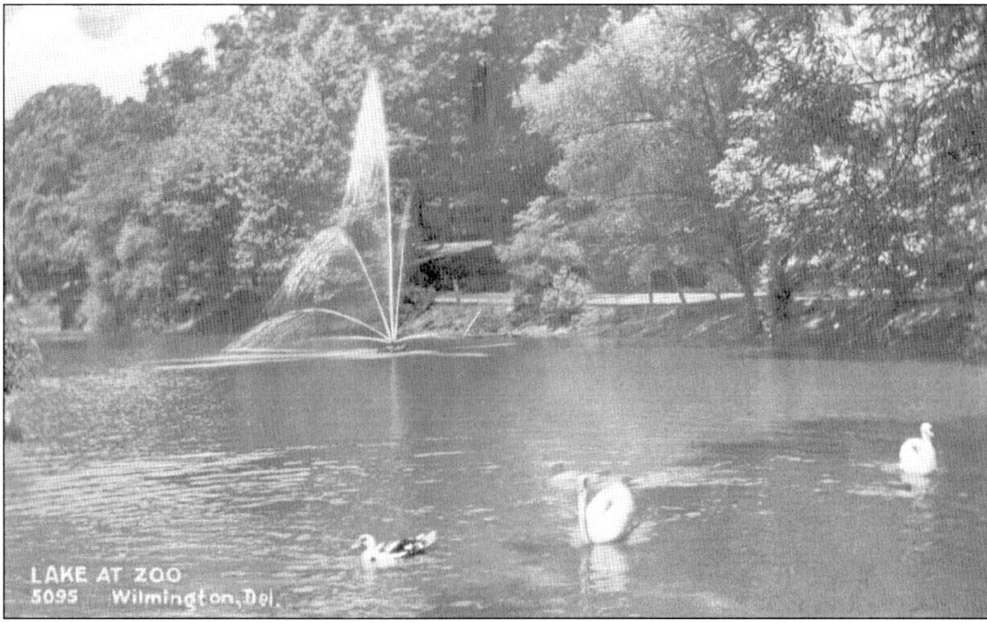

Along the Brandywine near the Baltimore & Ohio bridge runs North Park Drive and what used to be Tatnall's Woods. The area is now the Brandywine Zoo. A group of citizens headed by Samuel H. Bayard established the Brandywine Zoo in 1905. Originally, it was called the Wilmington Zoo. Its chief supporters were the Wilmington Board of Park Commissioners and the Wilmington Zoological Society. Above, the lake at the zoo is shown with some waterfowl. The postcard below shows the pavilion that acted as entrance to the zoo and two cannons placed in front of the building.

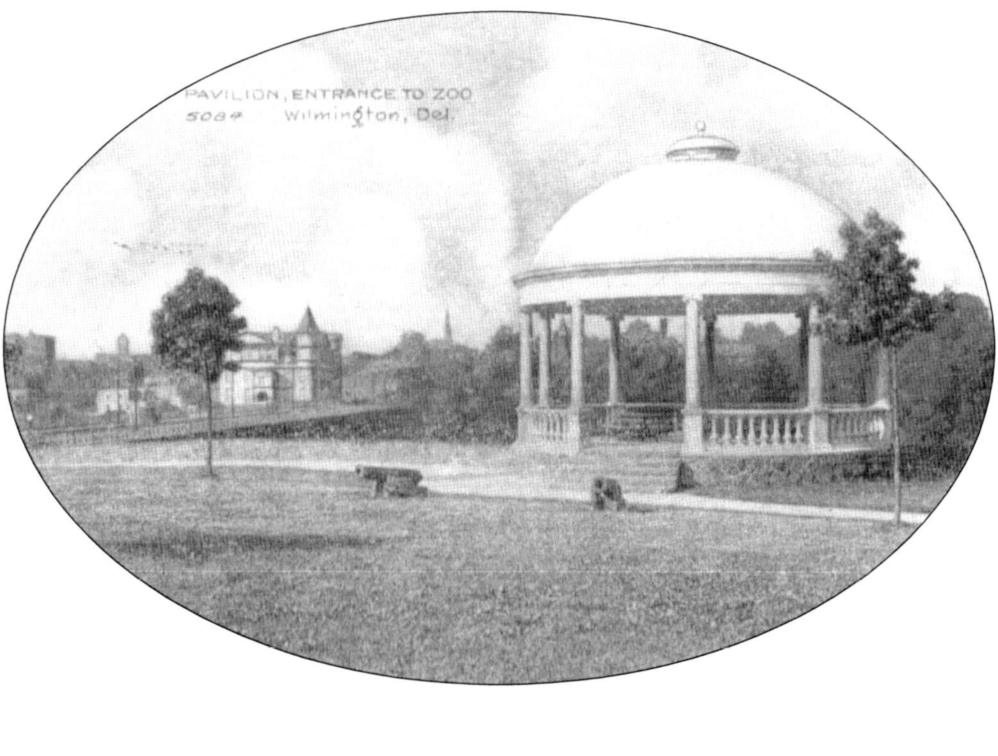

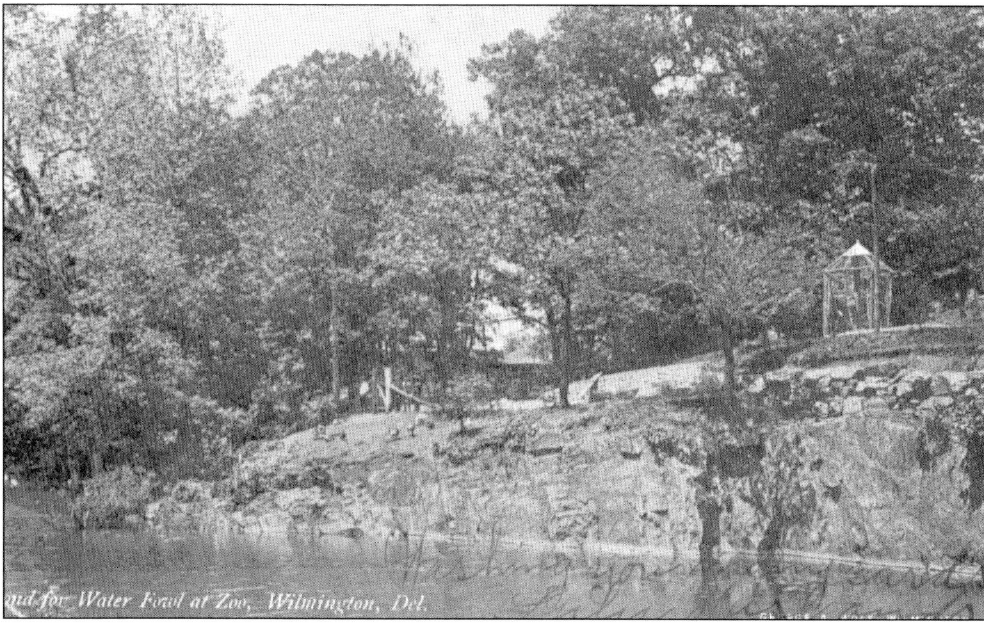

In 1969, the New Castle County Department of Parks and Recreation took over the responsibility of the zoo and it became known as the Brandywine Zoo. The zoo, with the help of the Delaware Zoological Society, offers a variety of educational and conservation programs. The Delaware State Parks now has the responsibility of running the zoo along with the Delaware Zoological Society. The postcard above shows the pond for waterfowl at the zoo. The postcard below shows the pathway leading into the zoo from the pavilion. The zoo is the only one in Delaware.

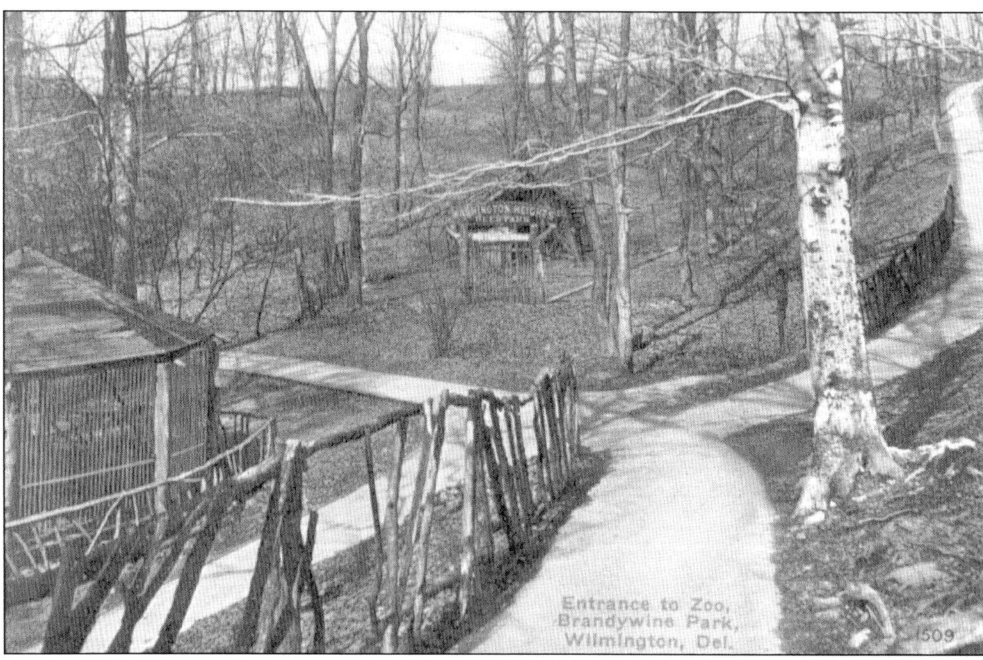

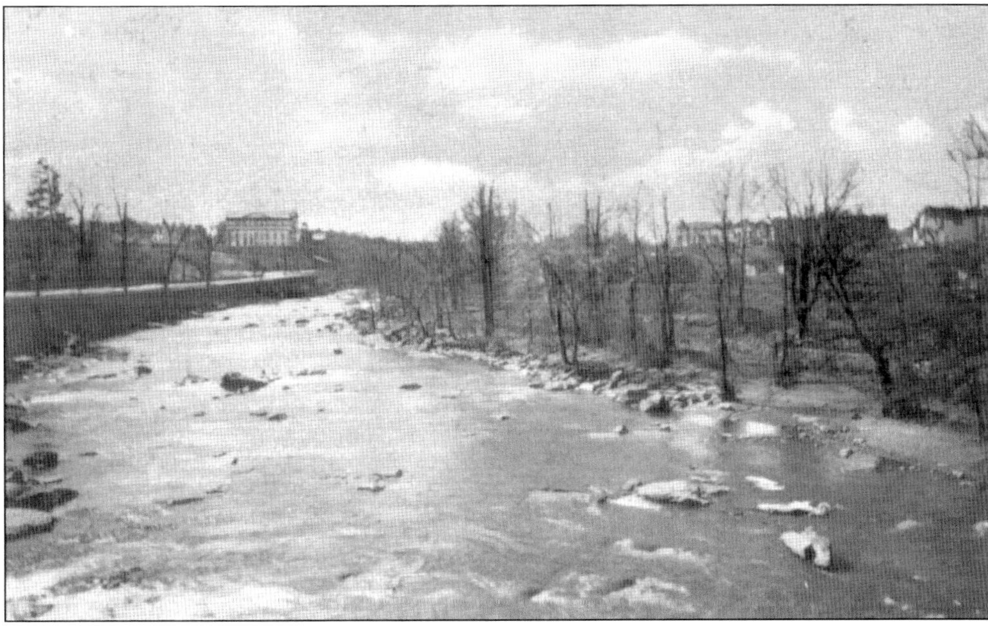

The farmers of the Brandywine area used to haul their grain to the mills along the Brandywine for processing. Many of those mills were near the Market Street Bridge over the river. In the scene in the postcard above, the Brandywine is viewed from the Market Street Bridge. The postmark is 1908. The card below says, "Old Bridge over Brandywine (Market Street), Wilmington, Del.," and was published by George A. Wolf. The card was sent to Francis R. Taylor in 1906 in care of the White Star Line steamship *Romanic*. The postcard welcomes him home to the "Land of the Free."

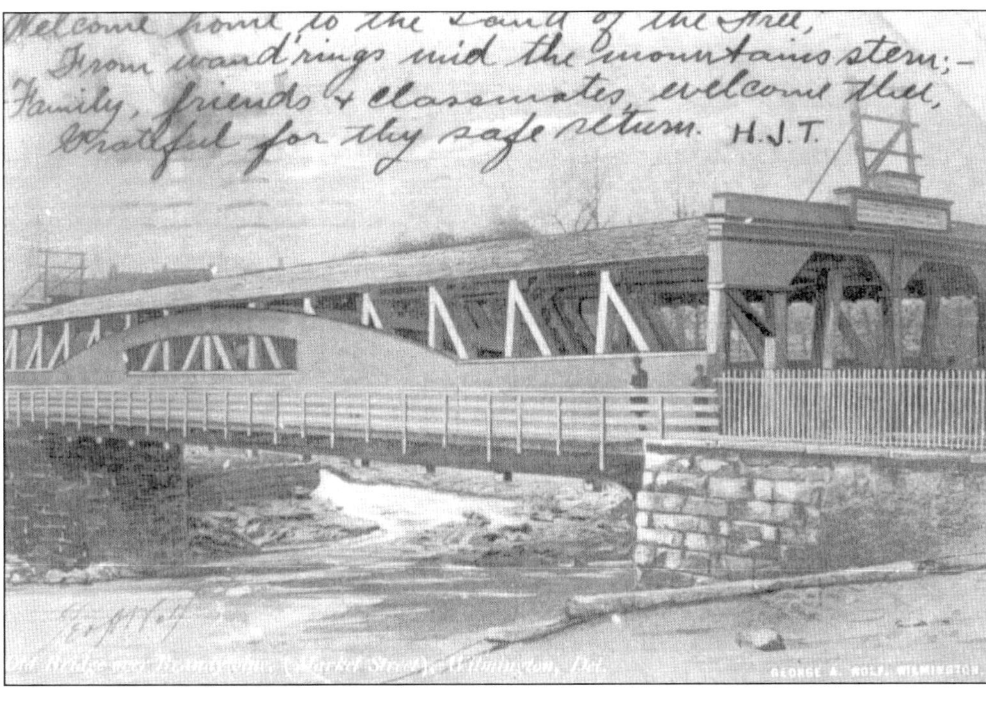

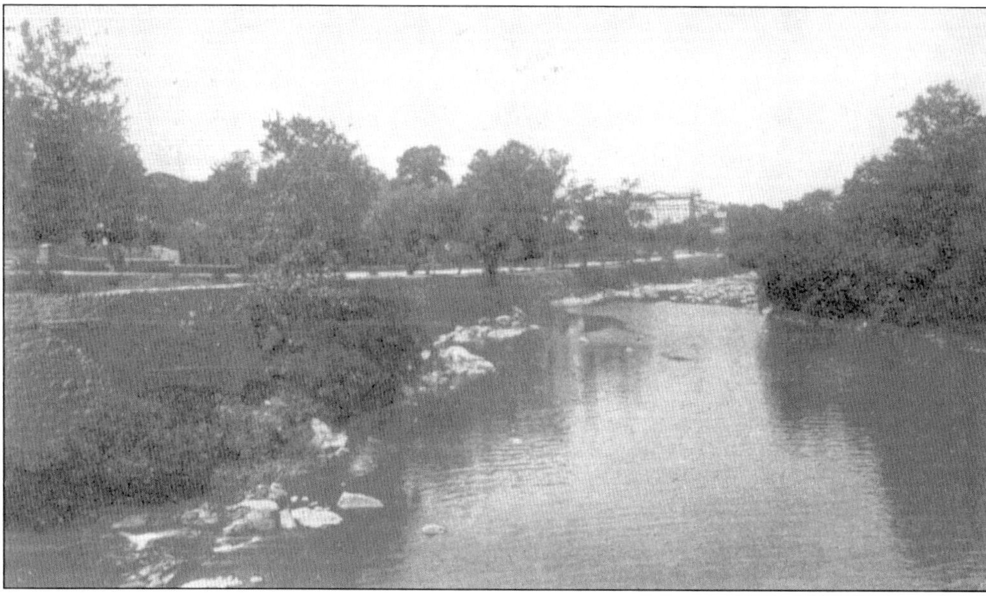

George A. Wolf produced the above card, looking west from Market Street Bridge, as part of the many postcards he published on the region. The card below has a different look at the Market Street Bridge. Much of the flour shipped from the mills in this area was sent under the trade name of "Brandywine Mills." The price of wheat and flour in our country was determined on the Brandywine at the end of the 18th century because of the efficiency of the mills and the quality of the product.

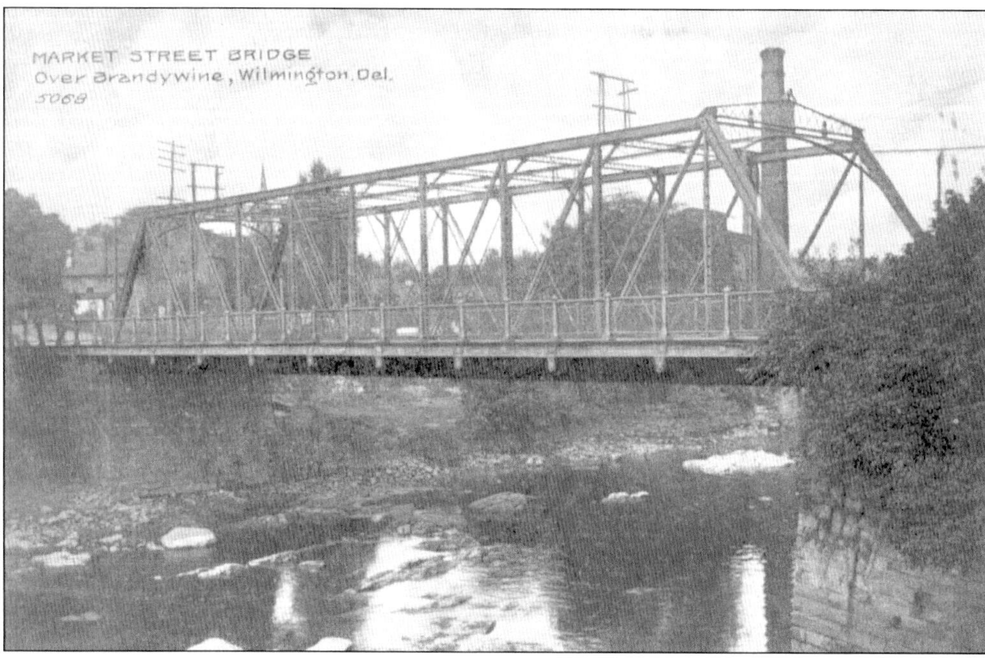

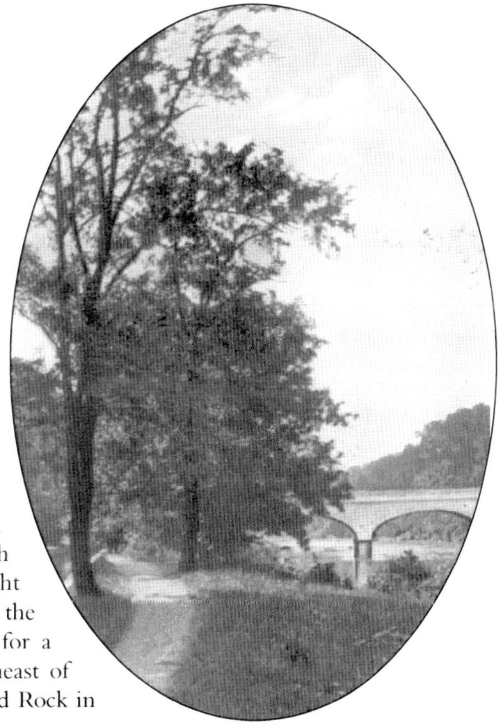

Brandywine Park, the first in Delaware, was founded in 1885. The park stretches along one mile of the Brandywine River and is admired for its classic bridges. It is also diverse, as its 178-acre area is home to 19th-century monuments, formal gardens, and open woodlands, along with the Brandywine Zoo. The postcard to the right is a scene in the park showing the river beyond the bridge. The message on the card details a plan for a strawberry-picking party in Boothwyn, just northeast of Wilmington. The postcard below shows Dog Head Rock in Brandywine Park.

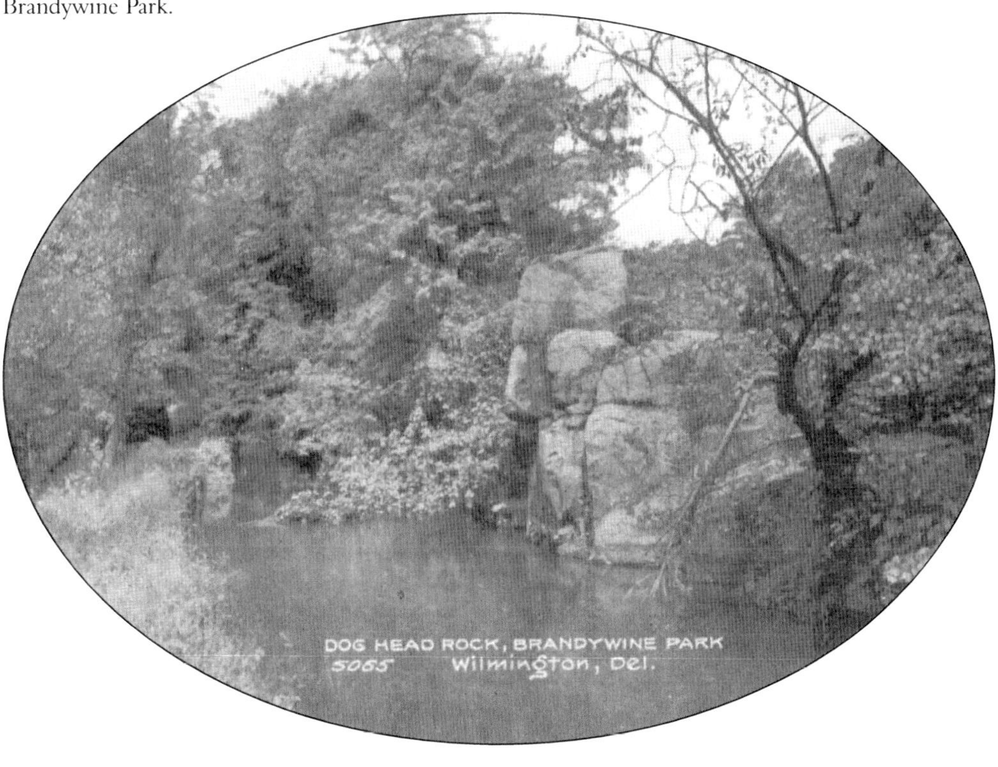

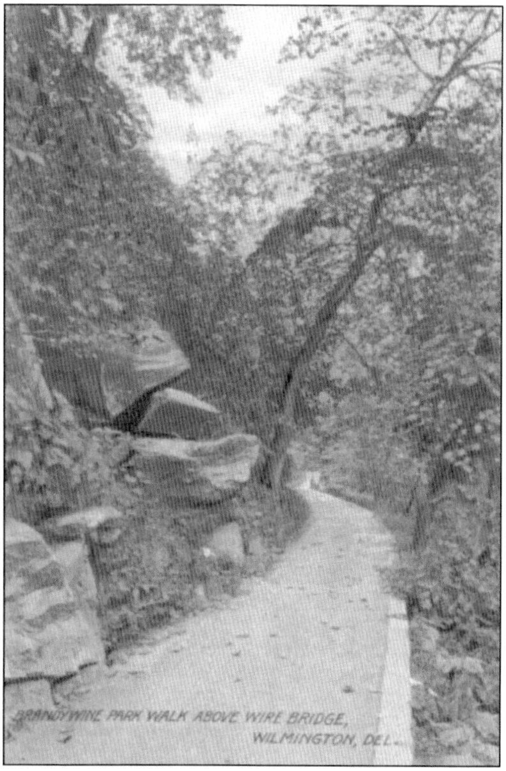

Brandywine Park utilizes the Brandywine River for all kinds of recreational activity, including fishing and kayaking. There are also many hiking and jogging trails that are part of Delaware's "Greenway" system. The trails are used for those keeping fit. The park also has a sensory trail where the visually impaired can join other park visitors to pause at stops to touch or smell a particular plant. Part of the walk in Brandywine Park above the wire bridge is shown in the postcard to the left. The postcard below has a 1913 postmark and shows part of the raceway in Brandywine Park.

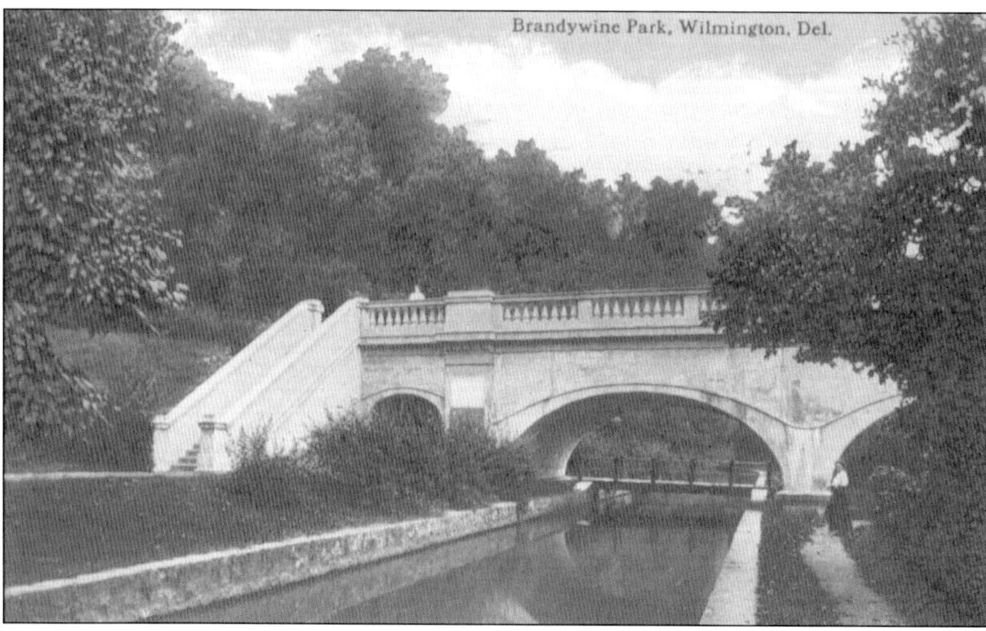

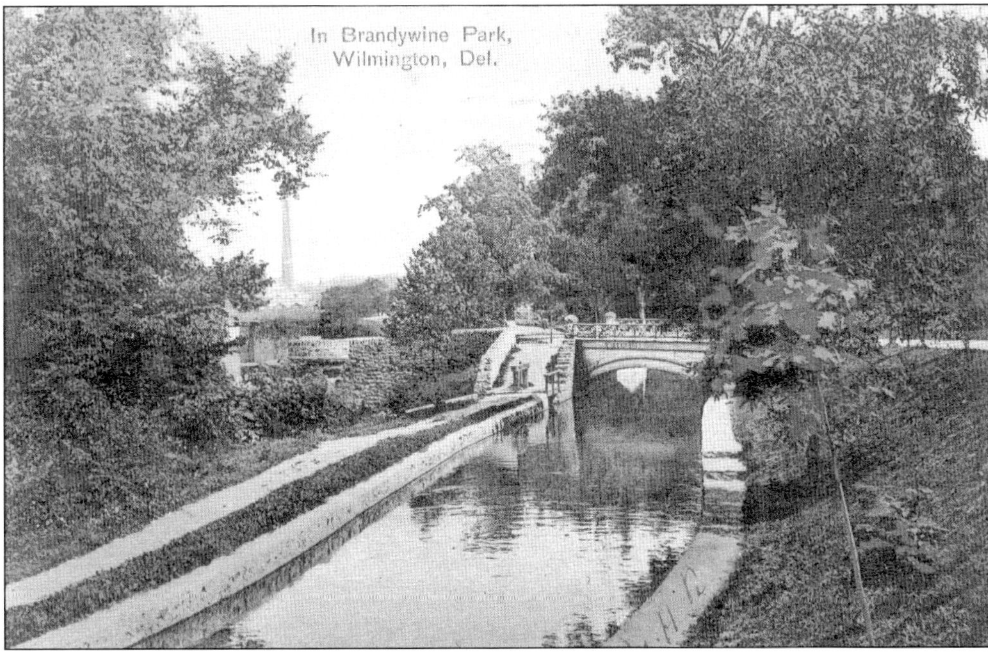

The E.S.R. Butler & Son Company of Wilmington published the two postcards on this page of the race in Brandywine Park. The cards have different views, but both have the same caption: "In Brandywine Park, Wilmington, Del." The card above, postmarked 1907, came from the United Art Publishing Company of New York City and was printed in Germany. It appears to have portions of the mill in the center. The bottom postcard, without a postmark, is No. D2449 in a series.

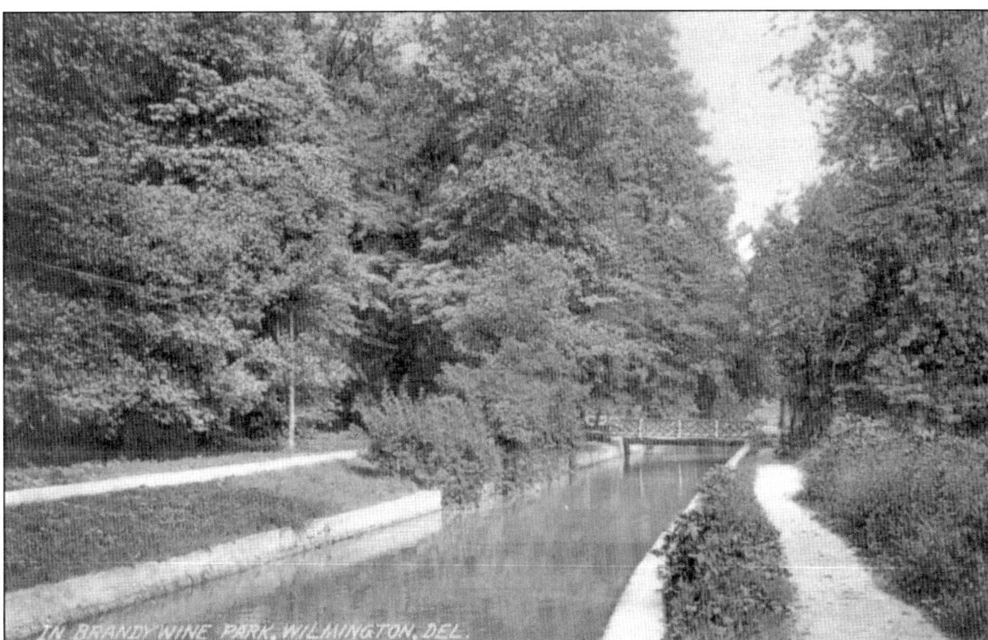

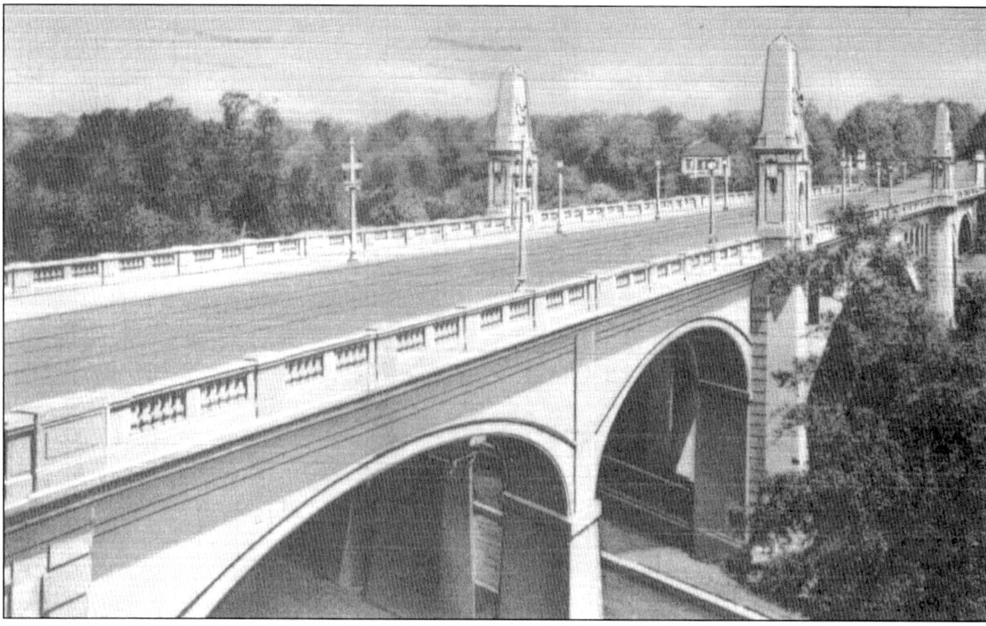

With all of the mills using the water from the Brandywine River for their processing needs, it is no wonder that the water supply was not always the cleanest. This is a troubling situation when the water is used for drinking. In 1873, members of the city's board of health did a study of the river and found it contained "water closets and hog pens." Their report stated that, for a long time, city residents believed that the water they had been drinking had impurity problems. The postcard above shows "Washington Street Bridge over Brandywine Creek." The card below has a concrete bridge crossing the Brandywine.

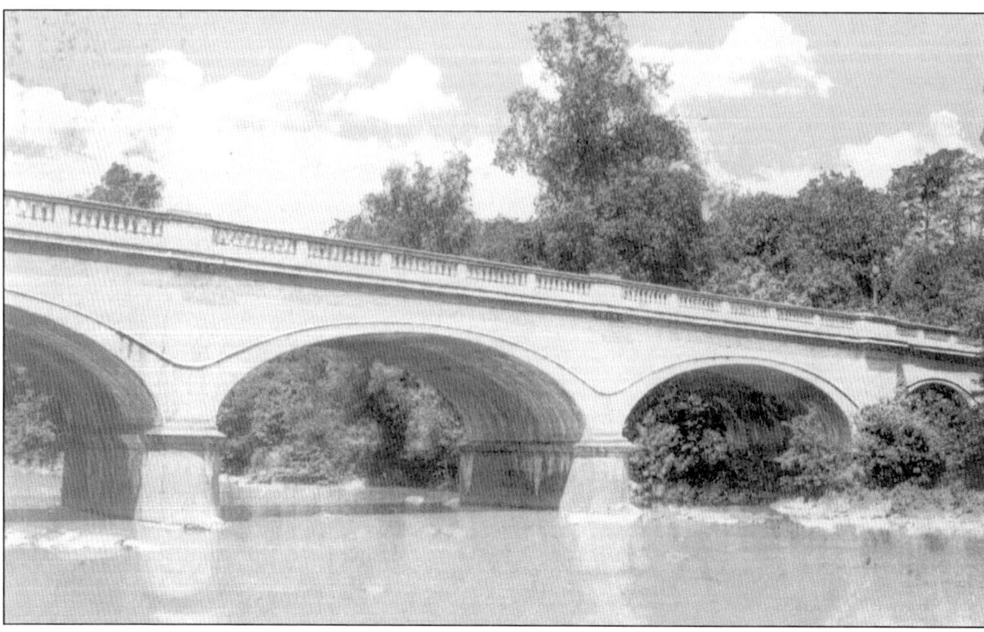

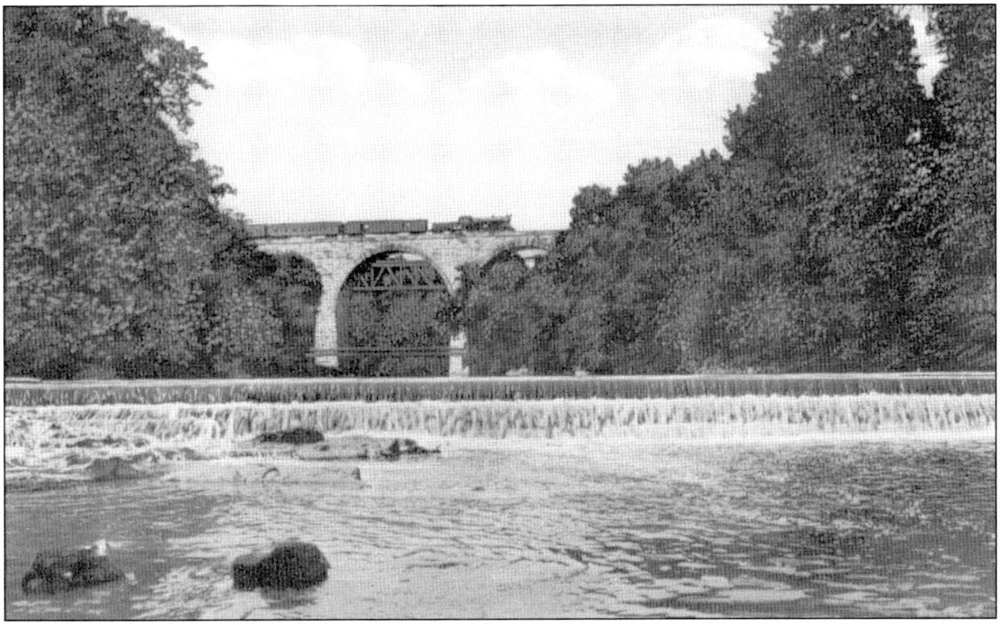

You can not believe everything you read on postcards. The above card was published by the Sabold-Herb Company of Philadelphia and depicts the dam and Baltimore & Ohio bridge on the Brandywine. The printed identification on the card says, "Here, September 11, 1777, was fought a severe battle between the British and German troops, 18,000 strong under Howe and the Americans numbering 13,000 men under Washington, in which the latter were defeated. The consequence of this battle was the occupation of Philadelphia by the British troops." Of course the Battle of Brandywine was fought near Chadds Ford, Pennsylvania, and not at Wilmington, Deleware. The bottom postcard shows the Washington Street Bridge.

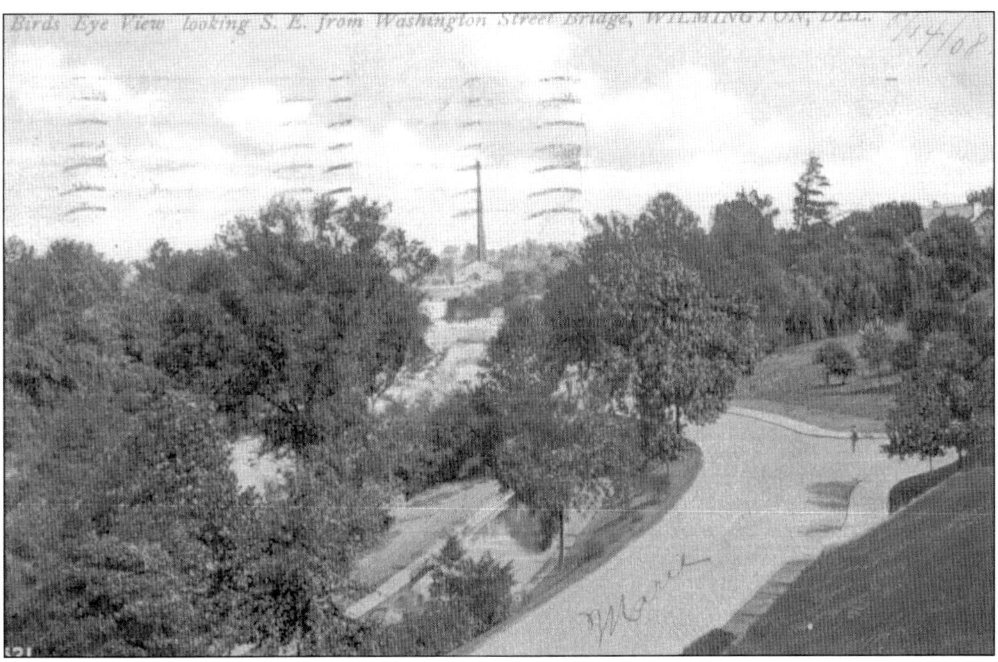

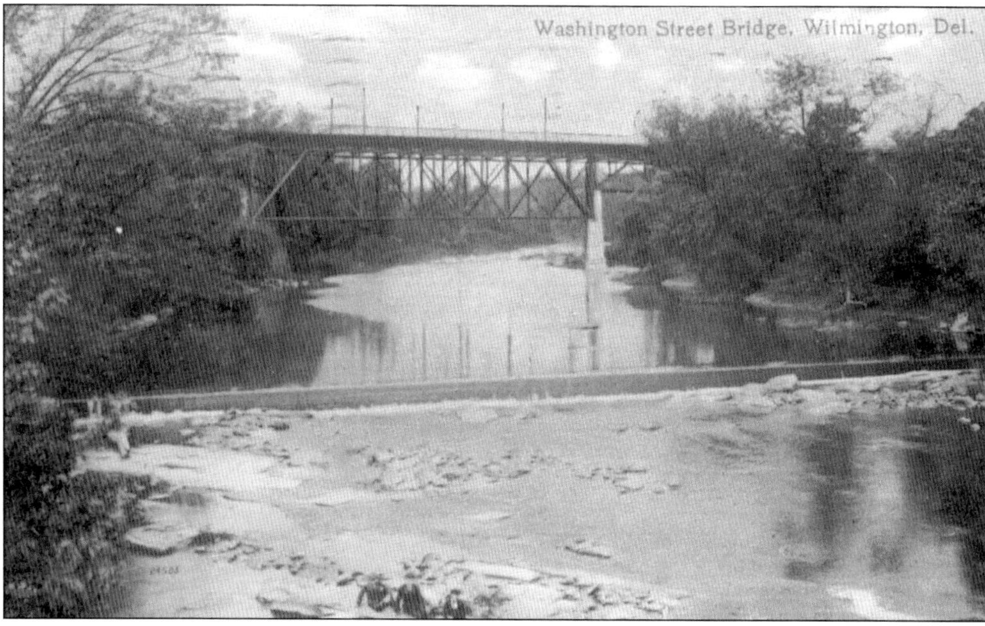

Not all of the messages on the postcards are accounts of good times, parties, and invitations. The card above carries the following message: "Dear Cousin, I tell you things are very dismal at home now days. It doesn't seem like home now since mother has gone, but we will have to make the best of it. Your cousin." Both of the cards are views of the Washington Street Bridge. The card below has the south race with several people walking along the path. It is one of the Julian B. Robinson cards.

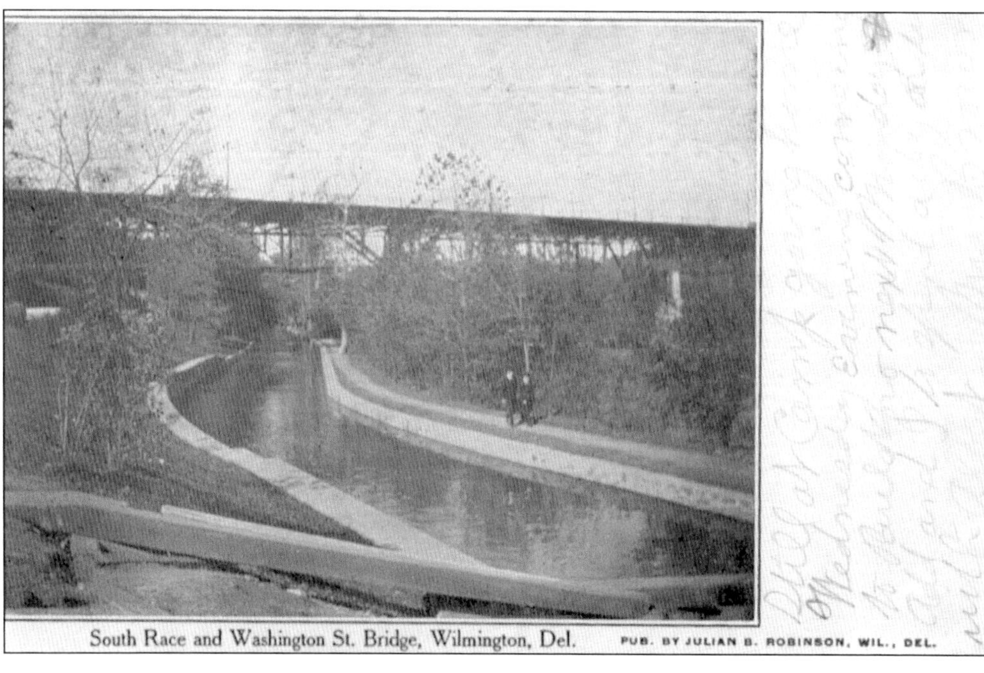

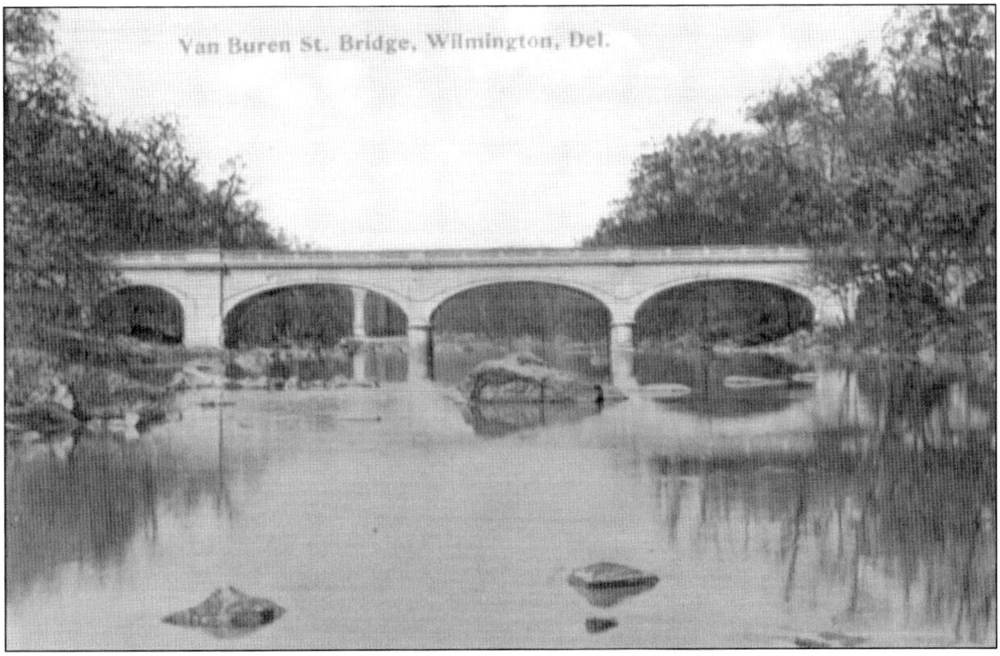

The mouth of the Brandywine grew from land between the Delaware and Christina rivers. There is a lost creek in this area called Black Cats Kill, and it is believed this is where the Brandywine was named. There are several possibilities for the origin of the name Brandywine. One involves a Dutch ship carrying kegs of golden wine that sank at the mouth of the river. Similar to that tale is the story of a keg-laden wagon that slid into the Brandywine and lost all of its cargo. The two postcards on this page show the Van Buren Street Bridge (above) and the Washington Street Bridge (below).

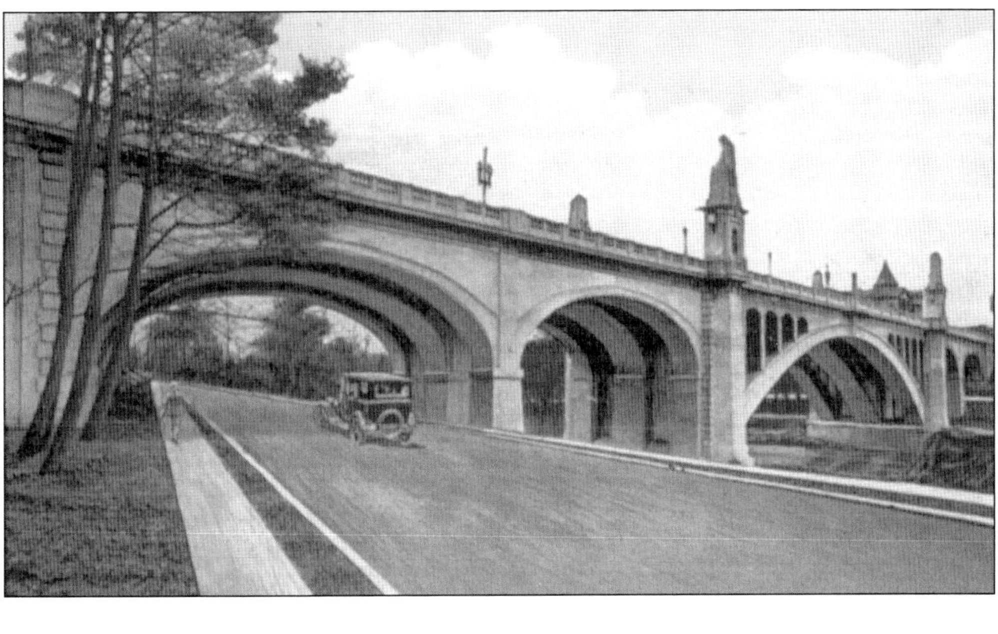

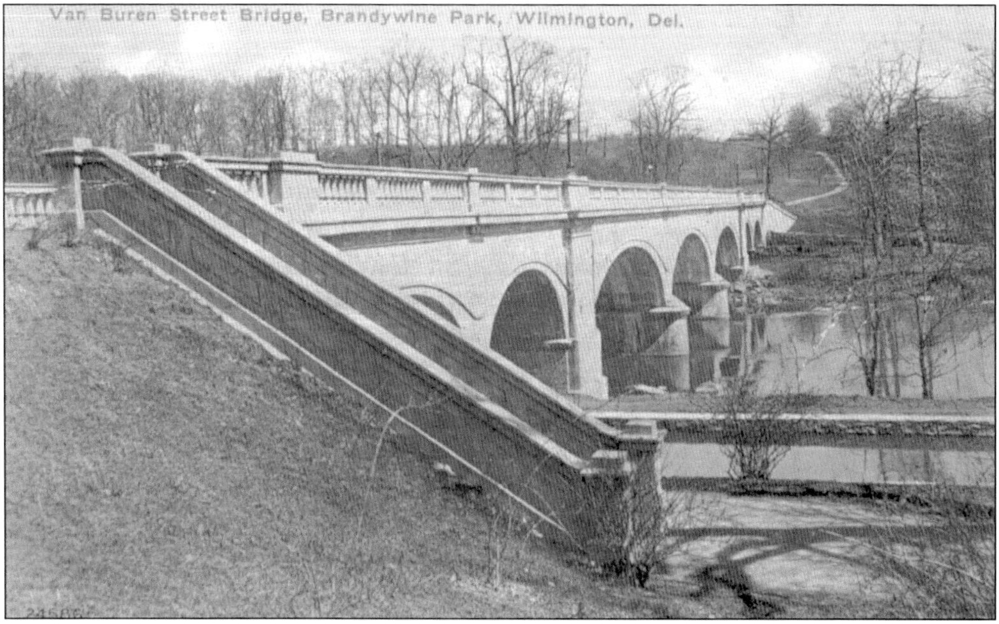

The name of the Brandywine, according to most historians, actually had nothing to do with wine or any other spirits. The river was named for a Dutch settler. The river at first was called Fishkill until Andren Brainwinde purchased 200 acres of the land on the south side of the creek in 1670. In time, Brainwinde's Kill became Brandywine. The postcard above shows the Van Buren Street Bridge in Brandywine Park. The postcard is postmarked 1913, and the sender says she drops something in to the post office almost every day. The Washington Street Bridge is shown below.

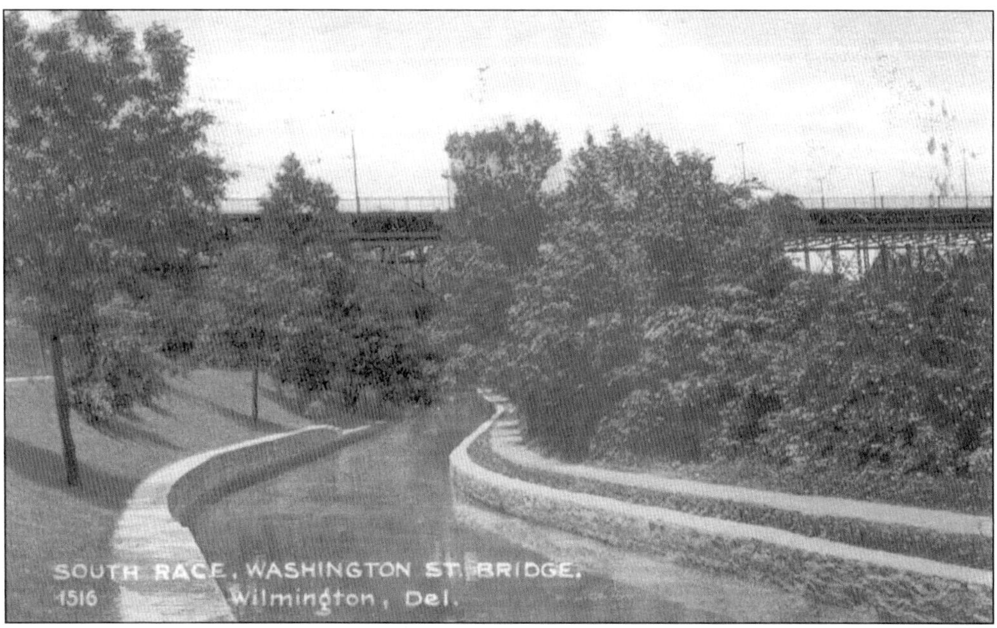

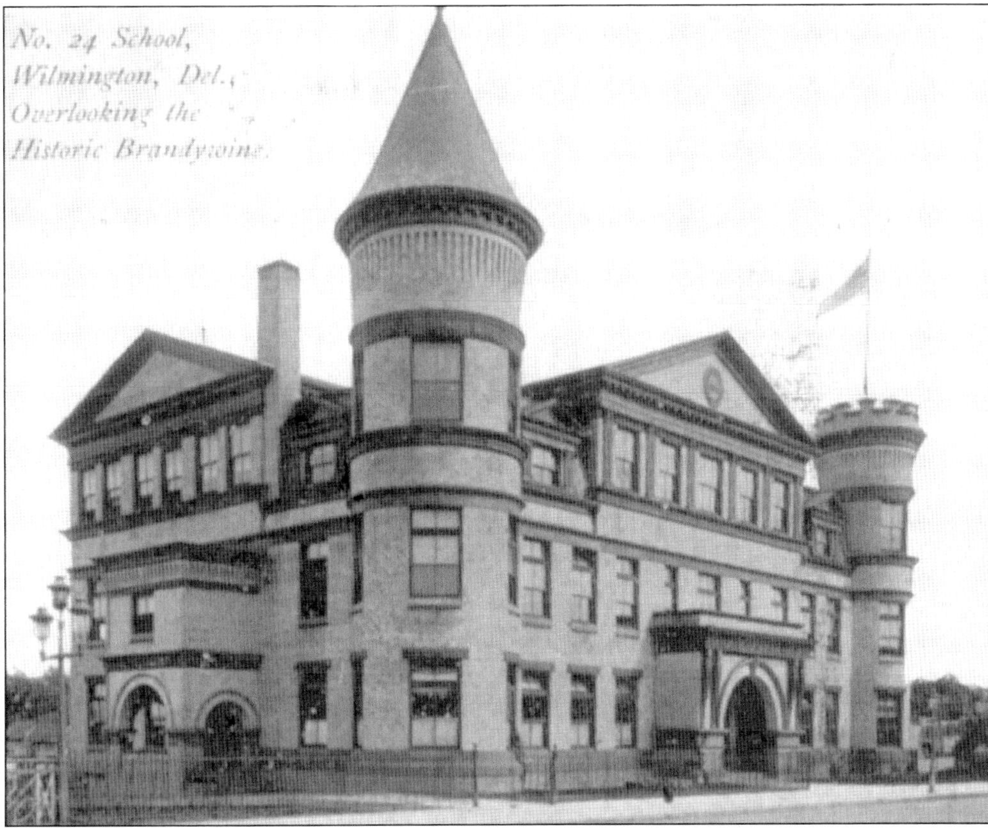

Building a structure along the scenic Brandywine River in the Wilmington section has been a desire of many landowners. Besides providing power for the many mills, the Brandywine supplies a pleasant location for homes and businesses. The postcard above says in its caption, "No. 24 School, Wilmington, Del., Overlooking the Historic Brandywine." The postcard carries a 1905 postmark. The postcard at the bottom of the page reads, "The Colonial Dames House and Park Drive on the Brandywine, Wilmington, Del." This postcard was published by another Wilmington company, Francis E. Gallagher of 2004 Market Street.

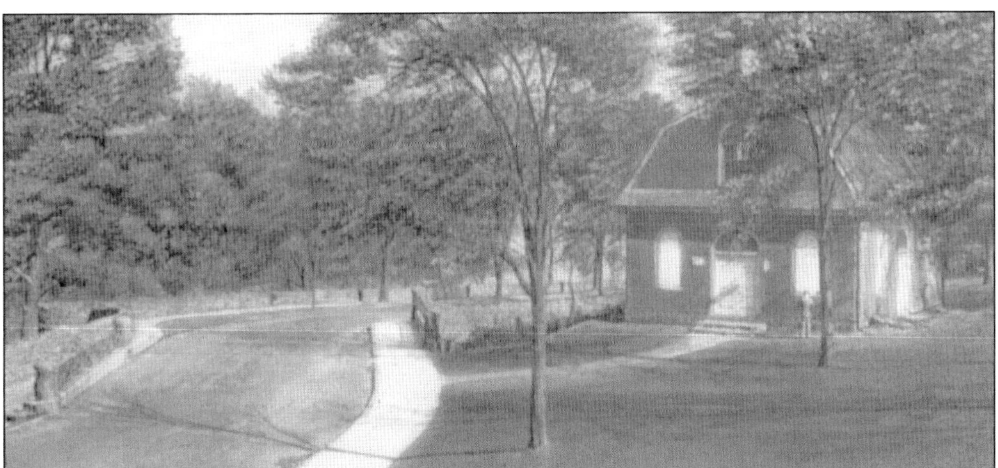

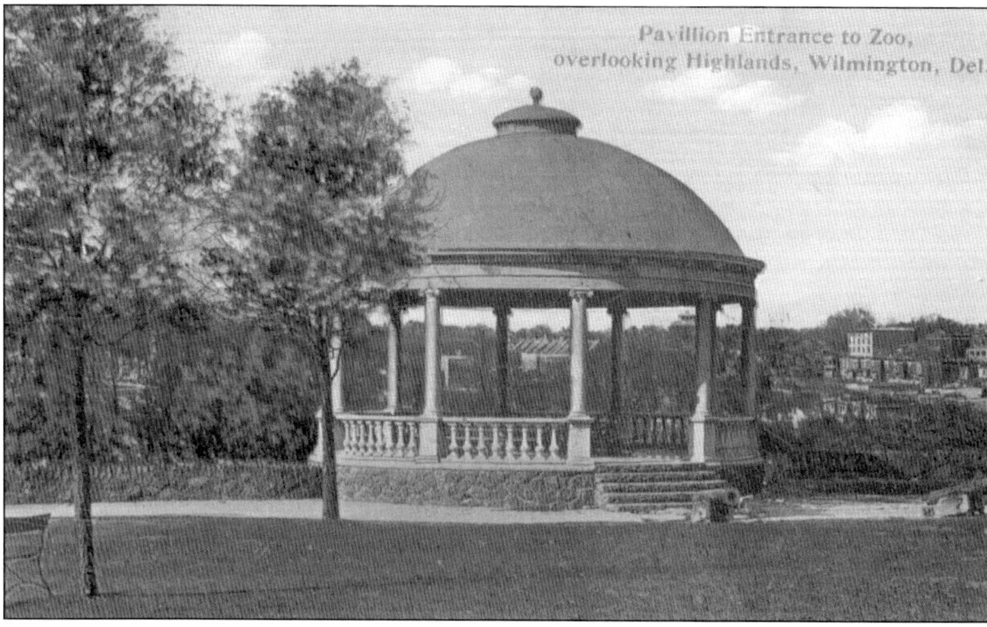

Scenes along the Brandywine River and in Brandywine Park also provide a sense of history for Wilmington residents. The postcard above, "Pavilion Entrance to Zoo, overlooking Highlands, Wilmington, Del.," shows a landmark that is known to those in the area. The bottom postcard shows both the Brandywine and the Baltimore & Ohio bridge. It is titled "Reflections on the Brandywine, Showing B.&.O. and Augustine Bridges, Wilmington, Del." There are many scenes captured by postcards of the historic Brandywine that will be remembered long after the actual scenes are changed by the passing of time.

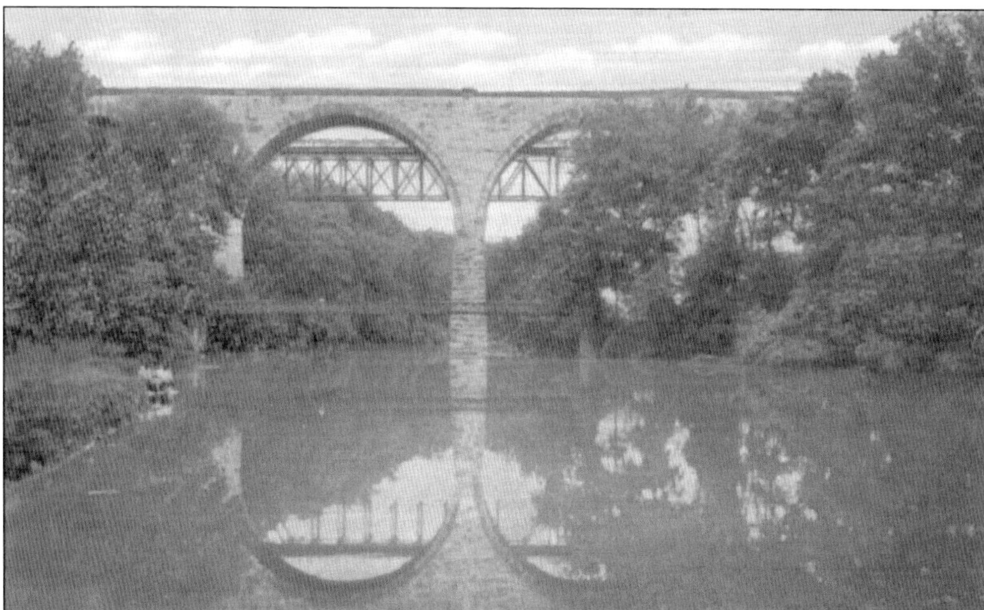

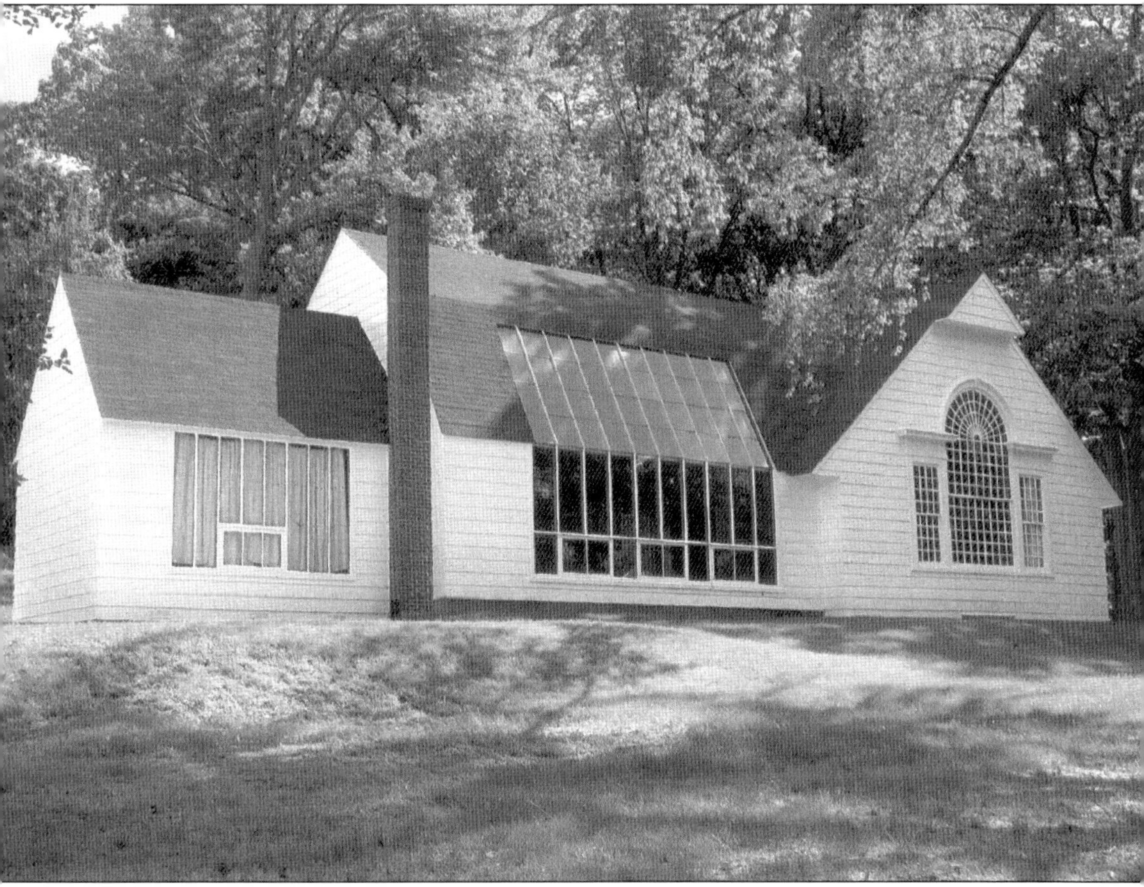

The Brandywine River is also responsible for new views that will in time fade into the milieu of historic places. Many of the classic scenes along the Brandywine have been painted by members of the Brandywine School, including Howard Pyle and N.C. Wyeth, two men who gained their fame along the banks of the Brandywine. Indeed, Wyeth's sons, daughters, and grandchildren have also interpreted the Brandywine Valley, a work of art itself, into works of art. The card above was issued by the Brandywine River Museum in Chadds Ford and depicts the N.C. Wyeth studio. The studio is open for tours by the public.

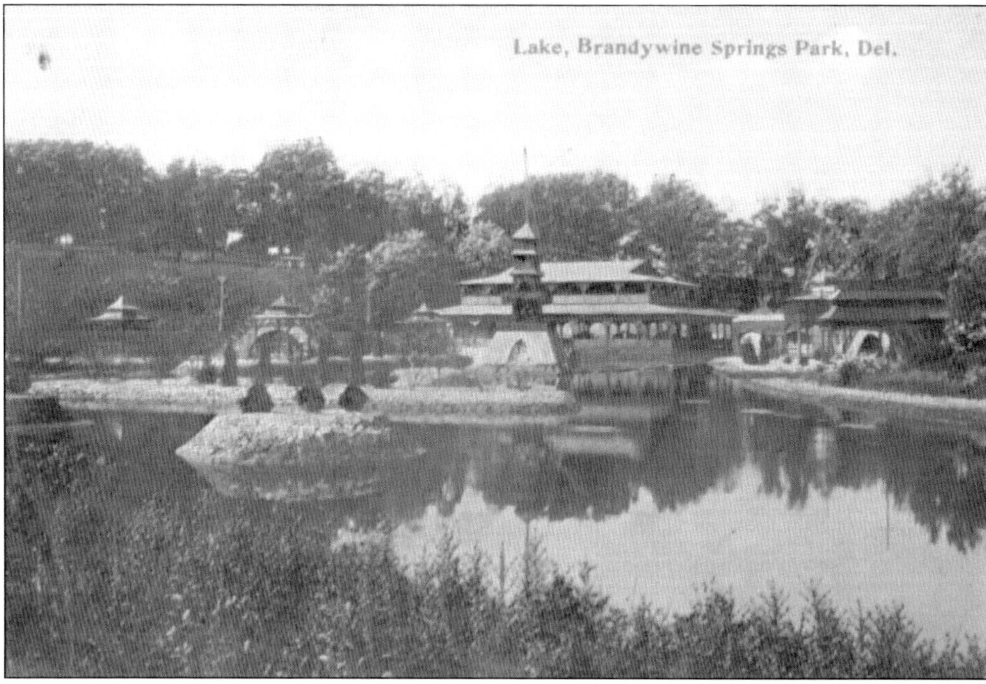

Although it is not located on the banks of the river, the Brandywine Springs Park is connected to the Brandywine by its name and location within the expanse of the Brandywine Valley. Like the amusement park at Lenape, the park's best days took place at the beginning of the century. The postcard above shows the lake, while the postcard below shows a creek view. The back of the bottom card says, "Official postcard of Brandywine Springs Park. Manufactured only by Geo. A. Wolf, Wilmington, Del." The spirit of the park, now closed, is kept alive by a group interested in its history. The location of the Brandywine Park is west of Wilmington near Hyde Run and the Red Clay Creek.

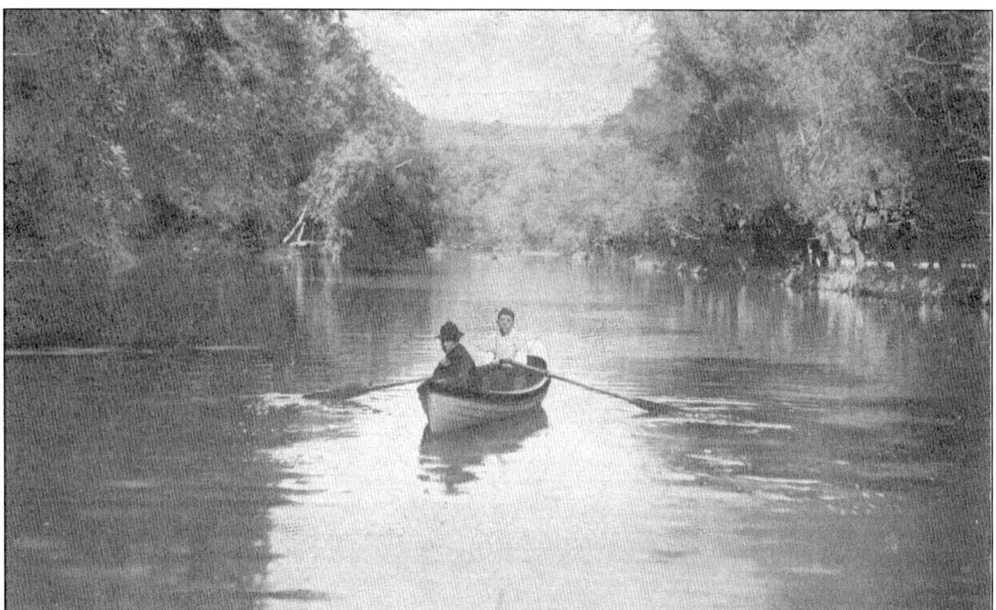

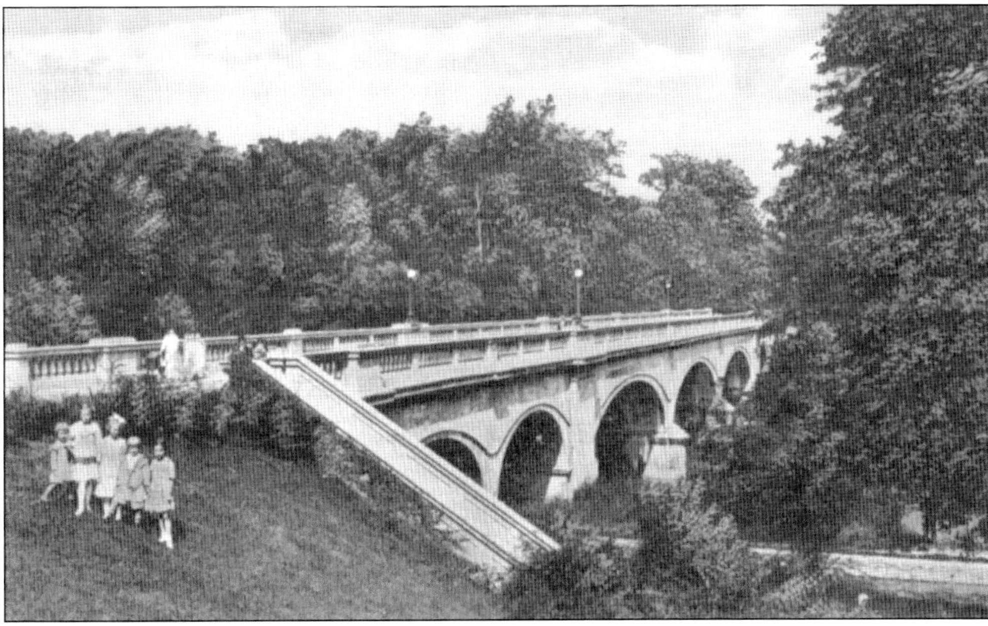

The above postcard is of the Van Buren Street Bridge with a young family standing on the grass. The bottom card shows a view of the new Washington Street Bridge over the Brandywine. Like everything, the Brandywine ends. The river flows into the Christina River, which makes its way to other larger water sources. The Brandywine begins in the Welsh Mountains of Chester County about 40 miles north of where it concludes. Making its way from the mountains to the Christina, the historic Brandywine flows through fields filled with American history.

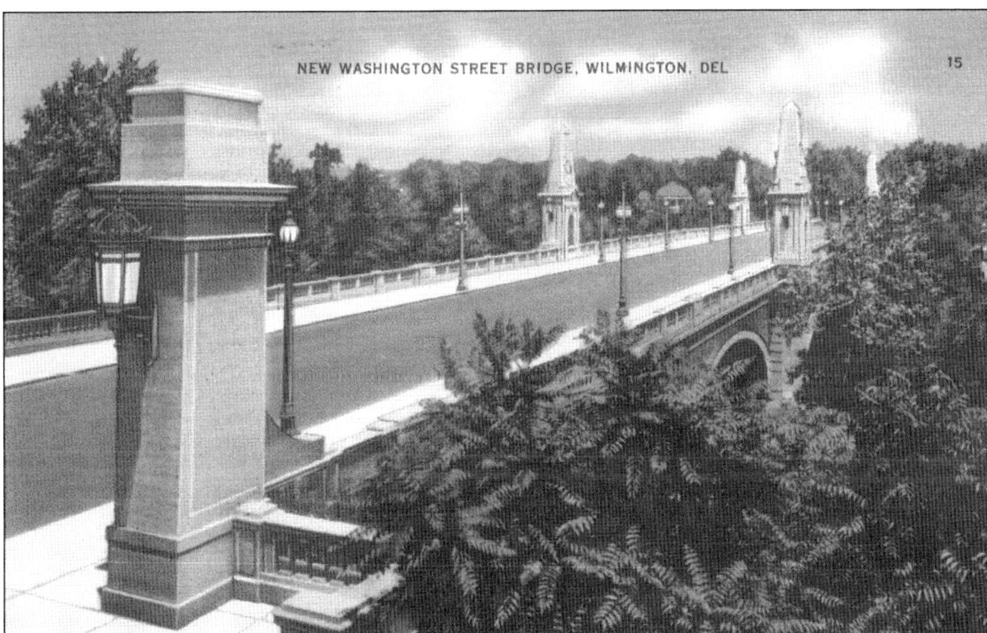

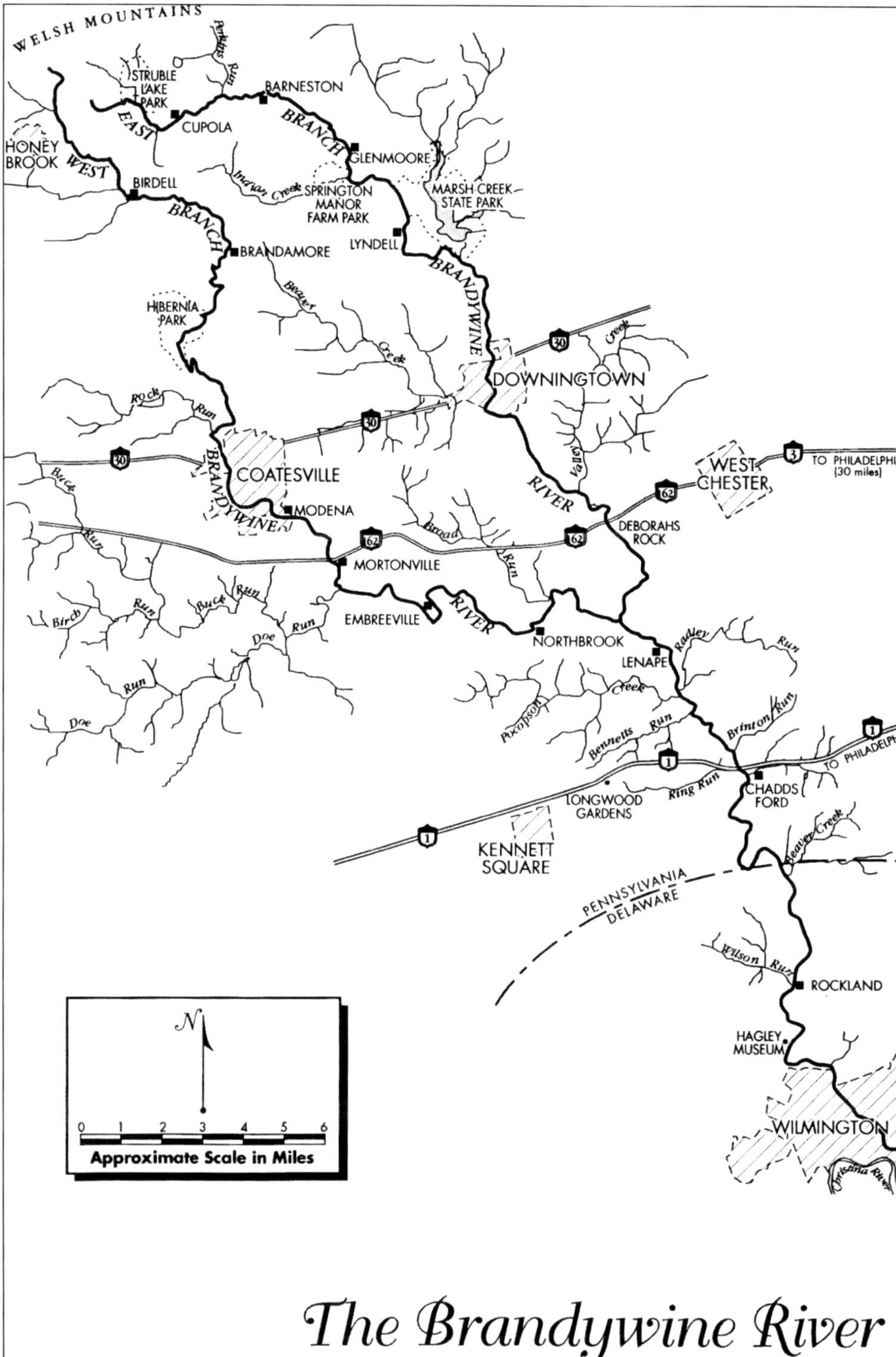

The historic Brandywine River begins in Chester County, Pennsylvania, and concludes in Wilmington, Delaware.

AFTERWORD

Vintage postcards give views of the Brandywine River that cannot be reconstructed by mere words or even recaptured by a current-day hike along its shores. The passage of time and the ravages of nature leave their marks on everything. The Brandywine River itself has changed course over the years, and man has, on occasion, intentionally diverted the flow of the river from its intended route. The only way to recapture the lost images of the Brandywine is by viewing photographs, postcards, like those included in *Along the Brandywine River,* or paintings by artists who have spent a lifetime along its shore, immortalizing the many scenic views.

There is no doubt that the vintage postcards and their irreplaceable images constitute the central focus of *Along the Brandywine River.* It is through the drawings and photographs on these postcards that the life of the early 20th century can be viewed. The clothing of the people depicted, their jobs, and the ways they relaxed all give clues to the life lived 100 years ago. Even modes of transportation, such as cars, trains, and wagons, offer insights into their everyday lives. Some of the places shown in the postcards, such as the cabins used as summer vacation homes that once existed north of Coatesville, no longer exist. Others spots have drastically changed in appearance.

The postcards can also call forth memories of childhood or even a first job as a youth. The park along the Brandywine at Lenape was the site where many area residents first gained youthful employment. Maybe a relative grew up along the Brandywine and talked about his youth to his children and grandchildren. These postcards show where those parents or grandparents may have spent their early years. Even the addresses on the postcards indicate a simpler time. Some of the postcards do not even list the city where it is to be delivered. The destination is assumed to be the city where it was mailed.

One wonders about the motivation of those who made the images for the postcards and sold them for pennies. Did they know they were leaving behind a visual history in their work that would become vintage postcards? George A. Wolf of Delaware gathered fine images for the cards he produced, as did the Parker Company in West Chester. The production of the postcards also added insights to our history. Germany was an important part of postcard production in the early 20th century, but a world war transferred the business to the United States. The quality of cards and their designs was transformed over the years as the tastes of Americans changed.

Along the Brandywine River is also a brief written history of the Brandywine. The stories of many of the individuals who purchased, wrote, and sent the postcards are revealed through some of the century-old messages written on those cards. Most of the verses are about wonderful experiences at the sites depicted on the cards. Others are used as notes to thank someone for his kindness or to give notice that a visit is at hand. But those members of generations past also had their sorrows. The relative who wrote about the passing of her mother and home not being the same since the death is a sentiment that can be felt today.

The Brandywine River is important to the early history of the United States. The nation might not even exist if a battle along its shores would have lasted another hour on the hot summer's day of September 11, 1777. Several British said if they had another hour of daylight, Gen. George Washington's troops would have been history. Washington himself escaped death after British captain Patrick Ferguson decided not to pull the trigger of his rifle when he had Washington in his sights. The river flows through one of the three original colonies of William Penn. Native Americans were already using the Brandywine as a source of life when the early European settlers moved to the area. The du Pont family made its fortune supplying black powder to the soldiers of our country's armies, and a major international company was formed. The river and those who lived along it made significant contributions to the development of the nation.

The Brandywine River is still enjoyed today. Canoeing on the Brandywine is common, and artists still use the river for inspiration. Perhaps *Along the Brandywine River* will inspire a trip to the river's shores, a visit to the Brandywine River Museum, Longwood Gardens, or one of the many museums in Delaware. The river continues to be living history.

SOURCES

Along the Brandywine River is intended to tell the history of the river. Every effort has been made to give factual information in the captions.

Bruce E. Mowday, the author, is a lifelong resident of the Brandywine River Valley and spent most of his professional life as a journalist. His profession has brought him into contact with many local historians and the thousands of newspaper articles and columns he has written supplied him with many of the facts used in this book.

As indicated in the acknowledgements, Elizabeth Humphrey, who wrote the book *Brandywine,* provided insight and information. Also, several Web sites were used for basic information on some of the cultural institutions in this book. Also consulted for some background was Mark M. Boatner III's *Encyclopedia of the American Revolution.*

Michael Kahn is a great photographer who illustrated the Humphrey book. Several of the postcards in this book have images he photographed. Also, the Brandywine Conservancy has given permission for use of several of their postcards.

BIBLIOGRAPHY

Boatner III, Mark M. *Encyclopedia of the American Revolution.* Mechanicsburg, Pennsylvania: Stackpole Books, 1994.

Canby, Henry Seidel. *The Brandywine.* Exton, Pennsylvania: Schiffer Ltd., 1941.

Humphrey, Elizabeth and Michael Kahn. *Brandywine.* Wilmington, Delaware: the Jared Company, 1990.

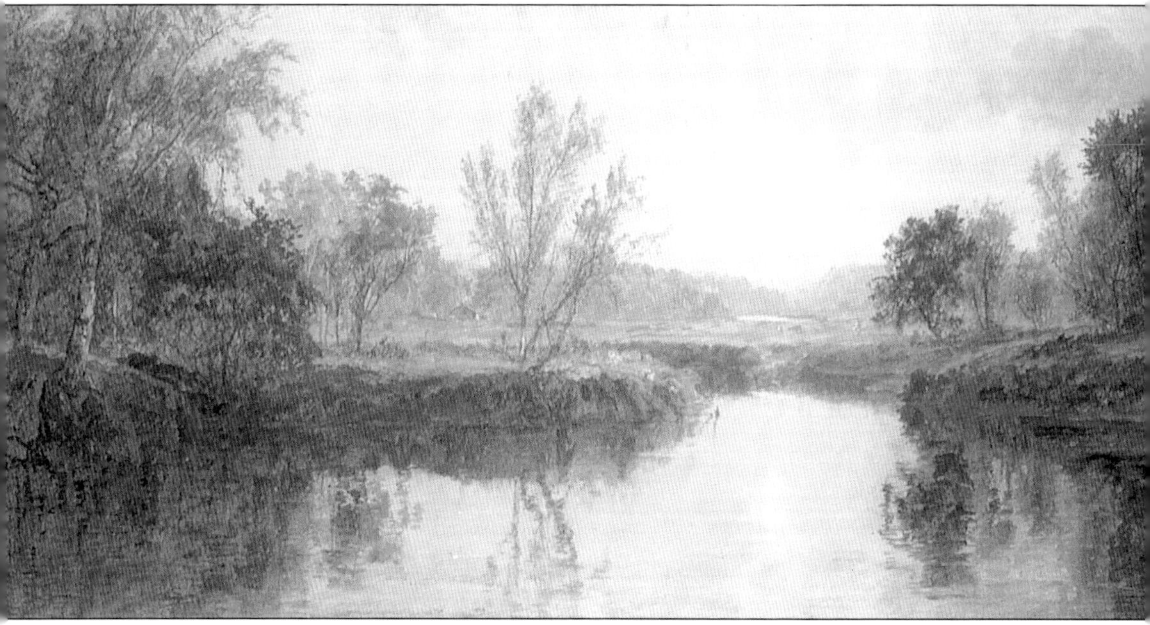

Jasper F. Cropsey captured the beauty of the Brandywine River in this 1887 painting. The postcard was printed by the Brandywine River Museum in Chadds Ford.